C000071180

Borana Folktales
A Contextual Study

Sahlu Kidane

Editorial Adviser
P.T.W. Baxter

HAAN

London, United Kingdom
New Brunswick, United States

transaction

Copyright © Sahlu Kidane 2002

Published by
HAAN Publishing
Southbank House
Black Prince Road
London SE1 7SJ

Distributed in North America by Transaction Publishers
390 Campus Drive, Somerset NJ 08873

ISBN 1 874209 39 1 (cased)
ISBN 1 874209 14 6 (paper)

All rights reserved. No part of this book may be reproduced, stored in a retrieval system, or transmitted in any form or by any means, electronic, mechanical, photocopying, recording or otherwise, without permission in writing from the publisher.

The Author hereby asserts his right to be identified as the Author of the work.

Typeset by MacStyle Ltd, Scarborough, N. Yorkshire
Printed and bound in Great Britain by Athenaeum Press, Gateshead

Photocredit: Front cover photo by Johan Helland, *Borana Elder (c. 1986)*
collection of PTW Baxter

PUBLICATION OF THIS WORK HAS BEEN SUPPORTED BY THE
GENEROUS ASSISTANCE OF THE CHR. MICHELSEN INSTITUTE,
NORWAY, AND THE ANDRZEJEWSKI TRUST FUND, AET, UK

Contents

---

1 Where ** appears by the title of a story, that tale is also presented in Borana in Part Three.

Acknowledgements

I owe much to my adviser, Dr. Fekade Azeze, who worked closely with me on the project from inception to completion. I am extremely grateful to my Borana mentor, Chachole Alakhe, who taught me tirelessly and to Boru Dida, my adoptive father. My sincere gratitude goes also to: Bule Arero Guyyo, Sintayehu Taddese, Siseraw Dinku, Teferra Mekonnen and to my sister-in-law, Alem. Thanks also to Dr. Johan Helland for assistance in bringing this work to publication, and to Dr. Paul Baxter for valuable editorial advice. Finally, I greatly appreciate the support of the Borana Office for Culture and Sports and the School of Graduate Studies at Addis Ababa University.

Sahlu Kidane
Addis Ababa

Editorial Note by P T W Baxter

These zestful narratives, which demonstrate and analyze the power that Borana give to wisely chosen words, are a shortened version of Sahlu's MA thesis, presented to the University of Addis Ababa, entitled *Borana Oromo Prose Narratives: A Contextual Study*. This book concentrates on the Borana texts and omits some discussion of the relationship of the prose narratives to folklore theory. I hope that Sahlu will publish his theoretical discussion in a specialist journal.

The translations of the tales avoid what Andrzejewski called the 'anti-English' of mind numbing word for word literal translation. As far as possible the English is 'bent' to carry the sense of the original, while remaining faithful to the original text. Sixteen of the tales are also presented in Borana in the form that Sahlu transcribed them from his tapes and in the spelling that he used then. To have altered the spelling to Kuube, three years later, in the study and far from the field, could only have introduced confusions, as would allusions to publications which were not available in Addis Ababa where this manuscript was written in 1996.

I worked among Borana in the early 1950s and was constantly frustrated by my inability to follow the speeches and asides of elders who were trying to adjudicate disputes. They and the disputants frequently uttered short quotations from folk tales, which I could not follow, but which had great impact on the situation. Even when friends were able to elucidate the meanings for me, I could very seldom place the folk tale allusions and references in the social and intellectual contexts from which their meaning derived and from which their impact depended. It was soon clear that the power of the elders lay in their hard won understanding, acquired through long study of the wise and elliptical words of their ancestors, and in their ability to adapt that understanding to contemporary contexts. But it was only very slowly that I came to realise, and then only in a bewildered and foggy way, that the elders themselves were in part controlled by the words which they used to control others.

If only Sahlu's findings had been available to me then.

PTWB
University of Manchester, October 2001

Part One
The Context

Chapter 1

The Borana, Fieldwork, and Translation and Transcription

This book is a contextual study of the prose narratives of the Borana branch of the Oromo people. Ever since their expansion from the south of Ethiopia during the sixteenth century, the widely dispersed Oromo have developed variations of dialect, religion and ways of life. Of all the Oromo people, the Borana alone still retain the old nomadic life and the ancient Gada socio-political system; therefore Borana Oromo folklore needs to be studied in its own social reality. Anthropologists like Asmarom and Baxter have pointed out that the Borana possess an immensely rich and systematic oral tradition which is highly active (Asmarom, 1973: 12; Baxter, 1965: 69). This study aims to reveal the complex yet most fascinating aspects of the narratives that can be discovered through enquiry into the communication process and local concepts, largely by using approaches developed by branches of the contextual school.

Three ethnic prose genres are defined and described in the context of performance. This is quite different from providing a large collection of tales with detailed analyses of their content and form – which is a fairly ambitious undertaking in its own right. The purpose of this chapter is to answer questions about the nature of Borana ethnic prose genres. Twenty-three *duri-duri* (children's tales), thirty *mamaksa* (adults' tales) and twenty-three *arga-ageti* (myths and legends) are given in English translation. In an attempt to enable the texts to reflect contextual practices they have been selected as representative of content and form, including variants, of a range of rare and popular tales that are affected by conventions of performance.

In order to show the general nature of each genre the tales' forms and content are analysed. Each genre is described according to its inherent features. In the formalistic description of the narratives some structuralist methods are used. Analytic terms are employed to relate the narratives to wider academic concepts in addition to the local taxonomies

The second chapter defines the genres and describes them in the contexts of performance. Later discussions on performance then become possible.

In the third chapter, issues concerning the identity of the performer, occasion, styles of performances and interaction between narrator and audience are discussed. The relationship between occasion and performance is so interwoven that delivery is greatly affected by the composition of the audience and the mood surrounding the performance. Especially with adults' tales, the occasion dictates the type of narrative to be invoked and the way the narrator edits his account to meet the demands of the occasion. Chapter three analyses the effect of the convergence of audience, narrator and occasion on what to perform and how to perform.

The fourth chapter focuses mainly on the genre *mamaksa*. It deals with functions, conventions and principles of usage in detail, with an ethnographic basis. This focus on the *mamaksa* is suggested by its very nature and, partly, to view the folklore communication process as the users perceive it. The *mamaksa* is the most widely and intensively used genre, for which conscious interpretation, principles of usage and locally recognized functions are available. Therefore, the researcher can discover these phenomena without imposing his own assumptions.

In the analysis of its mode of existence, the *mamaksa* is viewed as a language form. The user's attitude, aesthetic principles, functions and the many factors involved in relation to effective usage are discussed. Throughout, it is the user's point of view that I attempt to capture, and lack of local consensus and any disparities are described. Observed cases are presented to illustrate points and substantiate assertions. At the end an ethnographically detailed case study of a communicative event is provided, demonstrating some of the major concepts dealt with, and thus serving as a summary.

The Borana

The Borana people live in the area of southern Ethiopia from where, it is generally believed, the Oromo launched their northward expansion in the sixteenth century (Asmarom, 1973: 9). The present Borana population in Ethiopia is estimated at about 177,000 and there is a substantial population in northern Kenya. Legend has it that the Borana came from a place called Tullu Namaduri (hill of ancient people) in Balle region and settled in Liban, where today their important shrines are located. Eike Haberland maintains that the original homeland of the Borana was in northern Liban from where they were driven by the Guji Oromo into Dirre region (Haberland 1963: 779). At present they occupy the lowland area extending some 186 miles (300 kilometres) from Negelle town southwards up to, and across, the Kenyan border. They are flanked by the Guji and the Burji in the north, the Arsi and the Somali in the east and the Konso in the west. Borana relations with their neighbours, except for the Konso, are rather tense – often leading to open warfare.

The Borana speak Oromo. The distinct dialect, with its elaborate vocabulary is difficult to be understood by the central and western Oromo, to whom the same words often represent different meanings.

The Borana people are divided into exogamous moieties – the Sabo and Gona – which, in turn, branch into clans and subclans known as *mana* (house) and *balbala* (door) respectively. The number of divisions varies; for example, the Karrayu clan is divided into 36 subclans, while Mettari has only seven. These divisions are not localised but play a significant role in Borana religious, political and social events, such as marriage, conducting rituals, electing leaders and providing mutual assistance. An important aspect of clan divisions is resource utilization. During the long dry season, the deep wells become very important and their proper use and conservation a matter of intense debate (see Helland, 1980: 48–78) In periods of drought a well can only be used by members of a clan whose ancestors participated in digging it.

Gada

Borana society maintains its social and political order through a detailed and complex system known as Gada. Its practice involves many rites of passage and stratification into generation-sets. According to myth, the Gada law was given by God to a man named Gadayo who became the first Aba Gada, or 'father of Gada' (see tale A5). Every Aba Gada is elected and stays in office only for eight years then hands over power in a formal ceremony. The power of the Aba Gada is mainly judicial and ritual.

Religion

Around towns a small number of Muslims and an insignificant number of Christians are to be found, but most Borana practise their indigenous religion. They believe in one supreme God, Waaqa, who is responsible for the creation of all things. They pray to him for fertility and peace, and acknowledge no other spirit or demigod. Jaenan has described the Borana concept of God thus:

> Waka is a personal god also identified with the sky. Waka is personal in the sense that humans are supposed to be able to communicate with him and obtain divine guidance for the tribe (Jaenan, 1956: 183).

The Borana are a deeply religious people who pray regularly and frequently for peace, fertility and rain. They maintain that God forbids one to harm others for one's own good. This is the single most stressed mortal sin. They do not have a defined conception of an after life. A sinner is punished here on earth; either wrongdoing is paid for personally or the sinner's descendants will pay for it, and this notion is expressed in the saying: 'one meets his nemesis sooner or later.'

The Borana have many rites of passage and prayer rites conducted at shrines, which are specific localities occasionally marked by big sycamore trees and associated with some historical or mythical incident. In the fourth year of his term, every Aba Gada, together with his assembly which consists of hundreds of people and nearly all the councillors, commences his pilgrimage (*gooroo*) from Dirre towards Liban, where the shrines are located. It lasts almost a year and thousands of cattle are sacrificed. The ritual assembly visits the various shrines in a perfectly planned manner, staying at some for a month, at others for three days only, visiting some shrines twice and performing particular rituals at particular places and times. Members of the assembly take along their wives, children and cattle. The pilgrimage is a most arduous task and its successful completion is expected of every Aba Gada.

As well as the elected Aba Gada the Borana have two major and three minor hereditary spiritual leaders called Qallu, who are intimately associated with fertility and peace. Baxter noted that, 'without them the Borana would not have the "Peace of the Boran" ' (Baxter,1965: 69). Qallu judge major conflicts and, above all, play a significant role in electing the Gada leaders. The Qallu behave like women in many respects: they do not go to war, carry arms, defend themselves nor kill animals. They even style their hair like women. They symbolise peace, godliness and restraint.[2]

Economic Life

When Borana speak about the economy they speak about nothing but cattle – whose milk is literally the sole means of subsistence. Cattle may be slaughtered only during rituals and for very important guests. Possessing many cattle is a great source of pride, and the love of cattle can be seen from the great portion of Borana folksongs devoted to cattle . In the limited resources of Boranaland, keeping the cattle alive and well is a difficult task and men travel many miles each season in search of grass and water.[3] The major causes of war are cattle raiding, which is why the Borana say, 'cattle are men eaters.'

Every male child is given a heifer at the early age of one or two. By the time a boy is ready for marriage, that heifer should have multiplied to be the source of a considerable number of calves. Inheritance goes from father

---

2 For an analysis of comparable priestly attributes among the Borana speaking Gabra, who are neighbours of the Borana, see John Wood, *When men are women; Manhood among the Gabra nomads of East Africa*, University of Wisconsin Press, 1999.

3 For a resume of current conditions see Johan Helland 'Development Interventions and Pastoral Dynamics in Southern Ethiopia', pp 81–103 in Hogg, Richard, *Pastoralists, Ethnicity & the State in Ethiopia*, Haan, London 1997; and 'Institutional Erosion in the Drylands: the case of the Borana pastoralists', *EASS-REA Vol XIV, No 2*, 1998.

to eldest son, who is expected to share a portion of it with his brothers and his father's wives.

Though a wife can have her say as to how the family wealth should be spent, her role is subordinate – even to her son. At times her role in family life is defined as a responsibility to bear children, because it is the only way she can be respected, loved and considered 'normal'. Feeding the family and running all the home affairs, including raising the necessary money, rests on the woman's shoulders. Even house building is mostly a woman's job (see tale A8, and Dahl, 1990: 129–36).

Young children look after the calves and goats. The main task of a young adult is to take the cattle to far pastures (*fora*) and to water them. The main task of Borana men of about fifty years old and above is to act as guardians of tradition and to settle disputes (see tale M25).

Fieldwork

Methods and Problems

Kenneth Goldstien describes three categories of collecting stories and observing performances: natural, artificial, and induced natural settings (Goldstien, 1964: 87–9).

In the natural setting, the researcher does not affect the performance other than by being an unobtrusive participant. The artificial setting is an activity out of context organized by the collector. The third category – the induced natural setting – is where the researcher first discovers the natural context and then tries to bring it about.

For performance-centred research such as the work in hand, where the main goal goes beyond merely collecting stories, there is a need to capture performances in their actual settings. In my field experience, natural setting, despite its exceptional opportunity to observe the communication process in its purity, is not easy to come by as often as the researcher would wish. Therefore one is compelled to employ various strategies in addition.

The greater part of the research was conducted in Liban for the simple reason that I used to live at Negelle town and it is the area I know best. The survey was conducted with the help of two Borana elders, Boru Dida (then aged 65) and Alakhe Boru (then aged 70), whom I knew earlier and who used to take me to their villages frequently. Apart from offering me security and shelter, they introduced me to individuals admired for their eloquence and knowledge of tradition. Three months after the start, Alakhe Boru died. After a while, Boru Dida formally took me as his son, which was a very important development in the research process. Borana, with reason, are very suspicious toward non-Borana. Every time I am introduced to a new man, he has to be assured that I am harmless, that I am one of them, before he even consents to greet me. But as Boru's son, and introduced as such, they begin to chat intimately and cease to look on me as a stranger. I followed Boru, made new acquaintances and collected new stories or new versions. This process helped to widen the study.

The setting for collecting and observing varies according to the genres. Adults do not have the tradition of telling stories for entertainment or at request. It is difficult for the *mamaksa* to be actualized out of context; there has to be an issue of deliberation for the tale to be invoked. These occasions, though not rare, yield few tales. Wherever there is a speech-act, storytelling can take place. But the nature of the engagement affects the style of narration and the kinds of tales involved. So, however demanding it may be, one must visit the various scenes of engagement, be it work, assembly or leisure talk to observe the nature of communication and performance in its natural form from different angles.

Recording adults' tales in the natural setting poses difficulty. For example, at a village assembly a tale may be related at any minute, so a collector has to stand by, alert, to record one when it comes. Yet, if one is to understand the contextual meaning, the whole deliberation – which may last five to six hours – needs to be recorded. This indeed is a tedious and sometimes wasteful job. The solution I later adopted was to listen carefully and record only when a speaker is about to relate a tale prompted by the cue, 'There is one story.' Though this method saves time and money, occasionally it causes the loss of a very important detail which may put the whole contextual meaning into new light. I was able to avoid this by the simultaneous use of recording and taking short notes about the background. Once the principals established intimacy with me, they became oblivious of my presence and my recording machine.

Though 'natural setting' recording and observing the adult's tales offers a view of the narrative and of the performances in their working form, it does not yield as many tales as one wishes. So, even though this study is essentially performance centred, the short period of fieldwork time compelled me to arrange some stimulated or artificial settings.

The artificial setting can well be arranged by the fireside of a village house or under the shade of a tree. To provide liquor stimulates the occasion and encourages men to gather, and they also feel a sense of responsibility to pay off the collector. During such contrived occasions, the storytelling process is hard to initiate. When people are asked who the best storyteller is, they often point to the good public speaker or the man of great insight. When these persons are asked to tell stories they are disappointing at first. For one thing, they love to talk about the Gada system (which they expect me to ask them about). This does not mean that they look down on their narratives. But one never asks a Borana adult to *tell* folktales. 'How can I tell a tale without a case in hand?' is the typical answer. Occasionally one may manage to relate a tale or two outside the context, but cannot go further. This is the single most important problem the researcher encounters, even when conducting exclusive interviews with a competent storyteller.

Where the storytelling is slow to start, a helpful method is to ask for stories by theme: 'Do you know a story about an evil person who claims the property of other people?' for there are many on this theme. Once the first story is told, some element of that story triggers another story and can lead on to as many as four or five tales. Then without warning the subject melts into another discussion from where there is no return. Borana get bored telling tale after tale because that is not their way, and they see no reason in relating a string of stories aimed at nothing. In general, collecting adult stories is a difficult task.

With children's tales, the matter takes quite a different turn; here stories are told for entertainment. The children only have to be asked to recount and they respond immediately. At any time they are ready to provide tale upon tale. The normal performing hours are the daytime, when they are herding the calves, and the nighttime before going to bed. The style of performance between the natural and the artificial setting is not visibly different. But the knowledge that they are being recorded can make some children excited and others shy.

I had two assistants – Bule Arero Guyyo and Chachole Alakhe. Chachole, a high-school graduate in his early thirties, was brought up in the rural area of Yabello. Due to his inquisitive nature and great interest in mastering his tradition, he has developed a considerable knowledge of customs and history. His ability to translate and interpret cryptic lines and allusions is quite amazing. At Negelle town he used to organize sessions for me at which urbanized and educated men discussed issues I raised. Sometimes elders too participated at these sessions. These discussions are of great importance. First of all the educated ones tend to take a critical and interested attitude toward their culture. Moreover they are ready to give explanations. At times the arguments with the elders are revealing because they point out contradictions in their cultural practices. But the major contribution of the younger educated men lay in providing me with important questions that I should ask the elders.

There is a considerable problem in looking for local concepts, especially in defining and differentiating between genres. Often when a consensus is not obtained, one possibility is to describe the problem and adopt the dominant view. This, however, is not a difficulty that prevails in all the genres; children's tales are less affected than the myths and legends. Another problem is establishing the users' attitude toward the different genres. With children's tales, the question is whose opinion to consider, the children's or the adults'? Their opinions are not the same. A somewhat similar problem is encountered in the attitude towards the *mamaksa*, where a certain degree of variation is detected.

Another fieldwork problem is time. The graduate school of the University of Addis Ababa approves only a maximum of three months of fieldwork but to conduct research which requires one to record tales, observe live performances and understand usage within such a period of time is almost impossible. Therefore, I was forced to extend the fieldwork time to five months. But still such important issues as creation and transmission have to be left out because of the short period of observation.

Translation and Transcription

There are disagreements between those who favour literal translation and those who advocate free translation. Some, such as Andrzejewski, argue that literal translation produces 'anti-English', devoid of any linguistic reality, while others prefer closer renderings of words and structure (Finnegan, 1992: 189–90). Translators devise models appropriate for their purposes.

The translation from Borana into English was made with the help of my two assistants, so that contextual meaning might not be lost. The texts were first transcribed in the original language in order to get the opportunity to experiment with various modes of translation. Translating from one culture to another is obviously a difficult task. One of my predicaments was wavering between being loyal to the original and rendering it in standard English. The option I generally pursued is to be faithful to the original flavour as much as possible.

When discussing the artistic use of language in the narratives, the inadequacy of the English language, especially in carrying poetic expressions as they sound in the original, is pointed out. Clever turns of phrases and verses are composed by exploiting rhyme or alliteration or by using the same words in different contexts. Translation destroys these nuances. When the main virtue of a particular utterance rests on the verbal expression, the English is 'bent' to carry the sense of the original. My goal in translating the narratives is not to show what they would have looked like had they been composed in English, but to leave their local imprint on the English.

With transcription, the same objective of faithfulness is pursued. Except in a few cases, the narratives included are those recorded on tape, thus enabling transcription exactly as it comes from the lips of the narrator. Audience responses like 'eh', 'yes', or the echoing of the last word of the narrator after each sentence are omitted. Though these utterances are an important and natural element of performance, they appear parroty and tiresome on paper; the opposite of the purpose they serve during performance. Narrators usually proceed from direct speech to direct speech without stating who said what. At times they simply say: 'The other man said …', and 'the other man said …'. When exact transcription or representation of these on paper is felt to create ambiguity I add the name of the speaker. Children's tales contain highly repetitive lines and scenes. These are deliberate and therefore transcribed exactly as they are.

Finally, the titles of all the tales are ones that I have created. The letters D, M and A are used with numbering to categorize the tales; D standing for *duri-duri*, M for *mamaksa* and A for *arga-ageti*.

Chapter 2

Ethnic Genres: Descriptive Analysis

The problem of defining and classifying genres has been an issue of paramount importance in the history of folklore research. Indigenous interpretations of a particular genre, and why a particular tale belongs not to one genre but another are major issues. The researcher's ability to look beyond surface consensus helps in defining each ethnic prose genre. However, using local classifications is not without its problems. Native definitions and practice of the genres are not separated by definite and sharp boundaries. Some tales find themselves in more than one genre at a time.

Borana categorize their prose narratives into three genres: the *duri-duri* (children's tales), the *mamaksa* (adults' tales, including proverbs and folktales) and the *arga-ageti* (myths and legends). The purpose of this chapter is to define the nature of Borana ethnic genres briefly, because ensuing discussions on performance and communication are not otherwise possible.

The *duri-duri*

The *duri-duri* narratives consist of tales exclusively performed by children of about seven to fifteen – at which ages they are active performers. The term *duri-duri* means literally 'a long, long time ago' and in folklore is employed to indicate the unknown past. *Duri* means simply 'in the past' and here in the children's tales the doubling of the word *duri* is meant to stress the removal in time and space to the period when the world was different from today's – the period when animals and objects talk and interact among themselves like humans do. The *duri-duri* refers to a totally different space–time and the stories told cannot be replicated in the world we know.

Each tale begins with the phrase, 'It is said that a very long time ago (*duri-duri jedhen*),' which gives the impression that the story is set in a time when the realities of the world were distinct from the present. The phrase serves as a cue which tunes the minds of the audience to a referent world that can no longer be understood in terms of the world they experience.

To the children the *duri-duri* is simply 'a story told by children', which might be about how Fox fooled Hyena or how Hobgoblin came to eat people and got killed. It is difficult to be sure of conscious interpretation but the children consistently perceive the genre as humorous tales in which the small animal outwits the bigger. Children can differentiate between a tale that is *duri-duri* and one that is not, which may lead us to examine what they recognize in the *duri-duri*.

The *duri-duri* has many distinguishing features that set it apart from the other genres; tales are largely unified by subject matter, style, type and treatment of characters and structure. However, not all the unifying features are to be identified in every tale in the genre; not all the recorded tales are on the same theme or structurally of one type. But there are sets of themes, structures and characters that are manifested in the great majority of tales. Thus, viewed analytically, they serve as essential unifying factors. A tale collected from and known to a group of children becomes *duri-duri*.

The ensuing formal and thematic descriptions deal with inherent dominant characteristics shared by the majority of tales, and also takes into account the rare exceptions in the hope of revealing the nature of the *duri-duri* as a whole.

Themes and Types of Characters

Tales in the *duri-duri* are of varied themes with equally varying types of characters, ranging from lifeless objects and animals to humans. The tales can be categorized according to what they are about and whom they are about. The two become directly related when certain types of character are associated with specific themes. For example, there are trickster tales which still remain the same whether the characters are humans or animals. On the other hand, tales about hobgoblin, due to the presence of the character of hobgoblin, become of different content from the other groups. Therefore, thematic classification is not only based on what the tale is about but also relies on type of character, that is when a particular character is associated with a set of specified contents. In this way the major themes of the *duri-duri* are classified as: Trickster Tales, Hobgoblin Tales and Rescue Tales.

Trickster Tales

The majority of children's tales are trickster tales, about both animal and human characters, in which the trickster hero outwits or destroys rivals and partners. In the animal tales the trickster or the sly one, which is almost always Fox[4], deceives the dupes or causes their death in order to acquire their possessions. It is only rarely that other animals such as monkey or goat

---

4 For a full account of Fox in the folktales of the Gabra, who are Borana-speaking neighbours of the Borana see Kassem (1984); and *Africa*, 1986, 56.2, 193–209.

play the role of the sly. Such animal tales are found all over the world. They are 'the most popular and well known type of African narrative among many European collectors and readers', partly because, 'they fitted in with certain preconceptions about ... the supposed "childlike mentality" of Africans' (Finnegan, 1970: 353).

The trickster hero uses various ploys to serve its purpose, which are repeated many times over with variations. When the trickster is faced with many rivals, it deals with them one at a time. In D1 Fox causes the death of five of her friends and finally dispossesses them of all their cattle. When the dupe is only one, the trickster deceives it many times, whether the trickster is animal or human. Except in a few cases, the trickster embarks on its business motivated by nothing other than covetousness. One exception is the human trickster tale, D8, where the hero gets revenge against his brothers who killed his only steer. But even here the hero does not stop at revenge but proceeds to beguile other innocent people.

The dupes are often the bigger animals, such as the lion, elephant and hyena, while the sly is mostly the little fox. Somewhat similarly with the human trickster tales, it is the child or the youngest brother that outwits the grown-ups (see D8, D9 or D10). The portrayal of the characters is vivid and consistent, especially with the animal tales. Fox is depicted as clever and wily, and always exploits the weaknesses of her partners. Hyena is foolish and greedy. In D1 Fox proposes to Hyena, 'Let's eat Lion's calf.' They kill Lion's calf and she drinks only the blood while the hyena eats the flesh. Later when Lion finds out the crime, Fox incriminates Hyena. But when Hyena denies involvement, Fox says, 'Beat us and you will know the truth.' Lion beats Fox and nothing happens. When he beats Hyena the calf's intestine is discharged through his mouth and Lion kills him. Fox in this way exploited Hyena's greed to destroy him and inherit his cattle. Lion is depicted as brave and it is his bravery that is exploited by the trickster. In D4 Monkey shows Lion his reflection in a river saying, 'This is the one that took your shoes,' and Lion gets drowned attempting to fight his reflection. In D1 Fox rolls down a large stone wrapped with a hide and tells Lion that it is his ox. Lion gets killed trying to stop the rolling stone.

One important feature of the trickster tale is that the trickster hero always emerges successful, with all his intentions accomplished. Even when found out and captured, Fox still manages to escape before punishment is carried out.

Hobgoblin Tales

Tales about Hobgoblin constitute the second dominant group. The hobgoblin *(bulgu)* is a mythical character – a man-eating monster of human appearance. Tales about hobgoblin generally tell how it killed or tried to kill a member of a family and how, finally, it was killed. Hobgoblin, unlike trickster, is always punished for its act. The monster may manage to seize its

victim, or even succeed in killing it, but the monster's intentions are not carried out to completion by the time it is killed. A typical example is D12,
where hobgoblin comes to a woman whose husband is away. He asks her to
choose whether he should devour her or her heifer and dog. She chooses the
latter and sends for her husband. By the time the husband comes riding by
on his horse, the villain is preparing to 'fry' the wife. So the husband kills it.
Tales in this category always depict humans against hobgoblin. The villain
gets hold of its victims when they are alone, in the absence of other members of the family. In a few cases hobgoblin is presented as living with
humans. In D11 hobgoblin has a human wife whose sister is also living with
them. One day he sends the sister away and kills his wife. Then he tries to
make his sister-in-law eat his wife's flesh. However, the sister finds out and
later gets revenge by burning him to death.

Structurally the hobgoblin tales can take a number of slightly differing
courses, but initial success and eventual defeat on the part of the villain, and
revenge on the part of the human characters, are the essential features of the
tales.

Rescue Tales

Another major theme of the *duri-duri,* but less prominent than the two discussed above, is the theme of rescue. In tales of this theme, we see the troubled character wandering in search of help or offering something to acquire
help in exchange. The composition of characters occurs in any conceivable
form – humans, animals and objects interacting freely. The character in
search of help or the one who is about to be rescued undergoes many failed
attempts before finally acquiring the needed help. In D19 a boy throws the
squirrel's seashell into a river. Squirrel goes to the boy's father and asks him
to make his son retrieve the shell. When the father refuses, she goes to the
gazelle and begs it to graze the father's harvest to avenge her. Gazelle refuses.
Squirrel then asks hunter to shoot Gazelle and hunter refuses. Squirrel goes
on like this until finally she comes across Hyena who complies with her
demand. Here Hyena, as in the trickster tales, is characterized as greedy.
Similarly in D18 Coffeecup asks Camel to help her friend who is in trouble.
Camel says she has a duty to attend to. Coffeecup goes to a man and asks
him to solve the camel's problem so that Camel will be free to help her. The
man presents another problem. It goes on like this until finally she succeeds.

In cases where the troubled character does not wander in search of help,
say a character trapped in a cave or a well, the would-be helpers come to the
one in trouble. For instance, in D17 a man is trapped in a well. Many animals come, one after the other, to the place where the man is and ask him
for water. He interrogates each one, asking if they know how to summon
help before allowing them to drink. Many are turned away before the bird
who knows what to say comes and summons rescuers.

These are the major themes and types of character in the *duri-duri*. However, there are other themes, which are not found widely. For example, the theme of marriage is rare. In this respect, the stories of the defiant girl, Sule, in D20 and D22, and of the poor prince, in D23, are rare exceptions. In D20 Sule marries Lion. When the father objects and kills Lion she becomes very sad and refuses to be seated. As a consolation her father bids her to sit on Lion's hide. When she sits on it, the hide magically flies upwards (to where her husband is). At this point the etiological explanation adds: the sound of the flying hide became thunder, her shining teeth became a flash of lightning and her wedding sceptre became the rainbow. Though this tale is rendered with the characteristics of children's tales, it stands out distinctively for its subject matter and mythical element. (It is found in a different version as an adult's tale in A2.) In the other tale Sule's brother wants to marry a girl as beautiful as his sister. But he cannot find one. Then his father advises him to marry his sister Sule. Sule finds out this and runs away. She beseeches a very tall tree to become small and once she is on top, it assumes its original size. When all members of her family come one after the other and beg her to climb down, she refuses.

The story of the poor prince, D23, also deals with marriage. Prince goes to another country disguised as a poor person. There the King's youngest daughter chooses him for a husband. The King becomes furious and treats both his daughter and son-in-law badly. Prince uses his magic horse to perform many feats and finally reveals his true identity.

This discussion on theme and type of characters aims to give a general picture of the content of the *duri-duri* to serve as an introduction to the next sections. It would be difficult to raise issues of tone, style and structure without prior knowledge of the type of tales we are dealing with. It also helps to examine the relationship between theme and style and the limited types of themes.

Style

The styles of composition and structure of the text are important aspects of the *duri-duri* for they constitute the greater part of its essence. The stylistic analysis looks into the major forms of structural organization which further explain the nature of the genre. It also deals with the methods of execution and the premises which are found to be at the heart of the *duri-duri*.

The style of the *duri-duri*, in terms of its overall textual composition, is mainly repetitive and episodic. This is particularly true of the trickster and rescue tales, and also to some extent of the hobgoblin tales. The trickster tricks one character after another, or one character repeatedly and the story progresses from one scene to another. Each episode is complete and can stand as an anecdote by itself. That is why short and long versions of the same tale can be obtained, when narrators leave out some episodes or bring in extra ones from 'other' tales. For instance, D1 contains six characters and five episodes in which Fox deals with each character in turn. Fox deceives Elephant on three occasions (D2), Hyena on four occasions (D3), each of which forms an episode. A trickster tale has at least three episodes, either only loosely interconnected or not connected at all. Often, except for the first two, the rest are repetitions with variations.

Episodes are built on two bases. One variation is when the hero is involved with one partner; he outwits it twice or thrice until finally he is found out. If the trickster is found out a chase begins. He is captured, then escapes. This can also be subjected to repetition, as happens three times in D8. The second way of episode building occurs when the hero is engaged with many characters, one at a time. In such cases, the aim of the hero could be eliminating its rivals one by one (D1, D6), or exploiting opportunities as they are available one after the other, as in D9, D5 or D8. The wily Didd Flinch, D9, first deceives his friends, then Hyena, then a farmer and finally some merchants on different occasions. Sometimes these types of episodes become mere repetitions of the same incident with different characters. She-goat, D6, betrays a son, a mother and a father in exactly the same way, one after the other. Sule, D22, who refuses to climb down a tree, deals in similar ways, turn by turn, with five members of her family. In the hobgoblin tale, D15, the same incidents are repeated in the villain's encounter with four different characters at different times.

There are styles of composition in which groups of episodes are combined with other groups to form one tale. For example, D21, two sisters abandoned by their father find themselves in hobgoblin's house. While the wise sister escapes, the foolish one ends on the monster's plate. After relating this incident, the tale proceeds with another long story about the wise sister. Occasionally the two parts are presented as separate tales. In D5, a he-goat wanders from place to place challenging other animals to wrestle with him until finally Fox tricks him causing his death. The tale continues taking Fox as its heroine. In the ensuing episode a chicken eats a piece of meat that Fox has put aside. Fox demands more and more compensation and the story turns into a trickster tale. A third episode comes in when a snake takes away Fox's camel and Fox claims back her property. In this last episode, the tale manifests elements of a rescue tale. This tale is a combination of two groups of episodes and one anecdote. In D2, Fox deceives Elephant three times and escapes when Elephant is about to punish her. After the escape she comes to Wasp and manages to kill him and eat the food he has been preparing. The episode after the escape sometimes stands as a tale by itself; and forms part of another tale in others.

As most of the animal characters in the *duri-duri* manifest consistent characteristics, the combination and borrowing of episodes can easily take place. Harold Scheub speaks of a relatively similar practice about the Xhosa *ntsomi* performance. Although the *duri-duri* and the *ntsomi* are quite different forms of literature, they both use devices such as repetition, songs and interlocking of episodes, which arrange and re-arrange the many images and image segments of the tradition into a variety of *ntsomi*-performance. The *duri-duri* shares some of the characteristics of the *ntsomi*, which has, 'a vast number of episodes that are often interchangeable in a variety of narrative plots' (Scheub, 1977: 40–1).

Tales about hobgoblins are slightly different in style and structure from the other types, tending to form a class of their own. However, the fact that occasionally a hobgoblin tale can manifest some structural features of a trickster tale has to be kept in mind (see D15). On the whole they are composed as a tight plot, and separate episodes are less prevalent. The plot generally develops from the introduction of the villain through to the villain's death.

Comparatively speaking, these tales exhibit some structural elements of the European fairy tale. Propp's functions, such as Absentation (I), Interdiction (II), Violation (III), Trickery (VI), Complicity (VII), Villainy (VIII), Spatial Transference (XI), Struggle (XVI), Exposure (XXVII) and Punishment (XXX) can be found in some hobgoblin tales. (Propp, 1968.) Taking tale D13 as an example for comparison: the husband leaves home (I) warning his wife not to open the door for anyone (II). Hobgoblin comes and persuades her to admit him (VI). She lets him in (III, VII). Then hobgoblin buries her alive (VIII), and when the husband comes, he masquerades as the wife. A cow reveals the buried wife and the identity of the villain is known (XXVII). Finally the husband kills hobgoblin (XVI, XXX). In another instance, tale D12, the husband departs to visit relatives (I). Hobgoblin comes to the wife, devours the cattle and threatens her (VIII). She sends for her husband, who comes riding his rare-breed horse (XV), then he kills the monster (XVI, XXX).

Even from these two examples it can be observed that, of Propp's 31 functions, at least ten can be applied to the *duri-duri* hobgoblin tales. Some functions which are absent in one tale can appear in another. Even if some faint similarities are traceable the attempt here is not to equate the two separate types of tale, but only to show how hobgoblin tales can be stylistically distinct from the types discussed earlier. It is the fact that the villain is killed in the end that essentially distinguishes it from the other types and, to some extent, dictates the kind of structure shown above. However, as was stated earlier, in spite of structural differences between villainy (VIII), and death of the hobgoblin (XXX), a tale can employ stylistic elements of trickster and rescue tales. This further shows the unity of the *duri-duri* beneath its diversity. Another great unifying feature of the *duri-duri* is language, in particular the songs which are part of the style of the *duri-duri*.

Language: Recited Verses

The type of language considered here is that which appears in the tales as constant, unaffected by the skill and style of the narrator. The language of the *duri-duri* varies from one narrator to the other. However, as the performers are children, the language employed is plain language such as is used by children in their formal speech. What is special about the verse is that it must be delivered uniformly, and be unaffected by the narrator's style.

The verses are sung during narration and, from the performance point of view, are songs with varying rhymes. From a textual point of view, they are part of the language of the narratives, and their characteristics and significance need to be discussed.

The verses are unique features of the *duri-duri* and form one of its major hallmarks. Their presence in individual tales is so widespread and important that at times they form the main essence of a tale. Except in the human trickster tales, verses are found in all the tale types. Even in tales that are regarded as without verses, there will be two or three lines which, during performance, are delivered in a poetic rhythm distinct from the prose lines.

The verses are varied in nature and function. Some are short, some are long. Some are repetitive and others appear only once. They serve varied functions, from being dialogue between characters to carrying concealed messages. A discussion of their nature and significance uncovers their relation to a tale.

The first type of verses is repetitive. Each repetition builds on the last, adding a line or two, thus carrying the plot forward. As the repetitions are separated only by a few prose lines, they form the main interest of the tale. In such cases the verses are employed to present sequences of actions. For instance in D18, when Coffeecup finds her friend's ear hooked on a thorn, she searches for a rescuer. First she goes to camel, but when camel tells her that she is on her way home to suckle her baby, Coffeecup goes to a man and asks him to milk camel so that camel would be free to help her. The man presents another problem and she searches for another character who would solve the man's problem. Coffeecup narrates in verse the whole story to each would-be helper; and the tale goes on building up. After brief expository prose lines, the verses recited by Coffeecup are:

> Camel, Camel!
> Hare and I went to visit friends
> Hare strayed on the thorny way
> Her ear got hooked on a thorn
> I was unable to unhook it
> Camel, please relieve her.

Camel says, 'I can't, I have to suckle; my breast is overflowing.' Then Coffeecup goes to Man and says:

Man, Man!
Hare and I went to visit friends
Hare strayed on the thorny way
Her ear got hooked on a thorn
I was unable to unhook it
I asked Camel to unhook it
She said my breast is overflowing
Man please milk her.

Man then says, 'But I don't have a milking pot.' Coffeecup goes to Milkingpot – and the verse builds up. The repetition and sequence of events builds in this way as Coffeecup goes to various other characters and finally to Blacksmith. Thus the verse progresses from the six lines at the start to twenty at the end, as a result of six repetitions with additions.

The raising of the number of lines with each repetition is designed to show the worsening situation of the heroine. She needs to relate all that she has undergone to each character because events are interlocked. Camel is reputed to deal with thorn, (it feeds on thorny tree branches) and she is the only one fit for the mission. Therefore, camel's problem has to be solved at all costs. Similar phenomena are also observed in D5 and D19.

In the *duri-duri*, the switch to verses often occurs when a character sends an important message, gives a warning or interdiction, or expresses its plight. However, the verses do not always attain a heightened effect as in the example mentioned above; their purpose and nature come in different forms. What are termed as verses of message – which can be repetitive or not – describe the situation in which the sender finds itself. The language of the sender, especially in the hobgoblin tales, becomes less plain than that normally found in the prose. In D12, a wife who is endangered by Hobgoblin sends the following message to her husband:

[You Boran take this message.]
My name is Bokro, his name is Sarmo
His horses are seven kraals
His goats are seven kraals
His horse knows how to swim
My heart knows remembrance.

The reference to the number of goats and horses of her husband is to indicate that he is rich, and all his possessions are in danger of being destroyed. When she says, 'His horse knows how to swim,' the wife is making known to the messenger that her husband is in Dirre, across the Dawa river, and has to come soon. The last line, 'my heart knows remembrance,' is an emphatic way of expressing that she is badly in need of him. Such a level of obscurity in concealing messages cannot be found widely, but senders prefer not to express messages and warnings in direct language.

In D13 a father finds out that the character who is disguised as his wife is Hobgoblin. Then he urges his son, Wariyo, who is farther ahead travelling with Hobgoblin, to kill the hobgoblin. He shouts:

> Wariyo, Wariyo!
> Prevent the saddle from leaning
> Prevent the mother on the horse from going
> Thrust a spear on the horse
> That thing is beast.

The father warns the son not to let the saddle lean, which means not to allow the person on the horse to dismount or escape. The boy hearing this, when told to thrust a spear on the horse, realizes that 'the mother on the horse' has to be speared. The father travelling far behind tells his son in a rather indirect way to kill the monster. Similarly, in D13, a husband who warns his wife not to lose her guard says:

> Don't chew tree gum
> Don't make bracelets
> Don't weave the base of a tray

In a way he tells her not to divert her attention to playful things (chewing gum), not to be absorbed by herself (bracelets) and not to be occupied by housework.

Such indirectness in the language of the verses is often found in the hobgoblin tales. The need seems to come from the compulsion to speak in a language hobgoblin cannot understand. Though the monster is portrayed as the speaker of the language of men, the fact that he is not a human being seems to be taken into account.

We find verses employed in the form of dialogue. These are short, repetitive and rather direct, as in formal speech. In D22 Sule, the girl who ran away from home, deliberates with members of her family one by one. Each begs for her forgiveness and to each she states her refusal. Her mother comes and says:

> Sule, Sule!
> Sule of the beautiful neck
> Sule of iron woman's staff

Let's go together, be my companion
We will part with a farewell
Sule, please climb down.

Sule replies:
Mother, mother!
Once you were my mother
Now you are my husband's mother
I will not climb down for you.

This pattern is repeated five times in a dialogue with five family members. Repetitive verses along this line, or in a slightly different manner, are found in a number of tales.

Though it is quite evident that verses (or songs) play a major role in the *duri-duri*, it is difficult to deduce a formula that can indicate at which point they enter the narrative. Their importance varies in degree from constituting a major part of a tale to playing a marginal role; not to mention tales in which they are totally absent. But from general observation it can be seen that verses occur when very important and emphatic utterances are made. It could be said that the prose narrative switches to verse at a crucial point in a tale and the verse constitutes the main issue around which the narrative revolves. With some tales, one can only understand the whole story by looking at the verses. In D17, the sparrow which is sent to summon help cries:

The warriors campaigned
They went to a far country
They went to a country they didn't know
The warriors ate dog
Makk ate wild turnip
He is in a water well
He is alive
Go to him
With a horned ram and a cow
With a bullock and heifer
With an old man and woman
With a knife and a rope.

Even though these lines appear in the text toward the middle of the narrative, they contain very important information about the narrative. They might be said to encapsulate the kernel of the story. The verse, with its three repetitions, forms the core image of the tale. It can easily be memorized and form the main cue by which the story is remembered.

In the final analysis, even if a single and consistent function of these verses is not discernible and their formal feature is of varied nature, they remain a vital element of the form and its appeal for the children. The verses are primarily songs, and form part of the stylistic feature of the *duri-duri* when interconnected repetitive actions are presented. They are essential to the form. As songs they do not have separate existence out of the tale they belong to. A verse and its content bear a logical relationship with the rest of the tale. In some cases they are the tale itself.

Why some tales are without songs remains unexplained. But with the *duri-duri* everything is not the same everywhere. The major formal features are not found to be shared by every tale. The figures in the trickster tales are predominantly animals; but there are also human tricksters. Hobgoblin tales are structurally different from rescue tales, and yet there are hobgoblin tales with the styles of trickster tales, such as D15. Thematically D5 and D18 are not the same, but both are composed in the same style of 'verse build-up'. Tales may have songs, but the songs are of varied nature and rhyme. And there are tales with no songs. The trickster and the hobgoblin tales could be thematically and structurally different, but both types can have songs.

The *duri-duri*, though a distinct ethnic genre, do not show consistent similarity in theme, type of characters, style and form of language. And yet tales of different structures can show similarities in theme and type of characters. Two tales may have nothing in common; but with a third, both can display a point of convergence. Such are the connecting threads that run throughout the tales in the *duri-duri* and thus unify the genre.

The *mamaksa*

The term *mamaksa* is an ethnic taxonomy and, as a local genre of folklore, comprises a range of items from folktales and anecdotes to proverbs. *Mamaksa*, the term, is a rather ancient word whose origin and meaning seem to have been lost. Only a few 'learned' men are willing to trace its etymology. According to some, the term is derived from a combination of the words *amma* (now, or let's) and *akkasaa* (like it). According to others, the root word is *akeeke* (signify, imply) or *akkeesse* (impersonate, imitate). Today the term does not generally evoke any meaning other than denoting a form of folklore. The few men who furnished closely similar explanations stressed its illustrative quality. Presumably the *mamaksa* can be defined as 'an instance' or 'to liken'. It is apparently a case of deliberation and it draws a parallel or substantiates and comments on a situation or behaviour.

The reality of the *mamaksa* poses a difficulty in rendering it in an equivalent English word or standard analytic term. To begin with, besides being a narrative in the order of the folktale, it also includes proverbs, which are non-narrative and non-prose. Secondly, even the prose-*mamaksa* cannot be translated simply as folktale because the Borana have the *duri-duri*, which by definition is folktale. These two genres represent two different worlds that cannot possibly be served by the same term.

The *mamaksa*, it was said, consists of proverbs and prose narratives. These subdivisions are made only for analytic purpose, or for elucidation. The speakers do not make any conscious differentiations on formalistic grounds.

The prose-*mamaksa*, which we will discuss here, contain tales that sum up the values and beliefs of the society. Telling right from wrong, expressing wisdom, formulating conduct rules, and generally bringing the members into contact with the cultural reality they are born into and live in are the themes of *mamaksa*.

The reason why the Borana categorized proverbs and folktales into one genre is fairly clear. For them the categorization is mainly based on meaning and function. The proverb and the narrative part of the *mamaksa* are both used in the same way and for the same purpose. Both serve as common images with which one reasons and propagates valid ideas. Like proverbs, the narratives are used only in association with speech occasions or cases of deliberation.

In a descriptive analysis of the *mamaksa*, the features that help to explain it, by and large, are form and style. Searching for a unifying thread along thematic lines does not give a satisfactory result. Though there are cases where theme and structure relate, one may find more than one theme in a tale, and there are numerous themes in the *mamaksa* as a whole. Pursuing a description drawing on type of characters does not take us far either. Whoever the characters of the *mamaksa* may be, tales do not wholly dwell on the characters' identity, but aim at some kind of statement of truth or the essence of truth or morality. The *mamaksa* is predominantly engaged in presenting values, accepted rules of conduct and conventional wisdom. The way these concepts are rendered becomes a question of style, structure and language.

In grouping the tales, three basic divisions of *mamaksa* may be considered. These, for convenience, are termed as: morality tales, illustrative tales and anecdotes of speech. Morality tales portray good and evil; illustrative tales revolve around one aspect of character traits; anecdotes of speech differ from illustrative tales only because they focus on words rather than visual qualities.

Morality Tales

What distinguishes the morality tale from the other two types is not the injunction of a moral lesson; the illustrative tale too makes a moral point The distinguishing factor is structure. The morality tale follows a unified direction from the villain doing harm to the helpless victim, to his exposure and punishment by supernatural means. These functional elements are lacking in the illustrative tales.

Function in Vladmir Propp's words, 'is understood as an act of a character, defined from the point-of-view of its significance for the course of the action' (Propp, 1968: 21). The morality tale contains eight basic structural functions as follows:

I. Initial Situation or Exposition
Morphologically the initial situation is not a function but it plays an important role in the narrative. Whenever a narrative starts by setting backgrounds and initial situations, it always serves to enhance the moral message. For example, in M9, the villain gives the victim, who is his servant, a heifer. This heifer, for which the victim cares so much, breeds and populates the pen and the villain retracts his word and claims the cattle, which helps to enhance both the gravity of the villainy and the pains of the victim. The initial situation may also set the relationship or the status of the villain and the victim. When they are brothers as in M5, or poor and rich as in M4, it serves to strengthen the moral. Another purpose of the initial situation is to state how the victim came to acquire the property the villain covetously wants to possess or destroy. The object of contention is always the dearest possession of the victim. Therefore, even if it does not affect the structure of the tale, the initial situation is nevertheless an important morphological element.

II. Villain Wants to Possess What Belongs to the Victim or Wants to Harm Victim. (malice)
The motive of the villain is known:

1. Jealousy. M4 – The rich brother is jealous of the only ox owned by his poor brother.
2. Selfishness. M1 – Evil wants to be the sole owner of a camel which is collectively owned.
3. Covetousness. M2, M3, M6 – Villain wants to acquire what rightly belongs to the victim.

III. The Villain Makes a Move to Disinherit, Implicate or Deceive the Victim. (villainy)
This is the most important function in a tale and is where the real complication of the tale begins. Here the villain:

1. Destroys rivals. M3.
2. Denies what he has done or retracts. M9, M10.
3. Falsely accuses victim to dispossess or harm him. M5.
4. Claims what does not belong to him. M11.
5. Commits deception with malicious intent. M4.

IV. Victim is not in a Position to Prove his Innocence, Defend his Right or Check on Villain's Claim. (helplessness)

1. Victim has no witnesses to prove innocence when villain falsely accuses or claims what belongs to victim: M3, M5, M6, M7.
2. Victim is not in a position to validate villain's claim nor to discover villain's hidden motive.
   M4 – The rich man tells his brother to kill his only ox and to sell the hide in a land where a hide is worth a fortune.
   M8 – When a man dies the villain goes to the deceased's family and claims that the deceased owed him money.

V. Victim is Deluded, Convicted or Disinherited. (misfortune)
Here the villain's malicious or covetous intent is carried out successfully. This means harm is inflicted on the victim who is either dispossessed or banished out of the land.

VI. Misfortune Befalls Villain which Leads to Exposure. (exposure)
The villain's misfortune is caused by non-human witnesses associated with the crime or the crime scene. In M2, a rock he has been sitting on seizes the villain's buttocks; in M6, a lizard at the crime scene enters the villain's belly. Relief does not come until confession. When these witnesses cause the death of the villain, they do so in a way that exposes and proves his guilt. In M7, in which the villain has falsely accused the victim of raping his wife, the genitalia of the villain sink into the ground and he dies. See also M3, M5, and M8.

VII. Villain is Punished. (punishment)
Punishment of the villain is exacted in various ways:

1. The agents that exposed the villain cause his death or, if he suffers short of death and gets the chance to confess, he will give up what he illegally obtained. M2, M3, M5, M6, M7.
2. Victim personally punishes the villain. This happens when a victim receives help through function VI, which relieves his misfortune and then proceeds to revenge. M4, M9.
3. Villain is punished when he tries to reproduce the help required by the victim. M1 – The villain descends into a well where the victim acquired a fortune and there he dies.

VIII. Victim is Re-instated. (victory)
Once the villain is exposed and punished, the victim's innocence is established and he regains what is lost – be it status or property. In case of property the victim can acquire more than he lost.

Of the eight basic structural functions described the largest number a
tale can contain is seven. When the victim whose misfortune is relieved
through *help* personally punishes the villain, the *exposure* function
becomes absent.

In the morality tale, structure and the recurrent motifs directly affect the
meaning and shape it. They are employed to generate the desired message effectively. It was said that the first element, the initial situation, serves to strengthen
the moral, to give background information and to show that what the villain
desires is the dearest possession of the victim. The relationship between the
victim and the villain is as kinship or as master and servant; poor against rich or
brother against brother enhances the villainy. The local interpretation and the
cultural symbolism portray the society as members of one family.

An act of villainy is not supported by any convincing motive. The villain
embarks on his plan motivated by nothing other than malice and greed. The
victim is always helpless. He has no means to oppose nor discredit the villain. The only thing he does is invoke God. This is a recurrent motif. As the
victim is helpless, only God comes to his aid; and poetic justice is exacted.
The Borana say proverbially *Cubbuun tokko dhaqab, cubbuun tokko sirri-
iqa* (There is no evil act that remains unpunished, sooner or later).[5]

The manifestation of divine intervention is always realized through non-
human beings like stone, or animals. These agents are the only beings or
things who have first-hand information of the case besides the two litigants.
For instance in M6, lizard, who was on the tree to which the victim tied his
cow, slips into the belly of the villain through his anus and tortures him into
confession. Such kinds of intervention are effected, logically enough, by
agents (nonhuman) which have witnessed the crime. This could be interpreted as the omnipresence of God. Even the hero who personally revenges
the villain has to first receive God-given help.

Thus, these vital morphological elements and recurrent motifs show the
relationship between meaning and structure. Tales that bear similar structures and motifs operate with the same 'distinct fields of meaning'.

Illustrative Tales

Tales in this category are generally short in length. Their content illustrates
the virtue of positive values and the consequences of misconduct. The illustrative tales differ from the morality tales in meaning and structure. Even if
we find here too an evil and a good character, the former does not succeed
in carrying out his evil plan. Poetic justice meted out through divine intervention is a nonexistent element. For one thing, the hero is not helpless as is
the case with the morality tale. In the illustrative tale, he has the means and
the wisdom to defend himself and disgrace the evil doer.

---

5 Cf Ton Leus *Mammaassa Booranaa*, 1999: 61.

The illustrative tales concentrate on the individual's character traits. They demonstrate the moral and personal virtue of a character; positively, when he is depicted as behaving according to a culturally valid way, and negatively when he ceases to behave well. The virtues and follies involved are not moral aspects, but personal traits such as wisdom and ignorance. The single most recurrent aspect of virtue is wisdom. In M3 the rats, which were about to fall prey to cats, ask their elders for advice and escape unharmed. In M5 the seven monkeys, which were about to be overwhelmed by the many baboons, trick them into retreat. When the coward, the brave, and the wise came across the deadly hobgoblin, it is the wise that saves them all in M20.

When misconduct is demonstrated, the cause is generally ignorance, and the fault of the hero in failing to heed the culturally valid rule of conduct. In M12, soldiers disobey their commander and lose the case they brought against him. Baboon receives a nasty sting when he tries to attack bee who has been nice to him (M14). In M21 an impatient man is denied water for his cattle.

The illustrative tale is a demonstration of statements of belief. For example, in tales about wisdom the statement is, 'wisdom saves the day'. When it is lacking, the reverse becomes true. A tale illustrates these truths by taking examples and focusing on the way wisdom or lack of it is manifested. In other cases, the subject of illustration can be a moral virtue or belief which work at a grander scale, beyond the level of personal quality. In such cases, a tale substantiates an assertion that involves members of the society at large. In M11 a brave defiant warrior who can overpower many strong men becomes weak after being seduced by a woman into making love for the first time. The assertion is also clear here. In the tale about the power of harmony, M19, one man points to an empty field and speaks about a nonexistent prey. His hunt mate, without seeing anything agrees, 'I see it too.' And the prey pops into existence. For the purpose of contrast a third character is introduced who disagrees with them, impeding a repeat of the success. The point is 'harmony can work miracles'. These examples are illustrations of the society's beliefs and assertions.

The subjects of explanation in animal tales are the animals' unique behaviour or physical appearance, such as why baboon has a bald patch on its buttocks or why rats live in holes, as in M13 and M14. The tales, in the guise of furnishing etiological explanations, communicate moral and truth values. The explanations serve as a vehicle to transmit the moral. For example, baboon got its bald patch while rubbing his buttocks on the ground in an attempt to reduce the pain of the bee-sting he received while attempting to steal honey. The subject of explanation is always presented as a consequence of wrong. Though the etiological tales are stylistically similar, they do not operate on the same level of tone. Some are light and jokey. For instance, the he-camel's genitals came to be located in their unusual place because on the day God was distributing reproduction organs camel went past without stopping to collect, so God had to throw them from behind (M17).

On the whole the illustrative tales, in this sub-division, demonstrate
- virtuous personal quality and its reward.
- lack of good judgment and its consequence.
- culturally framed belief or assertion.

Anecdotes of Speech

Anecdote is defined as a short narrative of an amusing, interesting incident. The kind of anecdotes considered here are incidents of verbal utterances and are often presented as what someone has said in a particular situation. They are valued for the expressions made by the speaker.

So far in the analysis of the *mamaksa,* the issue of language has not been raised because in the kind of tales described, the language involved is not different from day-to-day usage. Moreover it varies from narrator to narrator. What makes the anecdote of speech unique is the emphasis on words. These words need to be reproduced verbatim during performance. They appear as a quotation and the exact wording must not be lost since therein lies its greatest merit.

Anecdotes of speech can be important for the truth and wisdom expressed in them, or simply for the clever way of expression. Whatever the content, verbal beauty is what is most important. For example Arero Bosaro, the famous Borana historian and diviner, is said to have quarrelled with his wife and insulted her (see M26). Although the anecdote is an insult, it has become part of Arero's 'legend' for its poetry and imagery. It is impossible adequately to convey the power of the original in English, for Arero exploits words of similar sounds and uses a highly localized imagery (see also the Borana text of M26). In the following snippet we can see the similar-sounding words in the original language. Arero discovered his wife's affair with a morally and physically frail man whom he despises.

> You feeble (*hurra*),
> You [ground] sloth (*lafa hurruma*)
> With bones (*lafee)* like elephant's
> Elephant eater like Wata
> Hovering over Wata like a vulture.

The Wata are said to eat dead animals, which means that the elephant mentioned is dead. The vulture hovering over a Wata is hovering over a carcass. Arero has equated his wife with the Wata and the vulture to say that she is visiting a 'lifeless' man; that her lover is 'dead' as the elephant and despised as the Wata.

Poetic expressions in anecdotes are charged with power. The husband whose wife takes in a lover and refuses to abandon him, sets out to the forest to prove his masculinity against big game (M29). When he returns home after killing a warthog, he chants in the presence of his wife, her lover, and others:

It is smaller than the bull, bigger than the bullock
My hunt-mates failed to identify my warthog
It is larger than the small, smaller than the large
My hunt-mates failed to name my spear
He hadn't asked for her hand
He hadn't paid the bridewealth calf
I failed to say why the womanish man is here.

When the lover hears this he flees away in shame. The brave husband, whose prey and the weapon he killed with defy classification – the man who bewildered his hunt-mates, is bewildered by the presence of a cowardly trespasser at his home. It is not only because the husband has proved his masculinity that the lover goes away, it is rather due to the power of the words. Similarly in M28, the young man who is despised by his age-mate peers for not killing beasts wants to show them his courage and strength. When he sets out for a hunt they follow him. He finds an elephant and charges it gallantly. But when he sees that the elephant is about to overpower him, he expresses poetically his need of help. His words summon the help of the onlookers before whom he has already proved his courage.

In the illustrative tale the utterances of the character who is faced with a problem can be taken as an illustration of wisdom that saves the day. The fact that the speech is composed of striking images and with depth of meaning makes it a demonstration of wisdom. The hero's problem is also solved with it.

In the anecdotes of speech we also find expressions of morality and values. In the story of the elder who enumerates the seven things he hates, people ask him for explanations (M25). He speaks about unaccepted social conduct with a discerning logic and clever turn of phrase. At one point they ask him why he hates a man in his forties who does not separate men who fight. He says:

A man of forty who does not pull apart two men who fight will never come to do it at any age. If he doesn't feel responsible [for the peace and order of his society] at this age he never will in the future.

Generally the *mamaksa* is a tale about the individual's rule of conduct in society. The analytic division into morality tales, illustrative tales and anecdotes of speech is purely formalistic. The users are not cognizant of such formal differentiations. What they are aware of is the fact that the *mamaksa* presents a culturally and socially valid view.

The researcher's attempt to categorize the *mamaksa* according to its formal or stylistic features is initiated by the analytic demand to describe what it looks like – its dimensions. Thematic categorization has been found inadequate for this. Therefore, the tales have to be grouped according to the most binding of the features they show. When this is done the three groups discussed above emerge. Such division, besides enabling us to discuss the *mamaksa* under a few categories, gives a good idea about the nature of the *mamaksa*. The formalistic description is made largely on structural and stylistic grounds. However, these grounds do not equally express every tale. For example, the shorter fables and anecdotes do not respond to a detailed Proppian morphological analysis. It is rather the overall style of composition that unifies and explains them. Therefore, where structural analysis makes sense, as in the elaborate morality tales, Propp's method has been used. Where this method cannot be successfully applied a more defining feature has been sought, such as style and field of meaning. As a whole the categorization or the formalistic description of the *mamaksa* enables us to grasp the genre's general characteristics.

The *arga-ageti*

The term *arga-ageti (argaa dhageetti)* literally means 'what had been seen and what had been heard'. Commonly the words are an expression of the process by which oral tradition is transmitted and preserved. In conventional understanding *arga-ageti* means oral history. When a person is referred to as a man who knows *arga-ageti*, it implies that he has a considerable knowledge of Borana history and tradition which, 'is a source of great concern and the learned men keep track of history to the depth of eight generations' (Asmarom, 1973: 194). As a genre of prose narrative, *arga-ageti* consists of tales that, analytically, can be termed as myths and historical narratives or myths and legends.

The difficulty the folklorist encounters in defining this genre is the disparity between the popularly held concept of the Borana people themselves and the analyst's deduction. In its wider context the society understands *arga-ageti* to mean history, which is mainly about wars, the deeds of Gada leaders and the roots of tradition. But many people are reluctant to think of popular legends as *arga-ageti*. For example, the very popular legends of Dido Gawole the warrior (see A9), or Abanoye[6] (see A8), are simply referred to as *tariki*, which on the face of it could be mistaken for a fourth

---

6 Variant spellings for this well-documented legendary character include Habanoye.

ethnic prose genre. The word *tariki*, which is not an Oromo term but of Arabic origin, means both history and story and may have been introduced into the Borana language in the late nineteenth century. The preference by some for the term *tariki* to describe certain legends is probably explainable. Historical accounts of the distant past concerning the life of the Gada leaders are mastered by very few men. Complete knowledge of Borana history is of great importance to the leaders because of their belief in the influence of history on the present course of events. Borana historians advise the leaders on what they ought to perform, be it ritual or war. These are the men who know *arga-ageti*. The rarity of such men and the rarity of their knowledge have given the genre the status of esoteric lore. On the other hand, some historical narratives about legendary warriors such as Dido Gawole have become very popular. Still, to many, *arga-ageti* is associated with the history of Gada leaders and some legendary figures. To reconcile this disparity a (perhaps unconscious) tendency has developed to separate the popular legends out from this genre. And yet no convincing new genre has been formulated for them, so the use of the term *tariki* – which word being itself a recent introduction to the language – may yet evolve into a new genre, and we may be witnessing that evolution. Andre Jolles maintains that, 'when the conditions for the existence of a genre change, the genre is transformed into a new type which corresponds in meaning to the earlier' (in Ben-Amos, 1982: 76). But there is no firm evidence for this.

Before examining individual tales we should ask why historical narratives and tales with characteristics of myth are categorized together.

Myth is often defined as a religious tale of origin, which is accepted on faith (Bascom, 1965: 9; Thompson, 1946: 9). The action takes place in the time before the world took its present shape and accounts for how certain things came to be as they are now. However, some scholars insist that all origin tales are not necessarily myths (for instance Finnegan, 1966: 34). In *arga-ageti* there are tales which conform to the widely accepted definitions of myth, such as tales which explain the origins of death (A1), the rainbow (A2), the sacrificial goat (A4) or the origin of the Qallu (A23). But from the point of view of the Borana, what we call myths are historical narratives. The stories of the myth-heroes like Gadayo, A5, who is believed to have founded the Gada tradition, are part of Borana history.

Borana historical narratives at times account for the origin of social and cultural practices. For example, the story of the female leader Abanoye, A8, who is considered a real historical figure, is often cited as an explanation for the supposed deceptive and seductive nature of women; thus the tale resembles both myth and legend.

History is not merely a thing of the past to Borana. As myth explains how the present is shaped, a historical account of great magnitude is also thought to have the potential to shape the future. The Borana conceive

history as a recurring force within a cycle known as *maqbasa*. Asmarom
says, 'The return of historical influence in accordance with *maqbasa* cycles
is a source of great concern for gada leaders' (Asmarom, 1973: 194).
Between two similar *maqbasas* there is a time gap of about 270 years. This
means events 270 years ago can have a direct influence on events today. For
example, A16 is about Wale Wachu the Gada leader (1772–80). The story
of his exile and return is considered as embodying a powerful consequence
(*dhaacci)*, which the current Aba Gada is attempting to avert. To clarify this
point, let us look at a case from Asmarom Legesse's *Gada*, which shows how
a native historian relates history in the framework of *maqbasa*. The native
historian Arero Rammeta explained to Asmarom that the period of Aga Adi
(1936–44) was directly influenced by the period of Abbayi Babbo
(1667–74). Abbayi Babbo was confronted by nine enemies. He married nine
wives, had nine children, he killed nine wild animals and he had nine kraals
of cattle which were all wiped out by disease. 'Everything regarding Abbayi
Babbo happened in nines. We Borana do not like the number nine.' Similarly
during the period of Aga Adi, '[Aga Adi] waged war nine times and ran
away from the enemy nine times. During the gada of Aga Adi, also, nine enemies penetrated Borana' (Asmarom, 1973: 198–9).

Here what happened during the *gada* period of Aga Adi was interpreted
as shaped by events about 270 years ago. In another way an historical narrative about Abbayi Babbo is an origin tale because the major events of Aga
Adi's period were caused and shaped by it. That is why we say the historical narrative, like myth, is an origin tale. Therefore, it is quite possible to say
that the Borana categorized myths and historical narratives together because
they conceive of them as one.

Historical narratives can be regarded as tales about famous individuals
and events, but there are also anecdotes specifically about bygone heroes
and rulers. These are often about what these individuals had done or spoken
in particular situations not connected with their heroic life; such as, what
Arero Bosaro is said to have said about his lackadaisical wife, or how Liban
Wata the Aba Gada once solved a riddle. The fact that such anecdotes are
about famous historical figures does not make them legends and the Borana
generally regard them as *mamaksa*. This is because *arga-ageti* in its historical narrative sense is conceived as deeds of heroes affecting the society at
large. The heroes are instrumental in waging wars and establishing customs.

Historical Narratives

The Legends are predominantly about war heroes who demonstrate unpar-
alleled courage and strength. They result from the Borana's incessant engagement in battles with neighbouring tribes. But the Borana conception of
heroism is not limited to battle. Wisdom and devoutness too are acts of heroism. Heroes are the great warriors (*janna*), the wise (*qaroo*) and the great
leaders (*mo'aa*), and in some instances individuals display a combination of

these qualities. Only brave warriors can rise from the common people to attain undying fame. Malda Doyo (A17), Shanu Qaru (A14), Dido Muke (A11) and Jarso Wada (A20) were heroes who held no public office. The quality of wisdom and leadership are treated as attributes of individuals who are already leaders. For example Liban Wata, the wisest man known to the Borana, and Wale Wachu the godly, are Aba Gadas.

Narratives about war heroes are set in their own time when the hero's remarkable qualities are demonstrated. The stories focus on: early rise, adult exploits and death. It is in relation to these events that the legend of a hero is told. A legend may focus on all three or only one, depending on the remarkable events in the hero's life. For instance the legend of Jarso Wada (A20) is recounted in relation to his death because he is remembered for the battle he fought and died at.

Early Rise: The early life of a hero becomes incorporated in his legend when there is something unique about his rise to heroism, or when as quite a young man he demonstrates signs of greatness. A17 tells how Malda Doyo, the weak boy, turned into a brave warrior. A10.1 and A10.2 tell how Dido Gawole demonstrated considerable wisdom and courage as a youth. A12 tells how Dido Muke avenged Dido Gawole's death at an age when he was thought to be not yet fit to fight battles.

Exploits: The second aspect depicted in a warrior's legend is the heroic deeds he performed in adulthood. There could be one or more stories, depending on the number of great exploits. There are heroes such as Shanu Qaru (A14) whose adventures are limited to what he accomplished in his late middle years.

Death: This becomes memorable when the hero dies an unnatural death, often killed in battle or betrayed into the hands of his enemies. Some heroes, like Jarso Wada, are remembered for nothing but the battle they fought gallantly and died at. Borana are especially concerned about the loss of a hero, remembering him with great anguish and the hero is celebrated for a glorious death more than in any other event of his heroic life A warrior becomes legendary due to the especial circumstances of his death. Enaye, A13, is said to be a strong and good fighter. But his exploits are not worthy enough to make him legendary. He is essentially remembered and became legendary for the circumstance of his death, which was caused by his wife's betrayal.

By contrast, consider Dido Gawole, the most legendary figure in Borana folk literature, of whom many stories are told beginning from his early childhood. Every trivial thing he did has entered the realm of folklore. But, when any male adult is asked to tell a story about Dido he promptly narrates the circumstances of his death. Dido, like Enaye, was betrayed by his wife and, when caught off guard, killed many of his attackers by striking them with calves. It is said that he received so many spear wounds that 'the sky could be seen through his body'. His body shook with such a fury that he sank into the ground.

Myths

Myth has been defined analytically as an origin tale which is believed to be true by the speaker. Origin myths account, in William Bascom's words, for the 'origin of the world, of mankind, or for characteristics of birds, animals, geographical features and the phenomena of nature' (Bascom, 1965: 9). Stith Thompson defines myth in terms of the type of characters as 'tales of sacred beings and of semi-divine heroes and of the origin of all things, usually through the agency of these sacred beings' (Thompson, 1946: 9). The two important subjects of myths are the root of customs and the origin of natural phenomena. A single myth can account for both. For example, A4 explains the creation of beasts and the root of the custom of animal sacrifice. A6 accounts for the origin of sleep and ritual prayer.

All aspects of origin are explained as a result of error made by the characters who deal with God. God is personified in all the myths and is portrayed as both merciful and exacting. The hero often makes mistakes and God punishes him for it. The punishment is expressed as a formation of a previously nonexistent natural phenomenon or aspect of human behaviour. Wayu Bano, A4, challenged God to a power show as a result of which wild beasts were created. The hero in A6 lied to God and sleep came into being. Sule, A2, stood in God's way and the rainbow was created. In the myths about the roots of custom the punished hero admits to his error and recants. Then God offers mercy. The hero will be given a chance to atone for his mistakes through observance of a custom. This is the point where custom originates. Thus Wayu Bano (A4), whose cattle were destroyed by the beasts God created, is made to offer animal sacrifice to demand God's help in times of crisis such as war. Gadayo, who carelessly lost the God-given book, is subjected to perform intestine reading, called haruspication (A5). The hero in A6, as a consequence of whose lie sleep was brought on mankind, is made to perform ritual songs during the night – his sleeping hours. A man spears the man cherished by God and the places where drops of blood fall from the wound become ritual shrines (A7).

The myths operate on the premise of wrong and its consequence, be it an offence of custom or natural phenomena. A result of wrong is transgression against God. An exception to this is the myth (A23) about the origin of the Qallu of the Karrayu clan who is said to have simply descended from heaven.

Common Motifs in Myths
The special characteristics of myths feature in many tales. They are:

Quest: The hero may lack something and departs in search of God in order to obtain it. The object of quest could be wealth as in A4, A5 and A6 or some other thing, such as a union with a dead family member (A2).

Test: The hero comes across a helper who greets, interrogates or tests him. The hero overlooks the helper and fails the test, as in A4 and A6.

Wrong Request: The hero comes across the donor (God) and puts a request with which the donor refuses to comply. In this case asking God for wealth or to stop the rain (A3) is the wrong request.

Help: The hero who has failed the test and whose request is declined is tested again and again by the helper. Finally he does the right thing and the helper advises the hero on how he should behave. The hero may directly go to a helper and ask for advice (A4).

Wrongdoing: The hero offends the donor; for example, in A6 he lies to God before receiving, or the hero challenges God's power after his wish is fulfilled. The wrong can be apparent in many other ways. The hero might violate an interdiction (A1), or behave wrongly when a request is turned down by the donor (A3).

Origin or Consequence: As a result of the wrong done, God proclaims punishment, dictates a new way of living, or a new nature phenomenon originates. For examples, in A1 the result is Death; in A2 Rainbow, Storm and woman's inferiority result; in A3 Sky recedes and Mule becomes sterile; in A4 wild beasts and animal sacrifice come into being. A5 tells of the origin of Gada and intestine reading; A6 tells how sleep and ritual prayer became necessary, and A7 tells of the causes of disintegration of unified people and ritual shrines.

These recurrent motifs may not be present in every tale. I have tried to explain the general nature of tales in *arga-ageti*. From the Borana point of view, the genre is generally conceived as tales about the life of great historical figures. Analytically the tales are found to be historical narratives and myths. In contrast to the genres *mamaksa* and *duri-duri*, *arga-ageti* is not a clearly conceived genre. And opinions differ as to the classification of the tales treated as myths – those about the origin of natural phenomena, such as A2 and A3. Some consider them as *mamaksa* and others as not. The legends of war heroes are not immediately associated with *arga-ageti*. Such confusion is seen much less in regard to the *mamaksa* and the *duri-duri*. One reason for the occasional violation of the *mamaksa/arga-ageti* boundary is performance or usage. During actual usage some narratives in *arga-ageti* are frequently employed to play the role of *mamaksa*. This will be explained more clearly when viewing the narratives in the context of performance.

The descriptive analysis of the ethnic genre, to which this chapter is devoted, has attempted to define the genres both from the user's point of view and the researcher's observation.

Chapter 3

The Narratives in the Context of Folklore Performance

Dell Hymes once described the new direction folklore study has taken as 'the movement from a focus on text to a focus on communicative event' (Hymes, 1971; 43). From the early 1960s a new wave of scholars of folklore have stressed the importance of examining folklore forms within the realities of social interaction and from the perspectives of the actors.

A discussion of the occasion of folktale presentation uncovers the grammar a society has devised for its performance. Occasion dictates the kind of narrative that should be presented and a change in occasion and audience composition could bring about a change in meaning and performance. As Finnegan put it well:

> To ignore these in an oral work is to risk missing much of the subtlety, flexibility and individual originality of its creator and furthermore to fail to give consideration to the aesthetic canons of those intimately concerned in the production and reception of this form of literature (Finnegan,1970: 12).

The most important contribution of the contextual study of folklore is its consideration of the users. The significant 'grammar of folklore' is formulated by the users, and it is only from them that one acquires the grammar along with the code or rules to understand it.

The following two chapters attempt to uncover the rules of communication the Borana formulated for their narratives. The simple question of who should use what reveals the dissemination of narratives on the basis of age and sex. This in turn leads into discussion of why the narratives assume different shapes, who is telling to whom, when where and for what purpose, and why certain narrative genres are the exclusive domains of certain members of the society. These are all complications of the folklore grammar. The users' attitudes to their narratives, the law which governs the use of a certain genre for a certain purpose, explain what they see in their folk-lore forms.

Let us consider the 'artistic canons' which govern usage, the functional importance they attach to tales, the process of composition and the rules to transmit and support. In studying rules of communication we are considering the speaker and his audience. The changing ability of the individual from childhood to old age, the way he or she acquires and builds on repertoire are also points that will be dealt with in relation to Borana prose narratives.

Performance and Occasion

The performance and occasion of use of prose narratives differ from genre to genre, age to age and between genders. There are children's tales performed only by children, and adults' tales performed only by male adults; so genres of narrative need to be considered primarily by identifying the performer.

Children's Tales: The Duri-duri

As has been stated, the *duri-duri* is exclusively performed and listened to by children. In African societies children may tell tales to children. But it is a rare phenomenon to find tales solely owned and performed by children. The only similar practice I have read about is the one recorded among the Dogon. Here there are stories *(elme* or *elume)* told to entertain children, often by the children themselves. These tales are not usually told by adults but by young people while they are herding (Lifchitz as cited by Finnegan, 1970: 365).

The occasions for reciting *duri-duri* occur both during the day and at night. Children of either sex, beginning from the age of about seven, spend the whole day herding the calves, camels and goats not far from their camps. This is expected of almost every child. The children pass the day playing various games both verbal and physical. There is no room for boredom. The sheer quantity of children's games is bewildering; among the many, one is story telling.

When boys reach about thirteen or fourteen years of age, they begin to bear more serious responsibilities. Some of them move far away to herd cattle in distant pastures *(fora)* for months, living on the milk of the cattle they look after. This experience, more than their early childhood days, provides great opportunity to learn and recount tales. Though the nights are mostly occupied by songs which eulogize the cattle, with much use of colourful language, there is still room for tale telling.

The night does not offer opportunities for story telling in equal measure to daytime. Many factors contribute to this. One is that the evening gathering by the fireside is made up of persons of all ages; therefore, the age-mate group feeling among the children is lost. During the night, in the presence of parents and grown-ups who may order the children to do something, a narration can be interrupted. Very rarely, when elders are engaged in serious talks, children may be told to keep quiet; but mostly they cease to play games and listen to the elders instead.

So, the evening session mostly lacks the relaxed mood, group feeling and opportunity to narrate uninterrupted, which are provided by day. There is another reason for performing *duri-duri* more frequently during the day time. There are children's games which are sanctioned culturally not to be played by day. One is riddle, which is never played by day. The explanations the children offer are: 'You will become a fool' or, according to others, 'You will lose your way home if you play riddles in the daytime'. This is what the children say they are told by the elders. However, today, the children pass this rule from one to another and no longer receive it directly from the elders. Nighttime is partly occupied by such games, which are restricted to this occasion only.

Nevertheless, whenever the situation permits, children recount *duri-duri* by the fireside of an evening, when, for example, parents from two or more houses gather in one house and children from the neighbourhood gather in a house the grown-ups have left. This brings in the daytime mood which they are accustomed to. But first we should look into some of the situations that lead the children into storytelling, especially during daytime.

Grazing the cattle is not something that requires the whole attention of the children all the day long; all it takes is to make sure the cattle are nearby and together. During the long sunny season the children gather under the shade of a tree. Someone proposes some kind of game and if agreed it is pursued. Most verbal and physical games have animal characters. These are the same animals that populate the *duri-duri*. So the name of each animal is a reminder in one way or another of a tale in which it is a character. Then, in the middle of a game, one may ask: 'Do you know the *duri-duri* about how the fox fooled the hyena?' Such questions are often put by the older children to the younger ones to test them. Whether the answer is yes or no, what follows is a tale. The one who is asked might tell it, or another child will say he knows, or the one who asked will proceed to tell. At times such questions are asked in order to laugh at children thought to be unable to tell a particular tale correctly. Sometimes, while the children are in the bush an encounter with some animal, naturally a character in tales, will bring to mind a song from a tale. The recital of the verses eventually leads to the story's rendition in full. The factors and cues which initiate the telling session are many, but there need not always be a lead in situation. The children may commence storytelling simply by saying, 'Now let's play *duri-duri*.'

Once the opportunity to start off the story telling occurs, the children might enter into a contest of who knows more or who recounts best. Say the storytelling is started by the senior child asking the youngest. If he tells it well, he could be asked for another or others may demand to be given the opportunity. If he does not tell it well, he is laughed at or if the error is slight he is corrected. A debate on versions can commence too. To avoid the probability of being laughed at, younger children do not start recounting to others until they are sure of having heard a tale enough times to remember it. I have often come across younger children who claim to know no *duri-duri*. The truth is that they are not sure whether they could tell a story properly. It is only towards the age of twelve or thirteen that the child attains perfection along with a rich repertoire.

During the performance of *duri-duri*, what first catches the attention are the style of narration and the audience–narrator relationship; a narrator always begins: 'It is said that a very long time ago...' There is always one person in the audience who is assumed to be the one to whom the narration is addressed, who either comes up willingly or is chosen by the narrator. This is a rule. A narrative is never recounted to an anonymous silent crowd. There must be one person who receives a message. This is also true of the way the Borana speak to each other. When the narrator starts: 'It is said that a very long time ago there was a boy named Didd Flinch' (in D9), the receiver responds: 'It is said so,' or in direct translation, 'They say it is said so' (*jedhan jedhan*). 'It is said that this boy has only a mother.' 'It is said so.' If the narrator continuous the whole narration by finishing each sentence with 'it is said' (in English it would begin each sentence), the receiver will echo, 'It is said so,' throughout the narration. A narrator may prefer to cut out the 'it is said', except at the beginning, and simply narrate. When this happens, the receiver repeats the last word the narrator speaks in each sentence.

The necessity of the response of the receiver, who is assumed to be, or is taken as, the single audience (carrying the rest behind him) is an assurance to the narrator that he is being followed. If for a moment the receiver fails to respond the narrator urges him to follow.

The performance of a *duri-duri* is a very lively dramatic moment. As most *duri-duri* are humorous and witty the narrator tries his best to bring out the humour clearly and draw laughter from the audience. Even if the audience knows the tale and the expression is fast becoming a cliche, the efficiency of the narrator certainly puts an old *duri-duri* into a new light. This is not in terms of meaning but performance. Even though the narrator is seated in most performances he is full of gestures and facial expressions. Important is the impersonation of characters' speech. Villains like hobgoblin, and dupes like hyena and lion are assumed to talk slowly and coarsely. The clever characters talk fast and persuasively to deceive and to demonstrate the sharpness of their wit. The narrator's ability to change his voice according to each character and the situation it is found in, for instance to demonstrate happiness, sadness, fear and so on, is relished and admired by the child audience.

Characters' dialogues are not normally followed by their names. It is mostly the change in voice which tells us who is speaking. Also admired is the narrator's fluency in delivery. The children appreciate their tale when told without any hesitation or loss for words. Especially there are tales such as D5, D18 or D19 which as a rule must be narrated speedily and crisply. Such tales are recited so fast that it requires a sharp ear to catch what is being said. These are tales in which sequences of events are repeated many times and the number of verses build up as the tale progresses. In the following example, D19, the lines of verses have grown from two in the opening verse to eleven at the end through ten times of repetition and progression:

> Cattle refused to trample on Ambush's spear
> Ambush refused to kill the children
> Children refused to kill Rat
> Rat refused to uproot Stump
> Stump refused to cut open Elephant's belly
> Elephant refused to suck Water
> Water refused to extinguish Fire
> Fire refused to burn Hunter's hut
> Hunter refused to shoot Gazelle
> Gazelle refused to graze Aba Garbicha's harvest
> And Aba Garbicha refused to beat his Garbicha into returning my shell.

These lines must be spoken very fast and the right order must be maintained during all the repetitions and progressions. Failure to recite fast and to maintain the right order are signs of a bad narrator. Depending on the gravity of the error it could cost him his 'narratorship.'

The performance of the *duri-duri* incorporates singing. The songs, which vary in length and frequency of repetition, also have different rhymes. Some of them are sung fully, some are half-sung or recited. Although the different songs in different tales have different rhymes, there are no recorded instances of the same song sung with a differing rhyme from narrator to narrator. The recitation is one of the highlights of a *duri-duri* performance. Unlike the tales with song found in many African societies, which are sung in chorus, the songs in the *duri-duri* are sung only by the narrator. The narrator sings with a vivid emotional feeling and becomes so absorbed that he stares at the far distant pastures or closes his eyes and moves to and fro as in dance. It is the prose that brings him once again face to face with the audience. Even the prose lines tend to be delivered with distinct poetic rhythm. This shows how fond the children are of songs.

The tale-telling session ends when the children seem after five or six tales to have had enough of it, or when something happens which interrupts it.

Occasion and composition of the audience directly influence the mode of narration, and depending on these and other factors, the narrator makes up his mind how best to tell the tale as befitting the situation at hand. Whenever there is narrative event a tale is recounted in full. The occasions of performance and the type of participants are well defined. The tendency to select suitable tales, to operate on the text, to elaborating or shortening it depending on the occasion and participants is less prevalent. If some children leave out some episodes, they do it from ignorance and not for some desired effect.

The mood surrounding the performance occasion has a noticeable effect on the narration. If the mood is relaxed, if the children are all by themselves, narration becomes elaborate, full of gestures and facial expressions. But in the presence of strangers and grown-ups the narrator becomes less excited. More importantly songs that should be sung many times are sung only a few times. Even the singing can turn into half-recitation, and the narrator skips some repetitive episodes. Adults do not listen to children's tales; a fact which the children know only too well and their presence causes a subdued mood. A full and lively rendition of a *duri-duri* is only demonstrated when the children are all by themselves, the natural setting for the *duri-duri* performance.

Adults' Tales: Mamaksa *and* Arga-ageti

In terms of performance what unites the two genres is the identity of the performers. Both are performed by male adults. To some extent occasion also unifies them. However, there are occasions where a *mamaksa* can be narrated but not *arga-ageti*. For example the latter cannot be related at occasions of dispute settlement and in most cases is limited to free discussions where people are engaged in talking about history and tradition.

Mamaksa, the most beloved genre, has complex rules of communication, depending on occasion, composition of the audience and the intention of the speaker. It took a deal of discussion to uncover them. The performance of *mamaksa* is not restricted by time and place. One may invoke *mamaksa* at a meeting to drive a point home and during light-hearted discussions to add charm to a speech. A father advises his son by relating relevant *mamaksa*. *But* when Borana speak of their *mamaksa,* what springs to their minds is its use at an assembly or in serious deliberations. That the *mamaksa* is associated with formal speech occasions is explained by its rules of performance. Adults do not recount tales taking the narration as an end by itself but in relation to a case in hand; a significant and frequent function is in association with dispute settlement. *Mamaksa* is perceived as a sign of knowledge and experience, it is the preserve of male elders, and juniors do not use it in front of their seniors.

Women and *mamaksa* mostly find themselves at odds. It is true that women can use proverbs with great subtlety, but it is difficult to consider them as the performers of prose-*mamaksa*. Women themselves speak without hesitation about their lack of the appropriate knowledge. As one old

woman answered curtly, 'Am I an elder [male] who would know *mamaksa?'*
(Ani jaarsaa ka mammaakssa beeku?) It has been difficult for me to find
women who, for example, could tell well the very popular legend of Dido
which many male youths of twenty can recount. It is something that
deserves an explanation.

The use of *mamaksa* is associated with court cases *(dubbii),* at which
women do not customarily sit, except when one appears as a witness, and
then she has to sit a short distance behind the men. Even if there is something that a woman must answer to, she is represented by her husband.
Custom prohibits her from being present at or organizing a meeting. After
the 1974 Ethiopian revolution women were required to form an association which enabled them to hold meetings entirely composed of women.
This was enough for the men to raise their eyebrows in amazement –
which compelled them to examine the times and concoct doomsday
verses.

Clearly the absence of women from assemblies hampers their development of eloquence, persuasiveness, sophistry and the ability to deliberate on
a single issue at length. Nevertheless opportunities occur time and again
where women listen when tales are related, be it in the house or on a journey. But, like the old lady, women assume that a woman has nothing to do
with *mamaksa* even when, as many do, they know the stories. The women
feel unable to narrate them. Even males who have a high degree of training
have to wait a long time before they become full-fledged performers.
Contrary to Borana practice, we find for example that in several, though by
no means all, Southern African societies story telling is mostly a function of
women. On this point, Ben-Amos writes:

> No doubt, cultural values, work pattern, ideas about speech and folklore
> and the respective conceptions of the roles of men and women in society
> could offer partial explanation for the association of forms with one sex
> only (Ben-Amos,1982: 157).

Light-hearted free discussions are another kind of occasion when both
mamaksa and *arga-ageti* are performed. The performance of historical narratives takes place when elders of experience and knowledge talk and argue
about their customs and history, which the Borana much love to do. The discussion mainly consists of jokes, witty parables and historical anecdotes.
The purpose here is more to generate amusement and add charm to one's
speech; but when a man of experience talks to young adults moral *mamaksa*
can be told. The situation is the same with myths and legends. For example,
an elder does not recount a legend of Dido, which is popular, at an assembly nor to his age mates just for the sake of telling it, but only if there is a
relevant issue in hand that evokes the legend.

When an adult relates a tale in a relaxed mood the narration is punctu-ated by different speech (skill) mechanisms which claim the attention of the audience. In some African societies we are told about the existence of pro-fessional storytellers; for example in Benin (Ben-Amos, 1982: 153). In Borana there are no professional storytellers but some people are known as knowledgeable storytellers. Eloquence and the power of speech are very much admired and every male attempts to acquire them, consciously listen-ing to the elders to 'learn how to talk'. Most adults are good narrators as far as vividness and details are concerned. After all narration is part of their life, as is evident in the highly active exchange of information which requires every Borana to observe and recount experiences with detailed and accurate recall. What differentiates the bad, average and good narrators is the effec-tiveness and richness of repertoire.

The main devices a good narrator puts in to his performance are pause, imitation of sounds, rising and falling tones and emotional rendition. Gestures and facial expressions come in occasionally and, as such, they are not considered tools of effective performance. Verbal qualities are more emphasized. This practice is in sharp contrast with the performance of chil-dren's tales.

Narrators make considerable use of pause. Long and impressive pauses punctuate the transition from one episode to another. Especially, the intro-duction of a new event or character is always preceded by a very long pause. This occurs mostly in high-toned moral tales and historical narratives. Pause, along with direct speech of characters, are the two major features distin-guishing formal speech from tale narration. In recounting experience during formal speech occasions the use of direct speech is employed. But in folklore narration, speeches of characters are presented with a change in voice from character to character. One can learn about the use of direct speech from the transcription of the tales, which are full of quotation marks. The narrator often goes from direct speech to direct speech without even saying 'he said', or 'she said'. The audience keeps track of the change in voice or understands logically from the assumption who could say what. When direct speech is transcribed on paper it can create confusion. But in actual narration this fea-ture gives it liveliness, immediacy and dramatic quality.

The sentences a narrator uses are mostly very short, often only a single word. This is because of the existence of a 'receiver' or an 'answerer'. As in the *duri-duri* a member of the audience is expected to respond at the end of each phrase or sentence by simply saying 'em', or by repeating the last word of each sentence. Again this breaks the monotony of the rendition, though the aim is to show that people are listening to each other. A closely related practice has been observed by Finnegan among the Limba, though they only use it sometimes (Finnegan, 1966: 67). With the Borana it is a rule, whether in story narration or formal speech.

The narrator now and then poses rhetorical questions to the answerer: 'Can one argue with God?' 'No.' 'The man is blind, is there a way he could see?' 'No.' The narrator's questions are mostly answered by 'No'. Another interesting question from the narrator is: 'What did I say now?' It comes now and then. With some it has turned into being a habit because they use it frequently, yet after asking 'What did I say now?' they never wait for a reply but proceed with the narration. Probably the effect is a kind of pause that gives the narrator an opportunity to think about the next sentence – a pause without silence.

During performance clever turn of phrases, verses, and maxims are often repeated by the narrator and even by the audience. The repetition is to the advantage of the audience since it forms the core of the story. Many tales are best remembered by the repeated lines, and at times they serve as a title by which the tales are referred. The repetition helps the audience to memorize them since they must be reproduced verbatim. Of course the narrator's intention sometimes could be to show what he wants to emphasize.

Narration at serious deliberations takes a slightly different turn from the occasions of free discussions. Here the seriousness of the issue being considered itself brings high-toned *mamaksa*. If the narrator believes the tale is a popular one and his citation is intended as a passing remark (or reference) he does not relate it in full. He only mentions it by its core message or some unique phrases it has. In most cases, only parables and some rare tales are the ones that are narrated fully. However, it all depends on the degree of the tale's pertinence. At a meeting, in contrast to the rendition of tales at pastime gatherings, the narrator recounts with subdued emotion and less detail. The tale is presented less as an art than an authoritative tool. The audience listens with maximum attention to see what the speaker is driving at. It does not matter if they know the tale already, for the interpretation is determined by the background purpose among other things. When I asked about the meaning of tales, Borana explanations used to begin with, 'For what purpose was it related?'.

Except in rare cases, such as when an elder is addressing a youth audience, the story of a *mamaksa* by itself does not form the area of interest. Therefore, even if the audience knows the tale, no-one can possibly say, 'leave it, I know it'. They know that a narrator relates not in the assumption that his audience does not know it but to say something special. If interactants are engaged in light-hearted discussions and a narrator makes some error he is promptly interrupted and corrected. However, this does not happen at serious meetings, for it is the highly experienced that most often narrate.

The relationship between occasion, narration and audience with respect to the text needs further consideration and illustration.

The text of a folklore piece is not static from the point of view of performance. The context determines the shape of a narrative, and the situation will be very carefully considered by the narrator. The adult narrator operates on his text to his own end. Once, at a meeting, a speaker, Gololcha Duba, said, 'It is like the case of the hares and pheasants. One party said "don't kill our leader", and the other, "don't destroy our home".' (see tale M18). As he was invoking quite a popular *mamaksa*, there was no need for him to recount it in full. On the other hand this snippet was enough to make his point known. After the meeting I asked him to tell me the tale. He told me how a man came across an assembly of hares and pheasants and asked them either to kill their leaders or destroy their communal life. Hares chose the destruction of their communal life and pheasants the death of their leader. That is why hares live separately and pheasants live in groups. He related simply, briefly and with few explanations. (I have also obtained a contradictory version of this tale.)

Quite accidentally on another occasion I found Gololcha as he was discussing with two young adults the importance of communal and family life. He took that same tale. After mentioning briefly the argument of the hares, he began to present the pheasants' view in detail:

The pheasants said: 'Kill the one leader we have, don't destroy our home. Leave the home. If you kill today our leader, leader is one man, it is this home that gives birth to a leader, don't destroy our home'. The hares said, 'Home without a leader is nothing. A home that has lost its leader is a destroyed home. Don't kill our leader'.

(After briefly presenting Hares' argument again he returned to the pheasants'. Gololcha is using the word *mana* (home) to imply family or communal life):

But the pheasants said, 'Kill our leader, leave our home. It is this home of ours that produces the wise, the brave, what a man learns – everything, education, agriculture, work, counselling. It is a thigh [penis] which begets a leader, this thigh cannot disappear, won't get emaciated, even if it gets emaciated it will grow fat again. Leader will be born but home won't be born; don't destroy our home kill our leader,' said the pheasants.

Note Gololcha's rendition on three different occasions and how he moulded the delivery to suit his intention and the demand of the situation. When he was advising the young men he elaborated on the pheasants' argument, which he sides with, to make it stronger. When a narrator emphasizes and expounds on certain parts of a tale he is showing where his interest lies, and by it the audience knows where sympathies should lie in interpreting the case in hand.

The other reason for expansion, contraction and deletion is dictated both by the interest of the audience and the aim of the narrator. If one asks why Abanoye (A8) was killed, the narrator expounds at length on how she ill-treated her subjects and committed a number of crimes, enumerating them at length. If the narrator wants to tell how she was killed, he only mentions a couple of her crimes and elaborates on the details surrounding her death. For example, by simply asking different men to tell me about Abanoye I have obtained versions where the story of the boy who solves her riddles and who was instrumental in her death is absent. These narrators must have wanted to tell me who Abanoye was rather than how the people suffered and planned her death. If we compare two renditions of the same tale by different narrators, it is as if we have two different versions. This happens predominantly with myths and legends, probably because they are longer and fragmentary.

The myths about the origin of death and disintegration of the Oromo are collected from the same man at different times a year apart. When he tells me about the origin of death, which has bits of biblical and Koranic elements, he recounted how Satan *(Shetan)* aroused the jealousy of Haway (Eve) into attempting to kill Adem (Adam) by making him eat the forbidden death-causer fruit. God intervenes before she kills her husband, and kills her.

A year later Boru Dida offered to tell me about the dispersal of the Oromo. He started with the story of Haway and Adem (A8). He narrated how Satan deluded Haway into believing that Adem visits another woman and how she gave Adem the fruit. Then he simply said, 'Haway killed herself,' and then proceeded to tell about the first Oromo who were the descendants of Haway and Adem. Despite cutting the story of the origin of death in half he seems to conclude the episode wrongly by saying Haway killed herself. In fact he means that Haway brought about her own death, or death in general. It is as if he is in haste to proceed to the second part of the story, which is his focus of interest. (He remembers telling me the first myth). He brought in the Adem-Haway story to establish the background as to why brothers began to kill each other.

So when a narrator tries to contract episodes he breaks the logic of a narrative and creates a version which can easily be dismissed as wrong or contradictory. This shows how the narrator's choice to edit and operate on his text is responsible for what the folklorist assumes at first glance to be a differing version. Though it is quite possible that, at the end of the day, such method of narration results in real different versions.

An even more interesting example of this kind of narration is the case of Dido's legend which Andrzejewski collected in the 1950s. Dido was a brave warrior but recalcitrant man. The leaders wanted to kill him but they were unable to do so. On the advice of a man who wanted his death, Dido travelled far and camped alone. There 'the enemies saw Dido and killed him' (Andrzejewski, 1962: 124). According to Andrzejewski's version the man directly responsible for Dido's death appears to be the man who sent him far away, near to the enemy's territory. This version does not have the story of how an enemy disguised as a fool entered Dido's service, how Dido's wife fell in love with the masquerader and let him into Dido's secret which he exploited to kill Dido. This long story, which shows that the person directly responsible for Dido's death is his wife, is missing. The man who told this legend to Andrzejewski has focused on Dido's recalcitrance and the leaders' attempt to kill him and wanted to blame the leaders as essentially responsible for Dido's death. Even though there is no contradiction between the two versions, the process of contraction, expansion and omission to generate a desired effect creates such discrepancies.

The Borana narrator does not recount the whole of a long and episodic story like Dido's, even if he knows every detail, because the tradition of storytelling for its own sake is nonexistent. A story has to be told only to serve a case and the narrator presents in light of his intention, not as he knows the tale. There is not one complete story of Dido that can be extracted at once from a narrator's mind. Even if one asks for the entire story of Dido from his childhood to death, one never gets such a unified story; for in the narrator's mind it is not found arranged in such a way. The story is stored in episodes and the episodes will be connected in various ways according to the intention of the narrator during the narrative event. (Since Dido's legend is found interesting in this respect I have put the different stories collected from a number of narrators as they were told. (See A10.1, A10.2, A11 and A12.)

To show how a narrator can recount Dido's legend in different combinations, here are four major episodes:

1. He demonstrated immense wisdom and courage as a young man
2. Recalcitrant Dido was at odds with the leaders
3. He was betrayed by his wife into the hands of his enemies
4. The Borana fought the Arsi to avenge Dido's death

Each episode is capable of forming a main focus of narrative by itself. Furthermore the narrator can combine them: 1–2–3–4, 1–2–3, 1–2, 1–3–4 or 3–4 to deliver it in many ways. Only combinations 1–3 and 1–4 do not work. Comparatively speaking, *mamaksa* are affected less by episodic narration than historical narratives. Historical narratives, as history, can cover a long time and incorporate many incidents.

As very long stories are not often delivered in full there are many tales of which young adults know only part. In an attempt to understand how far they have enriched their repertoire of prose narratives I used to play back earlier recorded tales for them. The interesting result of this investigation is that, of some tales, the young adults claim to know only certain parts. One instance is the story about the conceited man who wanted to 'fight' with God (A4). One man told me that he only knows the second half of the tale, which is concerned with the creation of beasts. He remembers how he came to hear it. Once in the company of elders a young man spoke in despair about why God created the destructive beasts. One of the elders proceeded to narrate the myth. But he did not start from the outset and explain how the hero came to acquire peace and wealth. The narrator only addresses the question.

Many elders know the story of Wale Wachu, A16, very well. But some people know only the first episode, which tells how Wale's wife subtly makes him realize that his people are not quite happy with him. They know this part because people frequently relate it as an anecdote about women's subtlety.

The nature of the communicative event, which includes the composition of audience, the occasion, and the narrator's intention, plays on the 'text' in these ways. With respect to adults' narratives one can hardly speak of a fixed text. Apart from the bare frame of the tale and some peculiar turn of phrases and verses which are reproduced verbatim, and stock expressions which are part of the communal conventional expressive forms, the rest is left to the individual narrator. The context of the narration plays the most significant role in determining what shape a delivery ought to take. However, as a particular context can never be repeated, no particular narrative can be repeated fully with the same effect. Every new rendition and interpretation is affected by situational contexts which involve both the narrator and the audience. What Wolfgang Iser said of the reading process applies to the communication process discussed above:

> The convergence of text and reader brings literary work into existence, and this conversion can never be pinpointed but always remain virtual as it is not to be identified either with the reality of the text or with the individual disposition of the reader (Iser, 1974: 274).

Examining the three Borana folktale genres in their context of performance and occasion we see a direct link between conception of a genre and its conventions of performance. The *duri-duri* is valued for the amusing story it tells and telling it 'correctly' becomes an end. The *duri-duri* adheres to conformity rather than individual style or originality. Though *arga-ageti*, like the *duri-duri*, is valued for the story it tells, the narrator considers the occasion and his audience to decide on the content of his text. From the point of view of performance, the *mamaksa* and the *arga-ageti* are united by the identity of the performers and by the fact that the narrator can shape the narrative according to the occasion and his intention. But a great difference lies in the kind of intention the two genres demand. In the case of *arga-ageti* the narrator decides the amount of information that should be included. Whatever the intention of the narrator the story he tells remains the centre of interest. But the *mamaksa* is not valued primarily for the story it tells as much as for its purpose of illumination. There has to be some issue to be illuminated for the *mamaksa* to be actualized. Therefore, on the part of the narrator, it involves a choice of relevant texts, defining purpose and anticipating response. The *mamaksa* needs to be judged against its function to understand its mode of existence. To understand the grammar of communication and to view the narratives as the users perceive them, the *mamaksa* has to be analyzed from the point of view of the function the society has attached to it. In this regard the *mamaksa* is so uniquely complex that it requires separate treatment. In the next chapter we will help unravel the detailed principles of the *mamaksa* usage.

Chapter 4

The Mamaksa: Function, Usage and Local Aesthetics

From the viewpoint of analysing communicative events the genre which most invites an in-depth analysis is the *mamaksa.*

Concepts such as function, usage, and local aesthetics are intertwined. A discussion of one aspect cannot be satisfactorily carried out without touching on the others; dealing with them separately results in delivering the picture in pieces or else in redundancy. For instance, persuasion is one of the functions of a *mamaksa* which, to discuss properly, one has to demonstrate when and how a narrative serves that purpose. But, in another way, this is a discussion on usage and, in speaking about usage, we are speaking about artistic canons of performance, that is, about the locally developed aesthetic theory.

On the other hand, the logical and methodological demand to treat these broad topics separately is evident. Even though usage and local aesthetics are closely related concepts, the fact that the Borana have developed a relatively well formulated aesthetic theory urges a separate treatment as well. An investigation into local aesthetics and thought, which Finnegan says is 'a study in its infancy', looks into the local concepts about composition, the principles of performance and systems of evaluation (Finnegan, 1992: 132). There are meta-folkloric expressions which comment on function, usage and meaning of *mamaksa;* and it is in the light of the cultural meta-folklore that the local aesthetic is examined.

Attitude Toward the Genre

The function a folklore form serves depends on how the society conceives it. Conventionally the function of a folklore form is associated with the question of belief. Borana have no problem in firmly identifying *arga-ageti* as factual. But with the *duri-duri* even the relevance of raising the issue of belief becomes questionable. First of all, if we are keen to consider the local interpretation, who is to be asked? The children or the adults? The children, who are the owners of the genre, say the *duri-duri* is factual. But, even if their opinion is the one that matters, they are not in a position to form a genuinely critical attitude toward their genre. Its factuality is taken for granted. On the other hand, the adults who no longer own the *duri-duri* look down on it, primarily because of its frivolity. Some are even reluctant to admit that they used to believe in it as a child. Ruth Finnegan writes:

> The degree of 'belief' in a particular narrative is one of the hardest things to assess. Even in a familiar society this is notoriously difficult – but it is even more difficult in unfamiliar cultures; it is made more difficult still in that investigators have taken very little interest in this question. (Finnegan, 1970: 368)

With the *mamaksa* the researcher is faced with this classic problem. As a narrative, the prose-*mamaksa* contains animal tales, moral fables, etiological tales and anecdotes about real historical figures. Then is the *mamaksa* factual or fictitious?

If the *mamaksa* consists of narratives as well as non-narrative items, such as proverbs, the question of its factuality appears to be absolutely meaningless. What creates the complexity here is the belief in the factuality of narratives in the *mamaksa* held by the culture members. Many Borana elders, when asked, regard animal tales and anecdotes about real people alike as factual. But when they are asked about particular tales, they assume a new attitude and dismiss the animal tales as fictitious, though they still do not cite factual *mamaksas*. But their views are not consistent among themselves, opinions are rather personal. These are people who consider themselves guardians of the Borana culture and, therefore, who have developed an especially critical outlook towards the beliefs of the common man. It is noteworthy that not a few men who took great pains to participate in and organize those rituals have been observed expressing heretic views about some rituals. Asmarom Legesse, too, was surprised by men who disparaged some traditional beliefs in private discussions, but who cited those very items with particular zeal and passion at serious debates.

It is particularly interesting to mention the incident between Asmarom and Guyyo Koto of which Asmarom says: 'Perhaps the most remarkable statement my Borana mentors made was made by Guyyo Koto, a famous Borana historian.' Asmarom asked about the origin of the Qallu:

G.K. Do you mean how was he first born?
A.L. Yes, I do mean that.
G.K. We do not know,
A.L. You must have some idea.

G.K. We thought you wanted to know about custom (*ada*) and law
       (*sera*), but now you are asking us to tell you stories.
A.L. Is there anything wrong with stories?
G.K. The people of old used to tell lies: if you want to hear lies, we will
       tell you.

'With this surprising introductory remark, Guyyo Kotto proceeded to tell
me about the supernatural aura surrounding the origin of the Kallu institu-
tion and the birth and death of the individual Kallu'. (Asmarom, 1973: 45)

This incident refers to a myth, believed by all the Borana; and the blas-
phemy was from a revered man like Guyyo Koto. Guyyo may have said the
story is a lie but once telling it, he recounted it with a serious tone. But is he
serious enough?

The question of belief, notoriously difficult as it is to unravel, is made
difficult by such learned men, to whom normally a researcher is bound to
listen, but who entertain such unorthodox views and behave differently
from what they explain. But to return to the animal *mamaksa*, at times a
performer starts a tale by saying, 'In the olden times they say animals could
talk', especially when relating a tale to young adults and strangers (for
example, me). Should this be interpreted as a literal statement or as nothing
more than a habitual expression? In M8 the narrator concludes the tale in
which the mule talked and revealed the wicked, with the statement: 'The
descendants of this boy are still to be found, only we do not know them.'
This could lead to the assumption of total belief. But deeper investigation
reveals a different aspect as to the root of the belief.

The search for this root leads into the complex maze of understanding
the traditional nature of composition and creativity, the function of
mamaksa and how it is defined. It touches the whole realm of folklore from
composition to interpretation.

Primarily, what the Borana see in their *mamaksa* is its ability to express
and interpret a situation. The etymology of the term itself is based on the
word 'to liken.' This ability to express a situation is in terms of drawing an
analogy, rendering personal understanding, passing judgment or familiar-
izing an issue by translating it into analyzable terms. *Mamaksa* is not
understood as a story by itself. Invariably when an elder is asked what
mamaksa is he gives the standard definition, expressed in meta-folklore as,
'*mamaksa* is the surgery of a case.' (*mammaaksi koobaa dubbii*), or as,
'*Mamaksa* is of two kinds: one brings a case; the other settles it'
(*Mammaksi lammuma: tokko dubbii fidaa; tokko dubbii fiixa*). The
mamaksa is not conceived as something that stands alone. That is why
Borana adults do not have the tradition of telling stories for stories' sake,
be it among themselves or as adults to children. There is nothing like a

storytelling occasion in the sense in which Finnegan describes among the Limba (Finnegan, 1966: 64). Only where there is a speech-act, an issue, can *mamaksa* exist. This is evident when an individual is asked to tell a tale and fails to do so. The typical answer is, 'You tell *mamaksa* in relation to an issue under discussion and not simply for itself' (*Dubbif mammaakan malee akkanumaan hin mammaakan*). Thus, it is best understood as a 'meta-speech' (to adapt Dundes term, 'meta-folklore'), a speech form which comments on a speech-act.

The other concept of *mamaksa* is associated with the method of composition. To relate *mamaksa* is broadly defined as relating what one has 'experienced or heard'. The 'experienced', in this case, is an incident the speaker witnessed or the experience of his father or grandfather; that is something he feels sure took place. He relates these by citing the relevant incident and the people involved in it. These are experiences related in the form of *mamaksa*. The 'heard' could be an age-old tale taking place in the distant past, including animal tales. The practice of relating anecdotes about real people and impressive experiences in the form of *mamaksa* in itself induces the idea that *mamaksas* are based on fact. If some tales in *mamaksa* are believed to be factual the assumption is that the others can be factual too. Here they are concerned with the *possibility*. So a Borana, even though he says all *mamaksas* are equally factual, is never seen using the animal tales for serious purposes, such as dispute settlement.

However, deep inside, the question of belief is the analyst's question. To the Borana it is simply a question of possibility which cannot be simply answered by 'no'.

Most of the points briefly discussed so far will be clearer when issues like effective usage and composition are dealt with.

Mamaksa as a Form of Language

The fact that the *mamaksa* is conceived as a form of expression and interpretation of experience brings in its function as a form of language. Discourse-centred analysis, which is an extension of the 'ethnography of speaking' approach pioneered by Dell Hymes, directs attention to the way cultural symbols and the particular resources of the language are *used* (Finnegan, 1992: 44). Hymes's approach is mainly action centred with a focus on the expressive view of language, on performance, and on detailed ethnographic observation of how people actually *use* language. The language of the *mamaksa* is literary language, which provides it with artistic and cultural images. When interactants express their views through *mamaksa* they are seeking a clarity of meaning. It is distinguished from other speech events, like conversations, by its ability to reduce ideas to common images. It enables interactants to attain similar pictures, a purpose which other speech forms may fail to fulfil. A *mamaksa* gives clarity of meaning, though varying degrees of under-standing cannot be ruled out. The Borana are well aware of this, and it is the first thing the folklorist observes about *mamaksa*. A proverb states 'One spits something by saying *a'kk* (clearing a throat). One speaks about something with *mamaksa*'. *(A'kk jedhan waa tufan, mammaksaan wa dubbatan)*. As an act of spitting requires throat clearing, certain views are best launched through the *mamaksa*. Because it represents common image and shared value, when diversified experiences and views are related through it, it succeeds in throwing the interactants back to a common cultural denominator. The concept of *mamaksa* as a tool of expression is clearly stated.

Apart from the purpose of making ideas substantive the proverb cited above indicates the utility of *mamaksa* as a form of language, which gen-erates multiple images that cannot be expressed as well and as easily through formal language. The use of *mamaksa* not only serves the purpose of attaining clarity of meaning, but at the same time aesthetic purpose is achieved; as expressed in the proverb, 'A food without salt and a speech without *mamaksa* are the same' *(Sagale soodda hin qabneefi dubbiin mammaaksa hin qabne tokko).*[7] The analogy between food without salt and speech without *mamaksa* emphasises the latter's ability to turn an oth-erwise insipid rendition impressive and memorable. To elucidate some of the above I will cite, with hindsight, a now famous case which I witnessed some years back, not as a researcher but as an ordinary participant.

In 1992 many Oromo political organizations were operating in Borana region. The Borana were in particular unhappy about one organization led by the self-styled General Waqo. A large assembly was held in Negelle town to solve disagreements. The district officials were trying to handle the matter delicately by playing down the causes of conflict and beating about the bush to prevent the possibility of open war. The Borana were insistent that the General should leave the region. In the mean time a furious man leapt to his feet, made a long speech enumerating the General's wrongs and then calmly related the following anecdote:

> The man has never been to a hunt campaign. He has never killed any-thing. But he sees his friends coming back from the hunt and then anointed [as a hero]. He also wanted to be a hero and pride to his wife. He set out into the forest determined to kill a lion after learning from his friends how to track a prey. As he was walking in the forest suddenly he

---

7 George Cotter takes the title *Salt for Stew* for his great collection of nearly five thousand Oromo proverbs from the saying: *dubbin mamakaa hinqabne itto sogidda hinqabne* (conversation without a proverb is like stew without salt).

saw the lion a few yards ahead. Then immediately he began to search for something on the ground. At this time another man came and asked him what he is looking for. 'I am about to kill this lion and I'm looking for his footprints, a hunter always follows the footprint.' [Then the narrator added:] Here is the culprit, we came for him, you [the mediators] know what he did, but here you are at a loss.

Huge applause erupted from the audience and the General left the hall. The speaker was applauded for his successful description of the situation they were in.

What the speaker related is a brief outline of a joke. The image of the hunter who searches for the footprints of a lion which is in clear sight, impressively expresses the state of the inquiry. Through this *mamaksa* the speaker is saying: 'the situation we find ourselves in is as ridiculous as the situation of the hunter'. It is for this very reason that he selected a joke, for he understood what was going on as a joke. His speech got its power when he used the image represented in the tale to carry his message. Until the time he felt an impasse had been created and related the *mamaksa*, his speech was nothing new and memorable. Like the analogy of the food without salt the anecdote transformed his rendition to artistic status. Probably no-one in the assembly had perceived the situation as ridiculous until the speaker interpreted it as such. The applause he received was a sign of agreement, because the tale appealed to others with an image which formal language might not have created so effectively.

As the views expressed in a tale are shared, it authenticates one's view by the background images and values contained in it. It not only renders strange concepts familiar but also ensures them the power of authority.

One day my assistant and I were discussing with two Borana elders the relationship of women and men. One of the elders, after stating that a man ought to handle a woman carefully, even limiting his relationship (including sex) with her, proceeded to recount a *mamaksa (M11)* about how a strong man, whom the people were unable to capture, was sent a beautiful girl who seduced him. It was the first time that the strong man had slept with a woman and she stayed with him for three days. On the fourth day, when the men came for him, he was weak and unable to defend himself. Here the narrator was using the *mamaksa* to substantiate his stated position.

On another occasion, in a light-hearted gathering, certain people were discussing four men who went to Negelle town to seek oil from the local relief organization and returned empty handed because they quarrelled among themselves. As they were discussing, one man said, 'It is not in accordance with custom for people who travel together to disagree. Two people who are together on one mission should speak with one mouth. Had they agreed:

"Look, a dead elephant!" "That is true!" They found the dead elephant. Quarrel with your mate and you end up losing what you already have.'

This piece of speech may appear incomprehensible. In fact the speaker is referring to a tale against which he wanted to relate the situation. As the audience is composed of elders and the speaker knows he is invoking a popular tale, he does not have to recount it in full. He is expressing a simple truth by making a casual reference. The *mamaksa* in question is M19, which tells that only because two men share a vision, they succeed in achieving the improbable. One says 'Look, giraffe' where there is none and the other responds 'Yes, I see.' And the giraffe pops into existence just because one agrees to the vision of the other. A third character is introduced in the tale who disagrees with them and causes failure.

The purpose of the allusion is slightly different from the intention cited earlier. In this case the invocation is not intended for persuasive purpose because no-one can possibly oppose his idea. Neither does he intend to validate his view with an illustration. He is simply making a choice to speak with the image and language of the *mamaksa*. The purpose of this allusion, practised very widely, is to give an old, traditionally provided meaning to the present situation. When he does this, he does not appear to be narrating a tale, he does not even suggest that he is referring to a tale but directly speaks with phrases taken from the tale. While the style shows how the *mamaksa* as approaching a formal language, the purpose is to enhance the gravity of error committed by the men who fail to agree.

Viewed as language the purpose of a tale may vary from clarification and interpretation to euphemism. As knowledge it is the means to relate one's idea to the wisdom and values accumulated since the dawn of history. The use of *mamaksa* is a sign of wisdom. Andrzejewski observed that:

> The adults though they normally do not recite fables or simple stories among themselves, are expected to know them intimately as a heritage of wit and wisdom shared by all and drawn upon as a source of knowledge and verbal imagery and modes of thought. (Andrzejewski, 1962: 116)

So we see the *mamaksa* as an expressive form, consciously maintained, which also has to be viewed in the context of dispute settlement. It is in this context that the esteem with which it is held, its power as a force at work, the range of social functions it fulfils and the grammar of usage are best examined.

The *Mamaksa* in Relation to Dispute Settlement

Persuasion

Even though it is used for purposes other than persuasion, this is the most serious and prominently practised purpose of the *mamaksa*. Nura Dida of

Negelle, gave this typical and very representative answer, which is reproduced here verbatim:

> Now they disagree. The Borana say one type of nemesis reaches soon
> [after the wrong doing] and the other catches up slowly. So as to make a
> person avoid the consequence of evil deed – for example a man kills a
> man, for such severe cases, cases which concern blood, the elders delib-
> erate. To calm and settle the matter you'll relate what you have seen or
> heard earlier. Now the man, to avoid that nemesis – for he has heard the
> consequence of evil he will think, 'Ah! I too can meet my nemesis tomor-
> row', and admits to his wrong.

The substantial role a *mamaksa* plays in dispute settlement depends
among other things on who the speaker is, on the kind of tale and the
timing. Many factors are involved and it does not mean that a disputant
promptly submits simply because a *mamaksa* is related against him. Nura
said, 'To calm and settle the matter you'll relate what you have seen or
heard earlier.' He is speaking about the *mamaksa*, which is assumed to be
the experience of the ancestors. During legal disputes carefully selected
tales are used against the disputant towards whom a mediator thinks the
evidence points. It is believed that once a very weighty and appropriate
mamaksa is related against a case, a direct connection will come into
force between the fate of the evil doer in the narrative and the concerned
disputant.

The *mamaksa* draws its power from being a collective expression of the
accumulated knowledge of the society, and to insult or bless a person
through *mamaksa* amounts to speaking with the wisdom of the whole
Borana. That is why the Borana take great care when they choose to speak
through *mamaksa*. Proverbially they say, 'A *mamaksa* hurts a man either
in the process or at the end of it.' (*Mammaaksi dhaqa nama tuqa gala
nama tuqa.*) The proverb refers to a *mamaksa* used when one man brings
a case against another and the *mamaksa* used when, in the end, one gives
up the case grudgingly. It means that any *mamaksa* hurts the feelings of
the person against whom it is directed. Even the *mamaksa* related after
one has admitted to wrong hurts. Viewed in the context of a dispute, it is
used as a powerful expression of one's unhappiness at the state of things.
The Borana greatly fear this power of the *mamaksa*, and when they argue
if one has related a *mamaksa*, the other may ask '*mamaksa* either hurts in
the process or at the end, why did you relate it?' This is simply a way of
making known how one is offended. Even if these people finally reach an
agreement, the latter still goes away deeply touched. In response to the
question of why and when a Borana uses the *mamaksa*, Arero Guyyo of
Yabello said:

When a case is brought, you relate a *mamaksa* to settle that case. If that case remains unsettled, you relate a *mamaksa* against it. These are the two types of *mamaksa*. Either a case is brought in and settled, or the guilty (accused) refuses to give in. If so, you reprove this man – by *mamaksa*. 'A *mamaksa*, be it the one that hurts in the process of deliberation or the one that hurts at the end, it is man that is hurt.'
So said the elder who is settling a dispute.

Effective Usage and Aesthetic Principles

The function of mamaksa in the context of dispute settlement greatly depends on the techniques by which persuasion is achieved. Uncovering these techniques leads to the question of usage and thence to the grammar of performance and the aesthetic principles. A discussion on usage based on actual observation gives a detailed picture of the grammar which cannot be successfully described by interviewing the users. For instance, it has been said that *mamaksa* serves as a means of settling disputes. This is a general statement. In practice we observe that there are some very popular tales and jokes which are not fit for that purpose. So, to gain additional understanding on the function of persuasion, it is necessary to delve into the rules and conventions of usage.

The primary and the most emphatically stressed rule of performance is the need to relate an appropriate tale for the appropriate case. Borana have many proverbs on the rule of appropriateness which shows its importance. One which indicates the right and aesthetically pleasing *mamaksa* reads, 'Mamaksa in accordance with the case, children who resemble their father'. (*Mammaaksi ka dubbii fakkaatu ilmeen ka abbaa fakkaattu.*) Appropriateness is a very difficult criterion which obstructs many adults from making use of the *mamaksa*. It is learned through experience and requires a degree of talent.

Another proverb indicating the direct relationship between a tale and the background case says, 'An issue brings in *mamaksa*, rubbing the genitals of an ox makes it urinate.' (*Mammaaksi dubbii fudha, goondolii fincaan fudha.*) It is for a medical purpose the ill ox is made to urinate and it is to interpret the difficult issue that *mamaksa* is invoked. If it is the issue that summons a *mamaksa*, logically the tale has to be appropriate to the issue. A similar proverb reads, 'An issue under discussion brings *mamaksa*, and *mamaksa* too brings an issue'. (*Mammaaksi dubbii fuuti, dubbiin ille mammaaksa fuuti.*) This proverb also shows the power of the *mamaksa* to redirect the course of discussion.

The technique by which a certain case and narrative are linked defies description. There can be so many connections. The rule for appropriateness is only a general statement; its effective execution is subject to no formula but something that is dictated by the demand of the situational context. The same tale can be used for many different cases. Sometimes a whole narrative will form the focus while at others only a certain part of the tale is focused upon. A narrator may relate only half the story, up to the point of interest. It is as pointless to assume rules whereby case and a narrative are combined as it is to discuss rules for writing a good poem or a novel. Whenever Borana attribute to an individual 'a knowledge of *mamaksa*' it is in reference to his skill in drawing unforseen parallels between a case and a *mamaksa*. Such a skilful narrator interrupts his narration now and then either to interpret and comment on the tale or to relate each point to the general situation and clarify his intention. To interrupt a narrative and revert to commentaries and explanations is the mark of a master storyteller. An example of this kind of narration and narrator will be given in the next chapter.

The second principle of usage concerns timing, what to use when. Borana generally divide their *mamaksa* into two categories: '*Mammaaksi lamuma: tokko dubbi fidaa, tokko dubbii fixaa'*, (Mamaksa are of two types, one brings a case, the other settles it.) The first type is usually employed with the intention of bringing an allegation. Its content states how someone wronged the other or behaved badly. This type of *mamaksa* is used either at the beginning by the complainant or at the end by the mediators when the loser fails to give in. In both cases it shows failure of agreement.

The other type is that which settles a dispute. This clearly comes at the end of a case or helps to end the conflict. Tales used at this stage show how righteousness pays or how an evil deed is punished. Such tales are used by the mediators in an attempt to reconcile disputants or to urge the person proven wrong into submission. Or, after a dispute is settled successfully, a *mamaksa* can be related as advice, as a warning and as a reference to the danger that has been avoided. In effect it makes enjoyable the peace that has been obtained.[8]

However, the division into *mamaksa* that bring a case and those which settle it is made complex, because it does not necessarily depend on the content of a tale. Based on the situation and on which part of the tale the narrator is focusing, the same tale can be used to generate either of the effects. Apart from the content of the tale and the timing, the main issue is the identity of the speaker and his intention. If the speakers are the disputants, their intention is largely to incriminate each other. If the speaker were a mediator, his intention would be to settle the case. The situational context has to be taken into account. That is, a mediator may reprove one or both of the disputants through *mamaksa* and yet the *mamaksa* would end the deliberation. This is an instance of pronouncing judgment through *mamaksa*. Here is an example of such a case which Bule Dabbasa told me:

---

8 Peace between people – *Nagaa Borana* (the Peace of the Borana) – has been a key Borana concept for as long as we have any record. It continues to be so, even among the isolated Moslem Borana of Garbe Tula in Kenya, as Mario Aguilar (1988) demonstrates very clearly.

Once a father and his elder son quarrelled over the sale of a heifer. The father wanted to sell it and the son strongly opposed the idea, all the same, the father sold the heifer. Now the son asked for some money but the father refused. By this time the son threatened to sell a she-goat and the case was brought to the elders. After some deliberations one man related the *mamaksa* M12: A commander sees a honey-bird and orders his soldiers to follow it. The soldiers refuse. The commander follows the bird by himself and comes back with the honey. Now the soldiers ask him to share the honey with them. He refuses and eats alone. Returning home both parties accuse each other. After a hearing the elders say, 'The bird sang and it was according to the custom. The commander ordered and it was according to the custom. You (soldiers) disobeyed and it was contrary to the custom. You (the commander) went after the bird leaving your soldiers behind and it was contrary to the custom. Then you ate alone which is not our custom. Only the bird was right and we don't discuss this matter any further.'

The narrator related this tale and said, 'This is all I have to say.' Immediately the other elders expressed their agreement and the meeting ended leaving father and son on their own. The point is that the son should have agreed with his father in the first place and the father should not have ignored his first-born's discontent. The analogy between the two situations, the representation of commander versus soldiers as father versus son is skilful. The narrator (mediator) by refusing to see their case and by judging both as wrong, indirectly made them feel ashamed and settle the matter between themselves. This *mamaksa* settles the case, as far as the mediators are concerned, but it is the type 'that hurts a man at the end'. In this instance both are hurt.

Though *mamaksa* plays a great role in persuasion and dispute settlement it is not invoked now and then throughout the meeting. In contrast proverbs occur abundantly, but tales are rare. And it is from this rarity that *mamaksa* partly draws its effectiveness. This has evolved from the user's awareness of its power and another convention of usage which is its employment by the highly experienced elders. In addition, one reverts to it only when he wants to present a unique view, interpretation or an approach from a new angle. The Borana say, '*Jabbiin bifa koormaatti mammaaksi koobaa dubbii.* (A calf has the looks of its father, *mamaksa* is a surgery of speech, or case.) Just as by looking at the calf one can tell its father bull, *mamaksa* enables one to show the truth. This recalls the Yoruba saying, 'A proverb is like a horse: When the truth is missing, we use a proverb to find it' (Dundes, in Ben-Amos, 1982: 138). For Borana to mediate a case is to interpret and dissect an idea to reveal the core of the problem. It is in this meta-folklore that we find expressed their reference for the *mamaksa* as a supreme tool of communication. So now let us consider the issue of the identity of the speaker.

Effective Usage and the Identity of the Speaker

People bring their cases to local and clan leaders or to elders who are respected for their knowledge and insight, but not to government courts. For instance the Borana hold a Great Assembly (Gumii Gaayo) only once every eight years.[9] This assembly lasts for several days and thousands of people take part. It looks into cases important enough to demand the attention of this highest body of conflict resolution. The elders inherit the wisdom of their fathers and take part at many hearings and develop remarkable skill in the wise use of the *mamaksa*. They are the ones who mediate and play a major role in deciding which course an issue should take. The *mamaksa* is an effective tool which elders exploit for this purpose. Often people prefer not to use the *mamaksa* in the presence of men who are senior in age or superior in knowledge, underlining its effectiveness as a means of persuasion.

The main user – the man to whom wisdom and eloquence is attributed – through experience and personal genius has developed an effective performance skill. The fact that the speaker is a renowned man, the fact that he can handle the *mamaksa* with skill gives weight to his folkloric utterances. One proverb goes:

> I am afraid of the wise one seated at an inquiry,
> I am afraid of the fool for he never forgives.

Borana admire subtle argument and the power of reasoning and eloquence. Gobba Alla, the Aba Gada from 1698 to 1705, committed a severe crime in refusing to hand over power. He was brought to the Great Assembly but he was such a speaker that he talked the assembly into justifying his action and avoided punishment. The Borana who condemn his action never fail to appreciate his virtue and skill. When it is said that the *mamaksa* serves to settle disputes what should always be remembered is the identity of the user.

To illustrate further the relationship between identity and effectiveness, related conventions of performance need to be considered.

When a speaker is about to embark on relating a *mamaksa*, he begins by mentioning the author or the person from whom he heard it. In the case of proverbs and wise sayings which are often composed as verses, the author can be known. There are many proverbs which are attributed to individuals dead as well as living. There are also anecdotes of speech which are turned into a tale by the first person who reports the incident. Here the author may be the man whom the anecdote deals with. But the longer tales do not have individual authors. The aesthetic principle on usage urges, 'a *mamaksa* for which you do not know the person who told it, is lame in one of its legs!'

---

9 For a full account of Gumii Gaayo see *I Borana: una societa assembleare dell'Ethiopia* by Marco Bassi, Milan; Franco Angei, 1996.

(*mamaaksa Abbaa hime ka hin beekne, mila tokkon naafaa*). During performance the name of the originating person has to be mentioned.

However not every *mamaksa* has its author nor every tale its known
teller. The very popular tales are heard by the audience many times over, so
it is almost meaningless to say, 'It is So-and-So who told me'. Citing the
source of a *mamaksa* is in a way an attribution to its rarity. It is also a way
of acknowledging the poets.

Experienced elders employ particularly rare and weighty *mamaksa*.
Then whenever a source is cited, it will be the name of a celebrity probably
known throughout Boranaland. Even the knowledgeable elite are bound by
the convention of citing a source. While the current narrator himself is an
important person, the systematic use of a tale which adds the name of
another important person gives extra weight to the tale. It enhances the persuasive capability, because the personality of the current narrator in addition to the eminent figure associated with it bends the will of the disputant.
Even when the current narrator is an ordinary man, citing the source serves
the purpose well. To give an instance of this: once a certain Godana Duba
related M6 after a minor dispute was settled. At the beginning as well as at
the end of the narration he mentioned his source, 'It is Wariyo Guyo Haro,
the father of Jilo Wario who told us this *mamaksa'*. He even mentioned the
son because though Wariyo Guyo is quite a well-known man, it is his son
who achieved greater popularity. The urgency to associate a tale with an
important person is quite evident here.

The practice on one hand is a way of attaching authority to the
mamaksa, while on the other, it can be equated to a way of bringing that
domineering figure in person. The narrator effaces himself and apportions
blame or approbation in the name of another person, thereby being forceful
but in the guise of mildness. The strategy amounts to saying, 'It is not me
who is saying this, it is So-and-So who once told it'.

Borana carefully follow the utterances of great personalities and when
something impressive is told, they soon make it part of their oral literature.
One interesting example is the saying, ' "*Ohoy*," said Huqqa Saritte when
he saw the sun setting', which is often said when something turns out unexpectedly. Huqqa is said to have said this when a case that had to be settled
that day was still unsettled by the time the sun was setting (meetings are not
held after sunset). There is nothing unique or memorable about the excla-
mation *ohoy*. But Huqqa, who died only some forty years ago, was a great
man and the circumstances of his utterance – his assumption of the sun's
setting as a strange phenomenon – is what makes it remarkable.

Popular tales or animal tales are not credited with sources, neither are
they invoked at serious disputes, because citing a source is a way of showing its worth. A tale without a source is less effective than one with a source.
That is what the Borana mean by a *mamaksa* without a source being 'lame

in one of its legs.' This ethnic grammar and aesthetic thought is a dictate of effectiveness.

Another method is to cite the source along with the particular situation under which the narrative is told. In this case a person may say, 'such a thing happened and So-and-So related the following *mamaksa'*. The situation under which the original tale is related and the current situation may share no similarities. The intention is to show the use of the *mamaksa* in a different context or appreciation of the skill of the antecedent narrator, or to remark in passing the importance of the former situation. This method is employed more frequently during light-hearted free discussions. On occasions of serious debate a source is cited along with the situation of utterance when that context is particularly similar to the current one. The narrator's allusion to that situation is not only to draw an analogy and create some kind of archetype so as to arrive at the same resolution, more importantly it is a move to define and interpret the issue in hand in the context in which the former situation was understood. This in particular is a skilful use of *mamaksa* because the narrator enforces his argument doubly, both through the *mamaksa* and by redefining the current issue against an incident that took place in the past.

Non-*Mamaksa* as *mamaksa*

Examining usage in the actual process of the communicative event reveals a different concept of *mamaksa*, which is not consciously acknowledged by the users. Borana categorize *mamaksa* and legends into different genres. The boundary between the genres, which is acknowledged outside the context of performance, is observed to be violated during performance. That is the case when legends are employed as *mamaksa*. Let me begin with an incident in which I was personally involved. Once, when I expressed my interest to be adopted as a Borana, Nura Yaya – a former policeman – related the legend of Dawwe (A21) twice in a single day. The legend of Dawwe is a story of betrayal and Nura suspected me of harbouring a hidden interest. Thus the narrator's focus was not on the story of a hero in its historical sense, but on drawing an analogy between the incident of betrayal and what he suspected was my motive. The narrator's intention was not to tell the story of Dawwe the hero, but to tell a story of betrayal, to use the legend as a *mamaksa*. The point is that such deviations from general conventions can only be revealed when examining the many facets of actual usage.

In a slightly different manner the practice of extracting certain episodes from legends to use them as *mamaksa* is another revealing aspect of usage. The extracted episodes are usually used in quite different context from that they originally have in the non-*mamaksa* forms. An elder, when speaking about the uselessness of deliberating on past events and the importance of

considering the future, extracted the following episode from the legend of
Abanoye (A8), the notorious female leader:

> As she said when the elders sent for her saying, 'Come immediately, we
> are faced with a serious matter,' [she replied] 'I am faced too with an
> equally serious matter, what has passed has passed; what has come we
> will consider together, handle it well till I come. I am dressing myself.'

The incident in the legend took place when the elders told her to come in
haste so as to make her come undressed and be disgraced. But she was wise
and realized their intention. Now when the speaker is 'quoting' this incident, it is said that 'he related a *mamaksa*' (*mammaake*). But he uses it, with
disregard to the original context, to express the uselessness of arguing about
past wrongs. The character in the legend made that remark not because she
meant it but as a pretext to take her time.

In this fashion episodes from historical narratives are used as *mamaksa*.
Even if there are folklore items which are known as *mamaksa*, the invocation of any item from the oral literature to express a situation is understood
as an act of using *mamaksa*. Even incidents from children's tales and verses
of songs can be used in this way, blurring the boundary between genres, spe-
cially between *mamaksa* and *arga-ageti*. An item that has never been
mamaksa, when used during a speech-act becomes *mamaksa* – even if only
for that moment – and attains the purpose and characteristics of *mamaksa*.

Chapter 5

Analysis of a Communicative Event: A Case Study

This case is intended to substantiate the major issues raised in respect to the performance of *mamaksa*. It focuses on the expressive use of language and how meaning is achieved or generated. It is based on a detailed ethnographic observation.

On 13 March 1995, fifteen men were gathered near Negelle town to deliberate on problems concerning a forthcoming ritual. The participants were *gada mojji*, men in the eleventh and final grade of the *gada* cycle. Men in this grade are seen as 'priests', concerned with blessings and performance of various rituals. After completion of this grade they retire by conducting a big ceremony to mark the occasion. On this day, they were only two months away from the ceremony of retirement and some problems had occurred when conducting the preparatory rituals. The meeting, which was held at the shrine Manquphsa, was called by one Huqqa Sarite (possibly the grandson of Huqqa mentioned on p.64), a diviner from the Karrayu clan. Huqqa had offered the 'heifer-of-rain', as is expected of him, to be sacrificed at the shrine. However, the sacrifice could not take place because most of the nearby *gada mojji* had not yet camped at the shrine. Only some had camped there and performed the necessary ritual before the sacrifice of the 'heifer-of-rain'. These men wanted to move to another area and demand that the heifer be sacrificed. But Huqqa, the heifer owner, wanted the presence of all the *gada mojji* according to the custom. Therefore, he summoned to a meeting both those that had already camped at the shrine and those that had not. Among those who had not performed the ritual *bararti*, five men failed to turn up. Both parties, those who wanted to move and those not yet ready to camp at Manquphsa, presented their reasons. At this point Huqqa Sarite related a *mamaksa* that expressed the situation, referring to those who failed to turn up, to those who refused to wait and those not ready to perform the *bararti*. Huqqa started by stating his discontent at the men who refused to answer his call:

It is I who called this meeting, isn't it in accordance with the custom?
It is. [there is one 'answerer' among the audience].

Come once again.
I came.
A message may reach its destination, and can fail to reach it too.
Yes.
Has this message reached [the men who didn't come]?
Yes.
To come is one thing; have they?
No.
To make known one's inability to come has its custom; have I got that?
No, you have not.
Peace be upon us! [all the audience say together: 'Peace!'] Let God help us to walk according to the custom!
Let it be so!
As a matter of fact, it was you [addressing the answerer] who once related this *mamaksa*, only you lost some points then

[Now the narrator recites]

They said, Kitte Ali Dida, the Worda, woke up in the middle of the night just after cock-crow. He rose and said:

'Awach!
Camel owners calm in sleep
Cattle owners travelled in the two cool hours'.

He kept repeating this until the bird that heralds dawn began to sing. When it was already morning, people in the neighbourhood rose to take out the cattle into the fields. They asked each other. 'Have you heard what Kitte was saying last night?' 'Yes, he was saying,

"Camel owners calm in sleep
Cattle owners travelled in the two cool hours".'

'What does he mean by that?' 'We do not know, shall we ask him?' 'Yes we will'. They went to Kitte. 'Kitte, what were you saying last night?' 'Camel owners ...' 'What does camel owners travelled ... mean?' [He answered] 'It is about:

The day cattle cease to give milk
The day men become women
The day conceiving takes place by fireside.'

[Here the narrator interrupts to comment]

Behold, the children are sitting by the fireside. What lesson would they learn? Do they respect their father? The elder son may pretend not to have seen what his father is doing but the younger is more dangerous and might think it is the right thing. He even goes on to tell what he sees or imitate his father.

Then Kitte told the men, 'In the future you'll come to see the day when:

Milk will be that of goat
Loading will be the ass.'

Isn't this the situation we find ourselves in?
It is.

Analysis

To see how the participants understood the tale it is necessary to explain the full range of meanings. First the meaning of the tale as it is, and second on the basis of its situational context.

Kitte, the character in the tale, said: 'Camel owners calm in sleep/Cattle owners travelled in the two cool hours'. Borana are mainly cattle owners. During the long dry season the cattle will be taken long distances to where water or better grass is available. To arrive there in time the cattle must leave home long before sunrise. They must reach the pastures before the day gets hot, for cattle do not graze in the scorching sun. Then when it is about sunset the cattle are taken on the long walk home. These are the two cool hours of the day the cattle owners travel by. As for the camels, they can live on tree leaves which are always nearby and can go without water for many days. Therefore their owners do not need to rise early. The reference to camel owners is to the neighbouring Somali and Gabra who are camel raisers. Borana who keep camels do so for transport and not for major economic support. In the tale, what Kitte meant is: 'as you are cattle owners why do you sleep like the camel owners?'

But when they asked him for explanation, rather than directly saying so, he encrypted it by stating the implication of the first two verses. So when they ask him for the meaning of his last night's speech he replied, 'The day cattle cease to give milk'. This is caused by the failure of the owners to give the cattle the necessary attention. Cattle are kept for milk and if they do not have it, it means they cease to be cattle, which in turn means the Borana have ceased to live and behave like Borana. The line, 'The day men became women', makes this clear. People no more behave as they ought to and have turned into what they used not to be. The reference to men becoming women is an expression of the decadence in social values. Men like women stay at home, where they do not belong. The third line. 'The day conceiving takes place by fireside', is an emphatic way of speaking about the decline of tradition and the death of prudence and responsibility. When the father makes love by the fireside, in front of his children, he betrays the secret of fatherhood. The secret of being father is to go through all the pains of hard work, to sacrifice himself for the care of his children. Then the disgraceful father, the man who does not know how to hold the secret of fatherhood, is the vain man who could not even feed his children and tell them right from wrong. The children will not find any reason to look upon this man as their father.

Kitte's interpretation of his final speech is presented through its implications. The consequence and meaning of the Borana cattle owner behaving like a camel owner is a reversal of situations, implying poverty and decadence. Kitte concludes by deducing the future they will face:

'milk will be that of goat
loading will be the ass'.

Vanity will have caused poverty. Living only on the milk of the goat, which normally only the little ones drink, means starvation. For Borana who greatly value cattle milk, not to have it is humiliation. The next verse states about loading the ass. Borana frequently move from one place to another and use camels to transport their belongings and the ass, which is rarely owned by them, is figuratively an expression of contempt. 'To use the ass for moving camp' is an indication of the degradation of traditional values – to succumb to the contemptible. It refers to the meagreness of one's belongings.

Briefly this is the meaning of the tale when viewed out of its situational context. It tells about the cultural and economic pitfalls caused by a failure to adhere to one's defined duty. When viewed in context, the tale as a whole may remain the same in terms of general meaning. But certain parts – the main current focus will be emphasised to generate a particular and suitable meaning for the occasion. The ensuing interpretation of the tale in its situational context is based on the narrator's intention, which I acquired from Huqqa the narrator himself.

At the meeting Huqqa used the tale's cultural implication as the background, against men who failed to observe custom. The lines, 'Camel owners calm in sleep/ Cattle owners travelled in the two cool hours', will come to mean that people who own strong traditions and men who have rituals to observe should pay the price it exacts. The Borana consider the neighbouring peoples as 'less traditional' and the narrator's intention is to say: 'we are not such people, we have strong, rich traditions that require observance that is not easy'. To use the tale in a different context by interpreting it anew, the narrator focused on the line, 'The day conceiving takes place by fireside'. He interrupted the narration to comment on this verse and hence gave it a new appearance. The commentary is about the bad lesson a father teaches his children and how he loses his respect. It is this new interpretation by the narrator which in effect pushes the tale towards the desired direction and creates a direct link with the current situation as Huqqa understands it. Now the question becomes, 'If we fail to observe our customs rightly what will be the fate of our children?' It is the future of the society that is at stake. He fears that the younger generation will not respect the elders and the culture in general. Accordingly the last lines, 'milk will be that of goat/Loading will be the ass', are a premonition of the situation that will face their children. The narrator is blaming the interactants as creators of that bad future.

These last verses are also given another implicit meaning. The prophecy which was made long ago, during the composition of the tale, is declared as fulfilled, since members of the group are beginning to behave contrary to custom. So it serves to explain the behaviour of the participants, including those who have failed to turn up for the meeting.

This is the contextual interpretation of the tale. Huqqa began as if invoking it against the men who ignored his invitation but in the end he related it to the situation as a whole, touching every participant. He wisely chose a particularly relevant tale which could generate wider meaning so that it could apply to all concerned. To persuade them he oscillated between urging, blaming and warning. The *mamaksa* more than expressing the situation is employed to highlight the gravity of their mistake and to control their future action. The subtlety of the speaker is demonstrated by his choice of a tale which is about the decline of tradition and its consequence. Huqqa is trying to interpret the tale in a way that could benefit him. Since the participants are a special group of elders, who consider themselves as upholders of tradition, found in the 'sacred grade' – sacred enough not to call things like spear and fire by their workaday names – they do not want to play a role in the realization of the prophecy.

After a long deliberation and compromise, the meeting was postponed to give a second chance for those who had failed to come.

This short tale has been chosen because it brings in many of the points discussed regarding usage, function and local aesthetics. The narrator started by citing the source, Kitte Ali Dida, who is thought to be a real historical figure, and chose a tale that goes along with the case. The narrator manipulates a tale to generate multiple meanings in order to initiate a wider and immediate effect. The analysis of the communicative event shows how selection of narratives depends on the occasion and audience composition. It helps to show how members of the society value and use *mamaksa* as a tool of persuasion. The tale itself is an example of how folkloric items can be deeply localized and impenetrable to outsiders.

Chapter 6

In Summary

One of the advantages of studying folklore from the native point of view is that it helps to avoid reading theories into the material of the study. At first instance this might seem a negation of the spirit of scientific enquiry which establishes order in research. But if we consider the variety of theoretical proposals, and sometimes contradictions, contextual study saves us from being torn between differing approaches and definitions.

An important aspect of contextual analysis is that it makes the description and understanding of the ethnic genres in their own right possible. Each genre dictates the terms for its description. The folklorist looks for what unifies an ethnic genre without imposing his or her own preconception. From the analysis of Borana narratives it can be seen that even describing concepts like theme, structure and language need not be indiscriminately applied to each genre. Tales in one genre can have a set of different themes, structures and language properties. That is why tales in the different genres are grouped into subdivisions according to the formal features they share. The formalistic approaches of Propp and others have led us to assume the presence of structural unity beneath each genre. This is not necessarily true with the Borana narratives.

The function of the *duri-duri* for the children, for instance, is obviously entertainment. The researcher may observe that it also serves the function of enhancing memory and broadening imagination. Beyond these simple conclusions, talk about function will be based on the analyst's deductions. On the other hand native interpretation of the function of the *mamaksa* is broad and defined and the analyst can observe it on the ground. Therefore, if function is discussed vigorously in relation to the *mamaksa* and not the *duri-duri*, partly it is to try to see the genres as the users see them, and partly to avoid speculative deductions. Through analyses of performance and occasion, we have been able to understand their relationship with the rest of Borana cultural life.

Studying the narratives in their own context has provided a natural way of looking at them that is nearer to an insider's view. But it is not without its problems. As one is bound to learn, the owners disagree in interpreting what they collectively own. The points of disagreement may be few compared to the points of agreement but they exist. In defining genres, the Borana are observed arguing over where a particular tale should belong. Further, during debates some prove others wrong and views will change. For example, the definition of *arga-ageti* was first obtained from a group of elders who were all of the same opinion. Then quite a different definition was obtained from one Arero. A few days later a session was arranged and the two parties came together. They argued and Arero convinced the others that they are wrong. But they were wrong in an interesting way – even interpretations that are 'proved' wrong need not be ignored. That a member of a group can admit that his understanding is wrong implies the possibility of obtaining other mistaken interpretations. This brings in the methodological question of how to decide who the folklorist should listen to. The best storyteller may not be the best interpreter; interpretations, however sound and logical, coming from the narrower circles of the society may not be shared by the vast majority. In the end, the lesson learnt from contextual study is that the folklorist has to be aware of the danger of considering the culture as a homogeneous whole.

Another difficulty presented by contextual study is the lack of local interpretations on some issues. The researcher hoping to base his study fully on the native's point of view demands explanation on every aspect; but most of his questions turn out to be something the people have never thought about before. Even though they own and perform the narratives, they do not often make critical examinations. Sometimes interpretations that have not been acknowledged verbally are revealed during the communication process. The actors are unconscious of some of their attitudes and practices. It is only from observing the communicative event that one can realise the relationship between effective usage and the identity of the speaker.

Part Two

The Narratives in Translation

Chapter 7

Duri-Duri: Children's Tales

D1 *The Treacherous Fox* **[10]

It is said that a very long time ago Lion, Fox, Hook (*ookko*)[11] Crane, *Soso* (milk-pot cleaner) and Hyena began to live together. One day Fox and *Soso* were out grazing the cattle. Fox said to *Soso*, 'Go to this [nearby] village and ask them for water.' 'I won't,' said *Soso*, 'they will take me away.' 'They won't, I will tell them that you are ours and take you back,' said Fox. So *Soso* went and the villagers, seeing her, said, 'We have got a *soso*,' and took her away. At night when the cattle returned home the others asked, 'Where is *Soso*?' Fox replied, 'She went to ask for water despite my warning and they took her away.'

The next day Hook and Fox took out the cattle to the fields. Now Fox said to Hook, 'Go to this neighbourhood and ask them for water.' Hook refused, 'I won't, they will take me away.' Fox said, 'They won't. I will tell them you are ours and take you back.' Hook went and the villagers kidnapped her. At night the others asked, 'Where is Hook?' 'She went to the village to ask for water and they took her away,' said Fox.

Another day they were grazing the cattle with Crane. Fox suggested that they should chew some tree gum. She gave some to Crane that she put in her mouth. Fox only pretended to chew. While Crane was chewing, the gum got glued to her teeth and she was unable to open her mouth. 'Crane!' called out the fox. 'hmmm,' mumbled Crane [her mouth being sealed]. 'Oh! You are making fun of Uncle Lion by imitating his voice. I will tell him,' threatened Fox. While they were returning home Fox hastened to tell Lion that Crane was impersonating him. 'You see for yourself, call her,' she said. 'Crane!' called the lion. 'Hmmm,' mumbled Crane. 'Are you impersonating me?' said Lion and killed her. The next day Fox went out with Hyena. As they were herding the cattle Lion's cow gave birth to a calf. 'Let's eat the calf,' said Fox. Hyena ate the flesh of the calf whereas Fox only drank the blood. Then they

---

10 Items marked with ** are also presented in Borana.
11 A stick with a V-shaped fork on one end and a hook on the other, which is the tool used for collecting thorn bush and building stock pens.

caught an antelope and returned home with it. The lion saw the antelope and asked what the cow had given birth to. The fox said, 'To a calf.' 'Who ate it?' asked the lion. 'The hyena,' said the fox. Hyena protested. But the fox said, 'Beat us both and you will know the truth.' Lion beat Fox and nothing came out. When Lion beat Hyena, he bawled and the calf's intestine came out through his mouth. 'You ate my calf,' said Lion and beat Hyena to death.

Now the fox and the lion went out herding. Fox took with her an ox's hide and climbed up a hill. She wrapped a big stone with the hide and pushed it down the hill. The fox on top cried to the lion below:

> Uncle Lion, Uncle Lion;
> My ox and your ox fought.
> Your ox is rolling down.
> Stop it with your chest,
> With your chest.

When the lion tried to stop it with his chest, the stone ran over him and killed him.

In this way the fox killed all of them and took for herself all their cattle.

D2 *The Fox Who Ate Elephant's Honey*

It is said that one day a very long time ago Fox was standing by the road side when Elephant came along carrying a pot full of honey. He said, 'Uncle, why are you standing here?' 'I have become poor,' said Fox. Elephant said, 'I will take you home,' and put her on his back. He then said, 'Don't open the honeypot.' Fox said, 'Uncle if you hear the sound *buuk* [the sound of opening] don't turn your head; it is the fart of a poor one. If you hear the sound of droplets, don't turn; they are the tears of the poor.' Then she opened the pot. When Elephant heard the sound and was about to turn his head, she said, 'Don't turn it is the fart of a poor one.' Again when the honey leaked through her fingers, she said, 'Don't turn, it is the tears of a poor one.' 'I won't,' said Elephant. Fox ate all the honeyand filled the pot with her excrement. She was full to bursting and became unable to jump down from Elephant's back. Now she said, 'Uncle, our people like to pass under a big tree. Please pass by a big tree.' When he did, she clung to a branch of the tree.

Elephant arrived home and said to his wife, 'There is a person on my back, open the door.' When she did so, he entered and said, 'Take down the man on my back.' 'There is no-one on your back,' said the wife. Elephant said, 'If I roll on my back and find him, I will kill you.' 'Kill me,' she said. He rolled, and there was no one. 'Forget it. there is no-one,' he said and opened the honey pot. When he opened, he found it full of faeces. 'She has ruined me,' he said and went back to get the fox.

When Elephant came back, Fox was still on the tree unable to come down. He seized her by the tail and struck her against the ground. This time she said, 'Our people are beaten with the root of an anthill, beat me with it.' The elephant began to dig under an anthill, but while digging, the anthill fell on him. He came back to Fox in anger and, when he was about to beat her again, she said, 'Our people are beaten with the root of the sun, beat me with the root of the sun.' He tied her to a tree and went to find the sun's root [where sun's ray hits the ground].

By this time a hyena had approached Fox and said, 'Uncle, what do you do here?' 'They tied me here because I refused to eat the fattened tail of a black sheep,' Fox said. Then the hyena said, 'I will eat,' and untied her and took her place. Now Elephant returned angry and unable to find the sun's root. He found Hyena there and beat him. While Elephant beat him, Hyena was crying, 'I will eat, I will eat.' At the same time Elephant was raging, 'Let you be eaten, what is it that you eat?' Elephant beat Hyena to death.

D3 Fox and Hyena in Search of Cattle

They said that a very long time ago Hyena and Fox set out in quest of cattle. Fox found a thin ox and Hyena a fat one. They took home their finds to kill and eat. Then again they set out to look for knife. Hyena found a double-bladed iron knife. Fox found bird's feathers.

When they returned home, Fox inserted *buri* [a juicy wild root like a sweet potato] into the anus of her emaciated ox. Then Fox said, 'Uncle Hyena, in order to see which ox is the fatter let's drive them up hill.' As they drove the oxen up hill the juicy potato in Fox's ox got squashed and began to pour down. 'Uncle look, mine is the fatter, the fat is coming out,' said Fox excitedly. Hyena begged Fox to exchange hers for his. 'Give me.' 'I won't.' 'Give me.' 'I won't.' 'Give me.' Finally Fox said in exasperation:

> I'm Fox, Hyena is you.
> You are a real fool,
> The fool of white shit. [hyena shit is white]
> Take, go to hell with it.

She exchanged her thin ox for Hyena's fat one. They returned home. Fox picked the feathers she got and she said, 'Uncle, if this one gets bent, I will use this one; if this one gets bent I will use this one; I have many. With what do you slaughter if the one knife you have gets bent?' Hyena said, 'Uncle Fox give me your knives and take mine.' 'I won't' 'Please give me.' Then again Fox said:

> I'm Fox, Hyena is you.
> You are a real fool,
> The fool of white shit.
> Take, go to hell with it.

And they exchanged the feathers for the iron knife.

When they were about to slaughter the oxen, Hyena was unable to cut his ox with the feathers. Fox saw this, came to his help and said, "Bring your knives, I will help you slaughter." Pretending to cut with the feathers, she quickly cut the ox's throat with her iron knife without Hyena discovering.

Now Hyena's children, fed on the thin ox's meat, grew thin. Fox's children who ate the fattened ox, grew fat. Hyena asked her, 'Uncle Fox, how did you fatten your children?' Fox explained, 'I boil water and when it bubbles I put my children in it for the whole night. By morning I take them out, saying 'My cheerful ones have bubbled' and kiss them. That is my secret.'

Hyena didn't ask further questions. He boiled water and put his children in it. Fox, who saw this, went to her home, covered a pot with a blanket, put it in bed and fled away. Hyena rose early in the morning and after saying, 'My cheerful ones have bubbled,' he opened the pot. When he was about to kiss his children, he realized that they are dead. He roared, 'She destroyed me,' and dashed towards Fox's house. He arrived at Fox's house and struck the blanket-covered-pot. When he saw the broken pieces of the pot he grew even angrier and went to pursue her. He went looking and at last sat at the mouth of a water well.

Fox saw Hyena and came over, first covering herself with tree barks (soso). She said, 'Water Owner, make me drink.' Hyena said, 'I may or may not; but who are you?' 'I am Mother *Soso*,' she said. Then the hyena said:

> My dear Mother *Soso*
> Go down and drink,
> Dip in your buttocks.

Fox went down, drank and bathed and went home. Another day she came covered with grass. 'Water Owner, make me drink.' 'I may or may not, but who are you?' 'I am Mother Grass.' Hyena said:

> My dear Mother Grass
> Go down and drink,
> Dip in your buttocks.

Fox drank, bathed and went home. Still another day she came covered with ash: 'Water Owner, make me drink.' 'I may or may not; but who are you?' 'I am Mother Ash.' He said:

> My dear Mother Ash
> Go down and drink,
> Dip in your buttocks

When Fox came out of the water, the ash got washed away. Hyena saw her and knew who she was. She ran away and he pursued. He seized her by the tail. But this time Fox said, 'You caught the soft, catch the stiff,' and defecated. Hyena released her tail and seized her pouring waste. And she escaped.

D4 How Monkey Destroyed Fox and Lion

It is said that a very long time ago Monkey, Fox and Lion were living together. Lion rose early one day and went to hunt. At home Monkey climbed on Lion's sycamore tree and began to eat the fruit. Fox came and begged Monkey to give her some. 'I won't,' said Monkey. 'Please, please give me some' begged Fox. 'I won't,' said the monkey. 'When Uncle Lion returns, if I don't tell him, I am not born!' 'Tell him, I am not afraid of Lion. And I will not let you eat this fruit. I am capable of making a stone shoe,' said Monkey. 'So you know how to make a stone shoe, yet the paws of Uncle Lion get pierced by thorn when he hunts,' said Fox.

In the evening, when Lion returned home, Fox told him what Monkey had said. Lion asked Monkey and she replied, 'Yes I can make a shoe from stone.' Lion said, 'Then make it now.' Monkey said, 'Well it needs additional material; if I get a fox's hide I can make it.' 'Fox's hide is no problem,' said Lion and cut off Fox's head. Monkey took the hide and said, 'It still needs another material, take me to a big river.' They went to a river. Monkey covered the stone with the hide and threw it down the river. Then she cried, 'Uncle, something big like you snatched it from me.' Lion came and saw his reflection in the water. 'Our people do not retreat from such things,' he said and jumped into the river and drowned.

In this way Monkey destroyed both Fox and Lion.

D5 The Wrestler He-Goat

It is said that a very long time ago there was one he-goat. He was so thin and emaciated that he could not walk. When the owners moved to a new camp, they left him behind. It was the dry season and the he-goat simply lay there in the hut barely alive. Then fell the rain. The he-goat drank water from the incense hole [a bowl-shaped hole in which incense is burnt] by the bedside. He grazed the grass from under the fence. He gained weight and became very big. Now he left the deserted camp.

He-goat came to Lion's house and bleated. Lion heard and said, 'Now, I have taken my goats to the fields in the morning; which one is bleating here?' Then He-goat said, 'It is me, He-goat, who thrived on water that gathered in the incense-hole and grass from under the fence. Wrestle with me.' And they wrestled. He-goat bounced Lion to the ground. 'I don't believe it, Let's wrestle again,' said the amazed lion. Again they wrestled and He-goat knocked Lion down. He-goat knocked down Lion twice and then he left.

He-goat came to Hyena's place. At the yard he bleated 'Now I have taken my goats to the fields in the morning; which one is bleating here?' said Hyena and came out to look. 'It is me, He-goat, who thrived on incense-hole water and grass from under the fence. Wrestle with me,' challenged the he-goat. They wrestled. He-goat knocked Hyena to the ground. 'I don't believe it, let's do it again,' said Hyena. Again He-goat knocked Hyena down. He knocked Hyena down twice and left.

Now He-goat came to Fox's yard. He bleated. Fox said, 'I have taken my goats to the fields in the morning, now which one is bleating here?' He-goat answered, 'It is me, He-goat, who thrived on incense hole water and grass from under the fence. Wrestle with me.' And they wrestled. He-goat knocked Fox down to the ground. 'I don't believe it, let's do it again,' said Fox. Again Fox was knocked down. Then Fox said, 'You knocked me down; but can you penetrate this wood cleft?' 'Yes I can,' said goat and entered into the cleft. He stuck there. 'I am going to die, go and call a medicine man,' said goat. Fox went. She didn't go far, but returned washing her face with her urine. She said, 'Look how the search made me sweat, look at my sweat; I couldn't find the medicine man.' 'Go and look for him again,' said He-goat. Fox went and returned, again pretending that she was unable to find the medicine man.

He-goat died. Fox ate it. One leg remained, and hanging it on a tree, Fox left. A chicken came and ate the hung meat. The fox discovered this and went to the owners of the chicken and said:

> I slaughtered a he-goat
> And hung the leg on a tree.
> A chicken ate the leg.
> Unless I am given the chicken
> I will not survive for a single day.

They gave her the chicken. Taking the chicken, Fox came to a woman making soup. The woman struck the chicken dead with the stirrer. The fox cried:

> I slaughtered a he-goat
> And hung the leg on a tree.
> A chicken ate the leg.
> They gave me the chicken.
> A woman who stirs soup killed it with the stirrer.
> Unless I am given the stirrer
> I will not survive for a single day.

The woman gave it to her. She went to goats, which were fighting, and put the stirrer in the middle of them. They broke it. Fox said to the owners:

> I slaughtered a he-goat
> And hung the leg on a tree.
> A chicken ate the leg.
> They gave me the chicken.
> A woman who stirs soup killed it with the stirrer.
> They gave me the stirrer.
> A he-goat broke it.
> Unless I am given this he-goat
> I will not survive for a single day.

They gave her the he-goat. She came across oxen fighting, and placed the he-goat between them. They killed the he-goat. Fox said:

> I slaughtered a he-goat
> And hung the leg on a tree.
> A chicken ate the leg.
> They gave me the chicken.
> A woman who stirs soup killed it with the stirrer.
> They gave me the stirrer.
> A he-goat broke it.
> They gave me the he-goat.
> An ox killed it.
> Unless I am given this ox
> I will not survive for a single day.

They gave it to her. She went to camels, who were returning home after drinking water. She put the ox in their way and said to them, 'Grey one, step over; red one, step over; white one, step over; brown one, step on it.' The brown camel at the end of the procession stepped on it and killed the ox. Fox cried:

> I slaughtered a he-goat
> And hung the leg on a tree.
> A chicken ate the leg.
> They gave me the chicken.
> A woman who stirs soup killed it with the stirrer.
> They gave me the stirrer.
> A he-goat broke it.
> They gave me the he-goat.
> An ox killed it.
> They gave me the ox.
> This she-camel killed it.
> Unless I am given this she-camel
> I will not survive for a single day.

They gave it to her. Now the she-camel was about to give birth. Fox called snake and begged it to mid-wife the camel. Snake mid-wifed the camel and took for himself the newly born and gave the fox the placenta. 'Give me the baby camel,' said Fox. But snake refused. Fox went and appealed to squirrel:

> I slaughtered a he-goat
> And hung the leg on a tree.
> A chicken ate the leg.
> They gave me the chicken.
> A woman who stirs soup killed it with the stirrer.
> A he-goat broke it.
> They gave me the he-goat.
> An ox killed it.
> They gave me the ox.
> A camel killed it.
> They gave me the camel.
> Snake took away my baby,
> Come and make him return it.

Squirrel came and said, 'Snake, give back Fox's baby.' This time snake said, 'I will pinch you with my pincers, go away.' To this Squirrel said, 'I will weave you into a milking-pot, return it to her.' Snake refused. They wrestled and Squirrel won. The defeated snake confessed: 'Fox's baby is in the little milking-pot.' Fox received her baby [little camel] and went home. Squirrel helped Fox in getting back her baby in this way.

D6 *The Sinner She-Goat that Brought Destruction*

It is said that a very long time ago there was one she-goat. A girl was looking after this goat. She-goat said to the girl, 'Milk me.' 'I won't,' said the girl. 'If you don't milk me I will commit suicide by squeezing myself into a tree cleft,' threatened the goat. The girl milked her. At evening they returned home and there the goat cried:

> In the field the herdgirl drains me
> At home my baby drains me
> How can I survive this dry season and reach the rains?

The father who heard this said, 'How dare you milk the goat?' and beat his daughter. The next day the son looked after the goat. 'Milk me,' she begged him. 'I won't.' 'If you don't milk me I will commit suicide by squeezing myself into a tree cleft.' He milked her and they returned home. Again she cried:

> In the field the herdboy drains me
> At home my baby drains me
> How can I survive this dry season and reach the rains?

The father beat his son. The next day the mother looked after the goat. 'Milk me.' 'I won't,' said the mother. 'If you don't milk me I will commit suicide by squeezing myself into a tree cleft.' She milked her. At evening they returned home. She-goat cried:

> In the field the herdswoman drains me
> At home my baby drains me
> How can I survive this dry season and reach the rains?

The father beat the mother too. The next morning the father took her to the grazing.'Milk me.' 'I won't.' 'I will commit suicide by squeezing myself into a tree cleft.' The father milked her into an upturned leaf. When they returned home she said:

> In the field the herdsman drains me
> At home my baby drains me
> How can I survive this dry season and reach the rains?

Now the father said, 'What I milked out of this goat is only this. She speaks evil. It is in this way that she harmed many people.' He showed the milk in the leaf to others. 'Evil She-goat,' he said and killed her. They took the meat home and ate some of it. Now came a guest, a son-in-law. When they saw him they said, 'Sorry, we have just finished the meat.' Then the meat in the kitchen spoke:

> Here is my head
> Here are my inner parts
> Here is the soup.
> They have slaughtered me.

They were embarrassed, and they threw the bones out of the house.

A boy who was going out to the fields saw a bone and struck it with his cane. When he struck it, bone spoke, 'I caught you, I caught you.' The boy was baffled: 'You Boran, I saw a bone that talks,' he told the people. 'What if you are lying, should we kill you?' 'Yes, kill me.' They came and struck bone. It kept silent. They killed the boy and buried him. When they were returning from the burial they struck bone just for fun. Now bone cried, 'I caught you!' 'Hey look, bone really talks. We killed the boy wrongly,' they said.

Evil She-goat destroyed many people in this way.

D7 The Slanderer

There were three people. These people left their village in search of jobs.
When they arrived in one country, they went to a rich man and spoke: 'We
need jobs. I am a thief without equal,' said one. 'I am voracious, I have no
equal in my voracity,' said another. 'I am a slanderer, people are tired of my
slander,' said the third. The rich man said, 'I will hire you. Come.'

The thief was entrusted with the garden. He stole and stole; he sold and
sold the fruits from the garden until he became sick of it. The voracious one
ate, and ate, and ate and became sick of it. To the slanderer the employer
said, 'I am going to work, watch my door; don't do any thing just keep an
eye on my wife.'

For a long time the man was guarding the house, and all the time he was
talking and gossiping about this and that until he had nothing to talk about.
Now having nothing to talk about, one time, at night, while husband and
wife were sleeping he poured a cup of water in the middle of them. When
the husband woke up, the sheets were wet. 'It is you who pissed on me.' 'No
I didn't.' Husband and wife argued. The guard was asleep, had he seen any
thing? Was it him who poured the water? In the morning when the husband
went to work, the guard said to the wife, 'Madam, you know my master
says you pissed on him.'

The husband returned from work. When he returned the slanderer said to
him, 'Master, madam said that you have pissed on her.' And then he said to
the wife, 'Madam now I will tell you something' – according to their custom
it is the wife who shaves the husband's pubic hair – 'I will tell you the way you
could find out what he has really said. When he returns from work, tell him
that you would like to shave his pubic hair. He will refuse and you will know
by this.' The husband returned from work. 'Master, madam said you've pissed
on her. If she asks you to shave your pubic hair, don't allow her to do so. She
has something in her mind.' Now when both husband and wife were at home,
the wife came with a razor. 'Let me have shave your pubic hair,' she said. 'Are
you going to kill me?' asked the husband and shot her with a pistol.

The man killed his wife and sealed her in a coffin. The slanderer cried,
'My mistress, no-one knows what happened to you. No-one has seen your
body.' The wife's relatives heard this and demanded to inspect her body.
When they opened the coffin they saw a bullet wound. Realizing that the
husband had shot her, one of them shot the husband. When the husband
died one of the husband's relatives shot the killer. Another man shot the
killer and that killer was shot by another.

In this way one slanderer caused the death of nine people.

D8 The Wicked Brothers

It is said that a very long time ago there lived a man who had seven wives.
The youngest wife had a son and this boy had a steer. The rest of his

half-brothers had a large number of cattle. They hated this boy. 'You! Shall we castrate your steer?' they said. He said,'OK.' They castrated it. The steer grew and became a big ox. Now they asked him, 'Shall we slaughter it?' 'Yes, and give me the hide.' They killed the ox and gave the boy the hide.

He travelled the whole day and climbed up a tree. The enemy who raided Borana cattle camped for the night under that tree. In the middle of the night the boy on the tree let the hide fall. It created a terrible noise 'Gwagwagwa.' The raiders said, 'The Borana are attacking us,' and ran away. The boy took all the cattle and returned home. At home he said to his brothers, 'Nothing can do good to a person like a hide does. Kill all your cattle.'

They killed all their cattle, carried away the hides and went. 'Do you buy hide?' they asked. 'Let God destroy you and your hides!' The people chased the brothers away. They returned home humiliated. 'We will burn your house,' they said to the boy. 'Burn it and give me the ash.' They burned it. He put the ash in a sack and went to another country. He passed the night in a house. He rose early in the morning and cried. When the people asked him what he is crying for, he said that they took his sack of gold and replaced it with ashes. The elders deliberated and paid him with cattle. He returned home and told his brothers, 'Nothing can do good to a person like ash does.'

The brothers burnt their houses, including the fences, and collected the ash into bags. Hoping to sell the ash they shouted, 'Ashes, ashes!' People who heard them retorted, 'Let God make an ash out of you,' and chased them away. They returned home and put their wily brother in a bag. Then they threw the bag into a river.

Along came a man who was seated on a mule and driving many cattle. Thinking he had got a bag, he retrieved it out of the water. When he opened it, there was a man inside. 'What are you doing here?' the traveller asked. 'Some people asked me to wait in here and they promised to come with something special. They will also give me a large amount of money.' When the man heard this, he begged the boy to exchange places with him. In return he would give him his cattle and the mule. The boy in the bag agreed. He enclosed the man in the bag and threw him into the river. Then he took all of his cattle and went home. At home he said to his brothers, 'Look what a river does. Look what I have got out of the river.' All his brothers ran in haste towards the river and all were drowned.

D9 The Trickster Didd Flinch **

It is said that a very long time ago there lived a boy named Didd Flinch. The boy lived alone with his mother. He looked after the cattle of the Borana.

One day he took out the cattle to the pastures early in the morning. There were other boys herding cattle. It was a holiday season and the boys had come with the holiday bread. Didd Flinch had got none. The other boys seated under the shade of a tree began to eat. Didd came to them with a kneaded lump of mud covered in a piece of cloth. He said, 'Let's eat yours first, and then we will eat mine.' And he ate. Then he said, 'Let me go and muster the cattle, I will return soon.' He went past the cattle and ran away. The other boys, who were a great number, pursued him. They seized him, tied him up and threw him into a hyena's hole.

At evening the cattle returned home. Didd's mother asked the boys about her son's absence. The boys told her that they have not seen him since morning. She went to look for him. She called out, 'Didd Flinch, Didd Flinch!' Hyena was listening to her. From the mouth of his hole Hyena too called out, 'Didd Flinch!' Didd Flinch, assuming the caller to be his mother, answered the call. Hyena took him out, put him on his back and went away. After a long run Hyena put him down and told Didd, 'Now I am Hyena, I am going to eat you.' The boy said, "You will have me alright, but go and call all your relatives. You will eat me together.'

When Hyena had gone, he collected stones and climbed a tall tree. When Hyena came back with his relatives the boy was not there. He called out 'Didd Flinch, Didd Flinch.' 'Yes!' 'Come down, we are come to eat you,' said Hyena. 'You will eat me, open your mouth.' When they opened wide, Didd hurled his stones into their mouths. He killed all but one. Didd had run out of stones. This hyena remained under the tree.

In the morning Didd saw a farmer come by, driving his oxen. He said, 'Abbo, I will be a son to you; kill this hyena.' The farmer killed the hyena and took the boy home. He told his wife, 'This is our son, take care of him.

Next day in the morning he took the boy to show him the farmland. Then he sent Didd back to fetch seeds. The boy came home and said to his mother, 'Father has said "kill both the he-goats we have and prepare the meat for us."' She killed the goats, gave the boy some meat to eat and the rest she sent back with him.

But Didd Flinch took the meat and ran away. As he ran away he came across a man mounted on a horse and greeted him. The man stopped and greeted him. Then the man dismounted from the horse to urinate. Didd offered to take care of the horse and, when the man was in the bush, he mounted the horse and rode away. As he rode he came across an old woman collecting firewood. The old woman said to him, 'Dear, come help me carry this wood.' Didd Flinch asked, 'To what am I to tie my horse?' 'Tie it to this tree,' said the woman. 'It is not the custom to tie a horse to a tree, but to a human leg.' 'All right, tie it to my leg and please put the wood on my back.' He tied the horse to her leg, put the wood on her back, and without untying the rope he mounted on the horse and went on dragging the old woman to the ground. Thus he killed the old woman.

When it was getting dark he made his way to some Borana houses and said to them, 'This woman is not well, I'll get her into bed, please get my horse into the stock pen. The next day early in the morning he rose and went out in the pretext of checking the horse. Now the woman is lying dead in the bed, and he knows that she is already dead. He cried. The neighbours came out running. He complained, 'This people have killed an old woman who is ill. I too fled for my life. That is why I am crying at this hour.' The neighbours talked it over and paid him the blood price.

Then he went on. He came across cattle merchants who had camped under a tree. From behind he climbed into the tree and let the horse's saddle fall from his hand. Frightened by the *bobobobobo* noise of the falling saddle the merchants fled away. Didd Flinch took the cattle and returned to his home.

D10 *The Lost Family*

There was a man who had a wife, two sons, two cattle and a camel. The family wanted to move to another place. They went in the direction of a river and crossed it. As they traveled, the children became hungry and the father killed a cow for them. Left with a camel, a cow, a wife and two children the man resumed his journey. Once again the children became hungry and the father slaughtered the camel. The father told his wife to fetch water, and picking up a pot she went, but she fell into the river and died.

When the wife failed to return, the husband wondered 'where has the woman gone to?' He went to the river, instructing his little son to take care of the meat. When the father was gone the elder son said, 'Just as Father has slaughtered the camel, I will slaughter you.' And he slew him. When the father returned, unable to find his wife, he found his younger son slain. He said to the killer, 'Why do you ruin me!' and went for him. The elder son ran away. He ran away to where his mother had gone. And running he fell into the river and drowned. Only one man was left and he belongs to god.

D11 *The Hobgoblin*[12] *who Took a Borana Wife and Ate Her*

It is said that a very long time ago a hobgoblin married a Borana girl. The girl had a sister who lived with her. One day hobgoblin said to her, 'Sister-in-law, I and my wife have something to do: please take out the cattle to the distant pastures.' The sister-in-law went off with the cattle. Husband and wife remained at home. Hobgoblin said to his wife, 'Please cut off your breast and give it to me.' 'A person whose breast is severed will die; I will not give you,' said the wife. 'I know why you will not die, give me,' insisted hobgoblin. She cut off her breast and gave it to him. 'Give me the other one too,' he said. 'I will die, I won't cut the other one,' she said. 'You will not die; I know that you won't die.' She cut it off and gave it to him. Soon she died. He ate her flesh. Then he went to the sister-in-law who was herding

---

12 *Bulguu*, translated as hobgoblin, are more malevolent than mischevious and often eat human flesh.

the cattle. 'Are the cattle in peace?' he asked. 'In peace.' Before coming to her the hobgoblin had laid the body on the bed, covering it with a blanket. Now he said to the girl, 'Your sister is not well, don't wake her and don't talk to her. There is roasted liver in the dish, eat it.' [It is her sister's flesh you know.] 'There is water in the pot, drink it. Go.'

The girl came home. She opened the pot to drink water. 'My blood, would you drink my blood?' spoke something out of the pot. It was her sister's blood. She left it alone. Then she picked up the liver. 'My liver would you eat my liver?' spoke the liver. She put it back. Then she saw the mortar on the bed. She sat and waited.

At night the hobgoblin returned home. He said, 'Sister-in-law, have you eaten the liver?' 'Yes, I have.' 'Have you drunk water?' 'Yes, I have.' Now, after the cows had been milked, he sat on the bed, and he said, 'If you hear a hyena crushing bones at the back of our home, shout, "I struck you with spear," ' [Now he is saying this in order to eat the bones of his wife.] Then he stayed in the bedroom and began to eat the bones. The sister-in-law, sitting in front of the hut by the fireside, heard the sound of the crushing and began to say, 'I struck you with spear'.

As she was sitting there she wove a rope and then tied the door tightly with it so that it would not open. She was outside the hut, which she then set on fire. Now the hobgoblin said, 'My sister-in-law deliver me out of the fire.' 'First you deliver my sister out of your belly.' Then he said, 'If you hear my liver explode, flee.' The liver exploded. She went away.

Soon she came across three lions. The lions said to her, 'We came when we saw this fire, what is it?' 'Three oxen were killed, but there are not enough people to eat them. I am going in search of men who would eat,' said the girl. One of the lions was blind. The two lions said to the blind one, 'Blind one, seize the arm of this girl, we will go and see. If she is lying we will come back and eat her.' The blind lion seized her arm. The girl took a club and put it into the blind lion's paw, withdrawing her arm. Then she ran away.

The lions returned: 'Blind one, the girl is simply lying. It is the house of Borana that is burning. Now where is she?' they asked him. 'Here she is.' 'Where?' 'Here, I am holding her arm can't you see?' He was showing them the club in his paw. In anger they took the club away from him and beat him to death.

In this way the girl who killed the hobgoblin also caused the death of a lion.

D12 The Two Lovers and the Hobgoblins

It is said that a very long time ago there were a boy and a girl. They were goatherds. One day while herding the goats they said to each other, 'When we grow up we will marry each other and no one else.' Time passed, they grew up and got married. The husband's parents were in Dirre, across the Dawa river, and one day he went to visit them.

A hobgoblin came to the house of the lonely woman and said to her, 'Shall I eat these heifers and the dog, or you?' She said, ' Don't eat me, eat these heifers and the dog.' At this time, a Borana man approached, talking to himself. She heard his voice and said to him [in song]:

Eh! You Borana, take this message
My husband is not here, he is in Dirre
My name is Bokro, his name is Sarmo
His horses are seven kraals
His goats are seven kraals
His horse knows how to swim
My heart knows remembrance.

'Please tell this to him.' The Borana man wondered, 'What am I hearing?' and listened carefully.

My name is Bokro, his name is Sarmo
His horses are seven kraals
His goats are seven kraals
His horse knows how to swim
My heart knows remembrance.

The message reached the husband and he mounted his horse. He came across a river and said to his horse, 'If you fail to get across this river, this whip will devour you.' To the whip he said, 'If you fail to thrash the horse well, this river will devour you.' and to the river he said, 'If you fail to swallow this whip, I will cut you apart.' The horse crossed the river and the river parted for if. The husband reached his home.

One of the hobgoblins was out collecting firewood. The second was ploughing, and the third sitting by the fireside ready to cook the wife. This latter hobgoblin was praying, 'My God, pour down my throat the blood of a red woman.' The husband came in stealthily from behind and killed this one. Then he shouted to the others outside, 'You are in danger, flee!' The hobgoblin collecting wood shouted back, 'Are you saying 'roast is ready, come?'' and came running. The husband waited and killed it with a spear. Again the husband shouted to the last hobgoblin, 'You are in danger flee; you are in danger flee!' The hobgoblin shouted back, 'Are you saying 'roast is ready, come; roast is ready, come'?' And he came running. The husband waited and killed this one too.

He destroyed all three in this way.

D13 The Hobgoblin who Buried his Wife**

It is said that a very long time ago there was a family consisting of husband, wife and a son. They say there was a hobgoblin in that country. The family had built a house. Father and son went to graze the cattle. The father shut the door keeping the mother inside and told her, 'Don't chew gum from a tree, don't make aluminium wrist bracelets, do not weave a fibre tray [ie do not act like a woman, as these activities are women's work].' Then the man made a hole in the roof and went out through it.

Hobgoblin came to the wife and asked her, 'Where is the entrance?' 'What?' 'I have a message from your family, show me the entrance,' said hobgoblin. 'Come in by the way of the roof,' she said. Hobgoblin climbed down through the roof and said, 'Shall I eat you or dig a hole and bury you?' 'Dig and bury me.' Hobgoblin buried the woman in the cattle enclosure.

Then hobgoblin swallowed the milking pot and waited. She was sitting when the husband came in. 'Bring me my stool,' he told her. Hobgoblin roamed all over the house [for she didn't know his stool]. 'Has the woman gone crazy, has the woman gone crazy?' asked the husband. She handed him the stool. Then the husband said, 'Hand me my milk-pot-the-full.' She began to go up and down past the milk-pot. 'Has the woman gone crazy, has the woman gone crazy?' he said. She went out. [He called her and] He asked her to lay out his sleeping hide. As she did not know which one is his, she walked out of the house. This time the son said, 'Father, this thing is not mother, this thing is not mother.' 'Has the boy gone crazy, has the boy gone crazy?' asked the father.

[The next day] They were about to move to a new camp. They put hobgoblin on a horse and began their journey. One cow, whose baby calf was dead, turned back to the house they had left. The cow began to the dig where the wife was buried. The cow dug and dug, revealing the wife. When the husband returned [for the cow] the wife was there. He dug, took her out and went back. On his way back he raised his voice and called out to his son:

> Hey! Wariyo, Wariyo!
> That thing is beast
> Unload it from the horse with spear
> Unload it from the horse with spear.

'What did you say? What did you say?' asked the son. The father returned:

> Hey! Wariyo, Wariyo!
> Prevent the saddle from leaning
> Prevent the mother on the horse from going
> Thrust a spear on the horse
> That thing is a beast.

While saying this, he caught up with them and killed the hobgoblin on the horse with a spear.

D14 *The Drunk Hobgoblin*

It is said that a very long time ago there were a husband and wife. The wife made beverages and the husband tilled the land. One day when he was about to go out for work he said to his wife, 'I have many enemies in this area; shut the door firmly. I will give you a password so that you can open only for me.' 'What is it?' she asked. 'I will sing this:

Aya Jile Boku, aya Jile Boku
I am back, open the door.

'How did you say it?' she asked.

Aya Jile Boku, aya Jile Boku
I am back, open the door.

The next day when he returned he sang:

Aya Jile Boku, aya Jile Boku
I am back, open the door.

She opened. He came in, she gave him food, he ate and went again. One day hobgoblin heard him when he was saying the password. The next day, when the husband was not in, hobgoblin came in and sang [in a heavy voice]:

Aya Jile Boku, aya Jile Boku
I am back open the door.

The wife wondered, 'This is not my husband's voice.' Then hobgoblin corrected his mistake and sang just like the husband and she opened the door. Hobgoblin entered and seized her. He put her on the chicken-bed [near the roof]. Then hobgoblin began to drink the beer. He drank his fill and slept by the fireside. The husband came and sang the song. The hobgoblin listened carefully:

Aya Jile Boku, aya Jile Boku
I am back, open the door.

Now he said:

Aya Jile Boku, aya Jile Boku
Something dangerous has caught me
Bang your gun and go to your homeland.

The husband lifted the gun and fired it. The bullet passed through the door and killed the hobgoblin.

D15 *The Hobgoblin who Ate the Herdboy*

A very long time ago it is said that a hobgoblin came to a boy who was herding camels. First it devoured the boy, then swallowed his milking-pot and finally it devoured the five camels. The father who came in search of the boy cried:

> Have you seen Aliyo's son?
> Have you seen his milking-pot?
> Have you seen the five camels?

Then hobgoblin replied:

> Aliyo's son is devoured
> His milking-pot is devoured
> The five camels are devoured.

[And he ate the father.]
Then came the mother of the boy and cried:

> Have you seen Aliyo's son?
> Have you seen his milking-pot?
> Have you seen the five camels?

Hobgoblin answered:

> Aliyo's son is devoured
> His milking pot is devoured
> The five camels are devoured.

Now came a woman pregnant with twins. She said:

> Have you seen Aliyo's son?
> Have you seen his milking-pot?
> Have you seen the five camels?

This time hobgoblin refused to answer. There the woman gave birth to a son and a daughter. The newly born son came to hobgoblin and asked:

> Have you seen Aliyo's son?
> Have you seen his milking-pot?
> Have you seen the five camels?

Hobgoblin answered:

> Aliyo's son is devoured
> His milking pot is devoured
> The five camels are devoured.

The baby who heard this struck hobgoblin with a spear and killed it.

D16 *The Qallu's Bird*

It is said that a very long time ago the Qallu went to war. He went off to a far-distant country, a country he did not know. It rained and he sheltered in a stone cave. A stone fell at the entrance and sealed the cave. Now a crow came and sat on the edge of a pond beside the cave. The crow said to the Qallu, 'Pond owner allow me water to drink.' 'I may or may not allow you, will you summon help for me?' asked the Qallu. 'Yes I will,' said the crow. 'How do you ask for help?' The crow replied, 'I will go to your village and cry *'Kaak, kaak, kaak ...'* The Qallu said, 'You know nothing, you will never drink from my water, go away.'

Now the crow went away and up came the sparrow. She said, 'Pond-owner allow me water to drink.' 'I may or may not allow you, but will you summon help for me?' 'I will,' she said. 'How do you ask for help?' The bird said, 'I will go to your village and cry:

> The Qallu went to war
> He went to fight in a far place
> He went to a place he doesn't know.
> It rained
> He sheltered in a stone cave
> A stone fell on him
> With a heifer and a cow
> With a horned sheep
> With thong of giraffes' hide
> With a belt of a woman who gave birth
> Go to him.

'Ah! you know it. What is your name?' said the Qallu. 'Mother grass,' she said. 'My dear Mother grass, dip into the water, swing your tail and go,' he said. The bird bathed in the pond and went to the village. She perched on the fence and said:

> The Qallu went to war
> He went to fight in a far place
> He went to a place he doesn't know.

It rained
He sheltered in a stone cave
A stone fell on him
With a heifer and a cow
With a horned sheep
With thong of giraffe's hide
With a belt of a woman who gave birth
Go to him.

The villagers enquired, 'Say who is talking, who is crying like this? Wait, wait.' And they listened. The bird sat on the door and once again raised the alarm. The villagers knew the Qallu was lost so they followed the bird. When they arrived at the Qallu's cave, they tied the stone at the cave's mouth with the giraffe-hide thong and pulled it. The thong snapped. Then they tied the stone with the belt and pulled it. The belt snapped too. And then they let the horned sheep butt against the stone. When the sheep butted it, the stone cracked and fell apart. And the Qallu came out.

On that day the Qallu went home taking the bird with him. The bird remained at his homestead and thrived there. It was on that day that the bird was named Bilee Qaalluu and that is how she came to acquire her name.

D17 The Bird Who Summoned Help

It is said that a very long time ago three men went to war. A dog was with them. They became very hungry and slaughtered the dog. When they killed the dog, one of them called Makk didn't want to eat the dog's meat. While they were roasting the dog, Makk was digging wild turnip. He came with the wild turnip hidden wrapped in his cloth. Now they gave him the meat. He put it aside and ate the turnip. They resumed their journey. They came across a well. One of them had forgotten his water bag at the place where they ate the dog and now returned to find it. There he saw on the ground the meat Makk had been given. He returned and said to Makk, 'Why didn't you eat your meat?' 'I did eat it,' said Makk. Now they knew he had not eaten it. So they said to Makk, 'We are thirsty. Go down the well and draw water.' 'No I won't,' he said. 'Why?' 'I am afraid that you will cave in the well on me.' 'We won't. We are Borana like you, go and fetch, the water' they said. He descended the well. He gave them the water. They drank and then rolled a stone over the well, leaving him inside. And they went away.

Hyena came to the well to drink. He said, 'Well-owner, allow me to drink water.' 'I may or may not, but who are you?' 'I am Father Hyena.' 'How will you summon help for me?' 'I will go to the village and cry *Wuuuy, wuuuy.*' 'Go away, you don't know,' said Makk.

Then came Fox. She said, 'Well-owner, allow me to drink.' 'I may or may not, but who are you?' 'I am Mother Fox.' 'How will you summon help for me?' 'I will cry *Biiq, biiiq*.' 'Go away, you don't know.'

Then came pigeon. 'Well-owner allow me to drink,' she said. 'I may or may not but who are you?' 'I am Mother pigeon.' 'How will you summon help for me?' 'I will cry *Kliiich, kliiich*.' 'Go away, you don't know.'

Then came sparrow. 'Well-owner allow me to drink.' 'I may or may not, but who are you?' 'I am sparrow' she said. How do you summon help for me?' 'I will cry', she said:

> Warriors campaigned
> They went to a far country
> They went to a country they don't know
> The warriors ate dog
> Makk ate wild turnip
> He is in a water well
> He is alive
> Go to him
> With a horned ram and a cow
> With bullock and heifer
> With old man and woman
> With knife and rope.

Makk allowed her to drink and she went towards his village. There people were eating roasted coffee beans. She sat on the coffee pot and said:

> Warriors campaigned
> They went to a far country
> They went to a country they don't know
> The warriors ate dog
> Makk ate wild turnip
> He is in a water well
> He is alive
> Go to him
> With a horned ram and a cow
> With bullock and heifer
> With old man and woman
> With knife and rope.

The people heard the song and said, 'Wait wait,' and listened carefully. Again she sang. They finished eating the coffee and followed the bird. They arrived at the well. They tied the stone with a rope and tried to remove it. But the rope snapped. They struck the stone with the knife. The knife got bent. The old man and woman tried to remove the stone. They failed. Then they let the horned sheep butt against the stone. The sheep struck the stone and crashed it to pieces.

The man was rescued in this way.

D18 *Hare's Ear Hooked on a Thorn***

It is said that a very long time ago Hare and Coffeecup went to visit friends. The hare strayed on the thorny way and her ear got hooked on a thorn. Coffeecup tried and failed to unhook it. She went to camel and asked her:

> Camel! Camel!
> Hare and I went to visit friends.
> Hare strayed on the thorny way
> Her ear got hooked on a thorn.
> I was unable to unhook it.
> Camel, please relieve her.

Camel said, 'I can't I have to suckle [my calf]; my breast is overflowing.' Then Coffeecup went to man and said:

> Man! man!
> Hare and I went to visit friends.
> Hare strayed on the thorny way
> Her ear got hooked on a thorn.
> I was unable to unhook it
> I asked camel to unhook it.
> She said my breast is overflowing
> Man, please milk camel.

Man said, 'Give me Milking-pot, then.' Then Coffeecup went to milking-pot:

> Milking-pot! Milking-pot!
> Hare and I went to visit friends.
> Hare strayed on the thorny way
> Her ear got hooked on a thorn.
> I was unable to unhook it
> I asked camel to unhook it.
> She said my breast is overflowing
> I asked man to milk her
> He demanded milking-pot.
> Milking-pot, please, let them milk with you.

'I won't consent to that,' said Milking-pot, 'If I get a bad smell, with what will you fumigate me?' Then Coffeecup went to *bedan*, the incense wood.

Bedan! Bedan!
Hare and I went to visit friends.
Hare strayed on the thorny way
Her ear got hooked on a thorn.
I was unable to unhook it
I asked camel to unhook it
She said my breast is overflowing
I asked man to milk her
He demanded milking-pot
I asked milking-pot to hold the milk
She said with what will you fumigate me?
Bedan please fumigate milking-pot.

Bedan said, 'I won't fumigate. If I get burnt altogether when you smoke me, who will put out the fire?' Coffeecup went to Sky:

Sky! Sky!
Hare and I went to visit friends
Hare strayed on the thorny way
Her ear got hooked on a thorn.
I was unable to unhook it
I asked camel to unhook it.
She said my breast is overflowing
I asked man to milk her
He demanded milking-pot
I asked milking-pot to hold the milk
She said with what will you fumigate me?
I asked Bedan to fumigate her
Bedan said who will put out my fire?
Sky, please rain and put out the fire.

Sky said, 'If much grass comes out when I rain, who will graze it?' She went to Elephant:

Elephant! Elephant!
Hare and I went to visit friends
Hare strayed on the thorny way
Her ear got hooked on a thorn.
I was unable to unhook it
I asked camel to unhook it.

> She said my breast is over-flowing
> I asked man to milk her
> He demanded milking-pot
> I asked milking-pot to hold the milk
> She said with what will you fumigate me.
> I asked Bedan to fumigate her
> Bedan said who will put out my fire.
> I asked sky to rain and put it out
> He said who will graze my grass.
> Elephant, please graze.

Elephant said, 'If I have to graze all that grass, who will relieve my belly if it is over filled?' So Coffeecup went to spear:

> Spear! Spear!
> Hare and I went to visit friends
> Hare strayed on the thorny way
> Her ear got hooked on a thorn.
> I was unable to unhook it
> I asked camel to unhook it.
> She said my breast is overflowing
> I asked man to milk her
> He demanded milking-pot
> I asked milking-pot to hold the milk
> She said with what will you fumigate me.
> I asked Bedan to fumigate her
> Bedan said who will put out my fire
> I asked sky to rain and put it out
> He said who will graze my grass
> I asked Elephant to graze it
> Who will relieve my belly, he said.
> Spear, please relieve it.

Spear said, 'Who will straighten me If I get bent when I try to relieve his belly?' Now Coffeecup went to the smith:

> Smith! Smith!
> Hare and I went to visit friends
> Hare strayed on the thorny way
> Her ear got hooked on a thorn.
> I was unable to unhook it
> I asked camel to unhook it.
> She said my breast is overflowing

I asked man to milk her
He demanded milking-pot
I asked milking-pot to hold the milk
She said with what will you fumigate me.
I asked Bedan to fumigate her
Bedan said who will put out my fire
I asked sky to rain and put it out
He said who will graze my grass
I asked Elephant to graze it
Who will relieve my belly, he said.
I asked spear to relieve Elephant
Spear said who will straighten me,
Smith, please straighten spear.

Now Smith said. 'I will straighten it,' and straightened the spear. Spear relieved Elephant, Elephant grazed the grass, rain put out the fire, bedan fumigated milking-pot, milking-pot was milked into, man milked camel, and camel unhooked the thorn on Hare's ear.

D19 *The Lost Seashell Necklace***

It is said that a very long time ago mole went to search for her lost seashell necklace, with a boy whose name is Garbicha. The boy found the seashell and dropped it in a river. Mole went to the boy's father and complained, 'Garibicha's Father, your Garbicha dropped my seashell into a river, beat him so that he retrieves it.' But Garbicha's father refused.

Then mole went to gazelle and said, 'Gazelle, gazelle of the bush; graze Aba Garbicha's [Garbicha's Father] harvest.'

'What is wrong with Aba Garbicha?' said gazelle. 'Aba Garbicha refused to beat his Garbicha into returning my shell.' said mole. 'I won't graze,' said gazelle. And mole went to hunter and said, 'Wata shoot gazelle.' 'What is wrong with gazelle?' Mole said:

Gazelle refused to graze Aba Garbicha's harvest;
Aba Garbicha refused to beat his Garbicha into returning my shell.

'I won't shoot,' said Wata. She went to fire: 'Fire, burn the hunter's hut.' 'What is wrong with hunter?' asked fire. Mole said:

The hunter refused to shoot gazelle.
Gazelle refused to graze Aba Garbicha's harvest;
Aba Garbicha refused to beat his Garbicha into returning my shell.

'I won't burn,' said fire. Mole went to water. 'Water, extinguish fire.' 'What is wrong with fire?'

Fire refused to burn the hunter's hut
The hunter refused to shoot gazelle
Gazelle refused to graze Aba Garbicha's harvest;
Aba Garbicha refused to beat his Garbicha into returning my shell.

'I won't extinguish,' said water. Mole went to Elephant. 'Elephant, suck water.' 'What is wrong with water?'

Water refused to extinguish fire
Fire refused to burn the hunter's hut
The hunter refused to shoot gazelle
Gazelle refused to graze Aba Garbicha's harvest;
Aba Garbicha refused to beat his Garbicha into returning my shell.

'I won't suck,' said Elephant. Mole went to stump. 'Stump cut open Elephant's belly.' 'What is wrong with Elephant?'

Elephant refused to suck water
Water refused to extinguish fire
Fire refused to burn the hunter's hut
The hunter refused to shoot gazelle
Gazelle refused to graze Aba Garbicha's harvest;
Aba Garbicha refused to beat his Garbicha into returning my shell.

'I won't cut,' said stump. Mole went to rat. 'Rat, uproot stump,' said Mole. 'What is wrong with stump?'

Stump refused to cut open Elephant's belly
Elephant refused to suck water
Water refused to extinguish fire
Fire refused to burn the hunter's hut.
The hunter refused to shoot gazelle
Gazelle refused to graze Aba Garbicha's harvest;
Aba Garbicha refused to beat his Garbicha into returning my shell.

'I won't uproot,' said rat. Mole went to the children. 'Children, kill rat with bow.' 'What is wrong with rat?'

Rat refused to uproot stump
Stump refused to cut open Elephant's belly
Elephant refused to suck water
Water refused to extinguish fire
Fire refused to burn the hunter's hut.
The hunter refused to shoot gazelle

Gazelle refused to graze Aba Garbicha's harvest;
Aba Garbicha refused to beat his Garbicha into returning my shell.

'We won't kill, ' said the children. Mole went to Ambush. 'Ambush, kill the children.' 'What is wrong with the children?'

Children refused to kill rat
Rat refused to uproot stump
Stump refused to cut open Elephant's belly
Elephant refused to suck water
Water refused to extinguish fire
Fire refused to burn the hunter's hut.
The hunter refused to shoot gazelle
Gazelle refused to graze Aba Garbicha's harvest;
Aba Garbicha refused to beat his Garbicha into returning my shell.

'I won't kill,' said Ambush. Mole went to the cattle. 'Cattle, break the shaft of Ambush's spear.' 'What is wrong with Ambush?'

Ambush refused to kill children
Children refused to kill rat
Rat refused to uproot stump
Stump refused to cut open Elephant's belly
Elephant refused to suck water
Water refused to extinguish fire
Fire refused to burn the hunter's hut.
The hunter refused to shoot gazelle
Gazelle refused to graze Aba Garbicha's harvest;
Aba Garbicha refused to beat his Garbicha into returning my shell.

'We won't break.' said cattle. Mole went to Hyena. 'Hyena eat cattle.' 'What is wrong with cattle?'

Cattle refused to break the shaft of Ambush's spear
Ambush refused to kill children
Children refused to kill rat
Rat refused to uproot stump
Stump refused to cut open Elephant's belly
Elephant refused to suck water
Water refused to extinguish fire
Fire refused to burn the hunter's hut.
The hunter refused to shoot gazelle
Gazelle refused to graze Aba Garbicha's harvest;
Aba Garbicha refused to beat his Garbicha into returning my shell.

Hyena did not refuse like the others. He went out and attacked the cattle. The cattle ran over the shaft of Ambush's spear. Ambush then attacked the children, the children killed the rat, the rat uprooted stump, stump cut open Elephant's belly, Elephant sucked water, water extinguished fire, fire burnt the hunter's hut, hunter shot gazelle, gazelle grazed Aba Garbicha's harvest and Aba Garbicha beat his son and made him retrieve the shell from the river and gave it back to mole.

D20 *Sule the Beautiful*

It is said that a very long time ago there were two children. They were sisters. One of them was called Sule and the other Gawile. One day they ran away from home. They came across the hobgoblins' house and dropped in. The hobgoblins were not at home. Sule began to clean the house and told Gawile to stir milk. After they had finished cleaning the house and stirring the milk the hobgoblins came. They said, 'Oh! we have got workers in our home.' The father hobgoblin had a lion friend. He went to the lion's house and said, 'I have got two persons in my home, one of them is beautiful, marry her and I will be father-in-law to you.' The lion married Sule and they began to live together.

When the children's father came in search of his daughters, he heard that a girl called Sule had been married to a lion. He went to Sule and said, ' What brought you here?' 'I married.' she said. 'Whom did you marry?' 'A lion.'

The father had always wanted to kill a lion. So he went away and returned at night. That night he killed the lion. Sule cried unceasingly. Now seeing that her father had killed the lion, she left. Sule's father skinned the lion, putting the hide in his backyard. Sule saw the hide, sat down on it and cried. Then the lion's hide lifted itself up and flew into the sky.

D21 *Qarote and Gawile – the Wise and the Stupid Sisters*

A long time ago it is said that two sisters called Qarote and Gawile, together with their father, went to collect wild fruits. While they worked, the father left to defecate. He defecated in a milk-pot and covered it with a turban. He went away. 'Father, isn't it time to go back home?' they asked. The waste in the pot answered, 'Not yet.' Qarote said, 'This is not Father's voice.' 'It is Father's voice; whose else can it be?' said Gawile. They went to see and they found the faeces in the pot. They walked off.

They simply walked, for they did not know their way home. They came to a hobgoblin's house. There was no one at home except a little girl who was cleaning the droppings of the goats and camels. When she saw the girls she told them, 'My parents will devour you, but if you clean the dung I will hide you.' They cleaned the dung and she hid them. Then came the hobgoblin. The girl said to her father, 'Father, today even if you killed for me the biggest camel, it would not appease me.' The father said, 'Say how come the little girl is so hungry she cannot be appeased?' and he killed the camel. Hobgoblin's daughter gave some meat to the girls in hiding. After a while she asked them, 'Qarote, have you had enough?' 'Yes.' Then she asked Gawile, 'Gawile, have you had enough?' 'I haven't, it is hardly enough,' said the fool Gawile. By this time, hobgoblin had heard their voices and he asked with whom his daughter was talking. 'This sharp knife cut my fingers,' said the little girl. He reduced the sharpness and gave it back.

The little hobgoblin girl gave the sisters some more meat and once again asked them, 'Qarote have you had enough?' 'Yes.' 'Gawile, have you had enough?' 'No, it is hardly enough.' Again the father asked his daughter, 'With whom are you talking?' She said, 'This knife of yours does not cut a thing.'

Now the mother hobgoblin came, and looked in the kitchen, and saw the girls. She said to them, 'Please go and collect firewood for us.' Then she hung a large piece of fattened meat on a tree and told them to take it when they returned.

When they were out into the bushes Qarote said, 'Let's run away.' 'No, I want to eat the meat,' said Gawile and refused to run away. Gawile turned back. When she got back, the hobgoblin family told her to eat the meat hanging on the tree. When she climbed the tree they made a fire under the tree with the wood she had brought. Then the tree snapped and Gawile fell into the fire. Just before her death she said, 'I was heedless of what sister Qarote warned me.'

Qarote, as she went, came across a lion seated on a tree. She found honey on the tree and said, 'I have got the gum of our land.' Lion said, 'I have found the girl of our land,' and took her home. Qarote took his honey and ran away to her home. The honey was dripping all the way. Lion followed the trail of the honey droplets and arrived at her village. There he urged the villagers to return his wife. The villagers brought together all the girls in the village, dyeing their hair with butter. Then they said to Lion, 'Can you tell your wife among these girls?' Lion said, 'If I pinch my wife she will say, 'Eeee!' When he pinched Qarote. 'Eeeeee!' she said. Her parents now said to Lion, 'We will give her to you only if you jump over nine spears.' The lion jumped over eight hurdles of spears and when he come to the ninth they killed him with it.

Now Qarote asked her father, 'Father, on what am I to rest?' 'Rest on that bed,' he said. 'The bed cannot contain me,' she said. 'Then sit on the chair.' 'The chair cannot contain me.' 'Rest on my lap.' 'You cannot contain me.' 'Well then, sit on the hide of your husband.' She sat on the hide of the lion. When she sat on it, the hide flew towards the sky. Flying, she cried:

Father, follow me on your horse
Pull me down by my belt.

The father followed her on his horse and pulled her by her hanging belt. When he pulled, the belt snapped. She rose high into the sky. She laughed, and her teeth became a lightening flash, the noise the flying hide made became the roar of thunder, and her staff became the rainbow.

D22 *Sule with the Beautiful Neck***

It is said that a very long time ago there was a boy. This boy said to his father one day, 'Father, find me a girl as beautiful as our Sule.' Sule was his sister. His father set out to look, but could not find one, and he told his son so. The boy sent his father out again; and again his father returned unsuccessful. Finally he said to his son, 'I will marry you to our Sule. Pretend to be ill and hide in the bedroom.' The boy went into the bedroom.

There was a small girl in the house. This small girl went to Sule and said, 'Sister Sule, I will tell you what our father has said about you; milk this goat for me.' Sule milked the goat for her. The little girl then told her what she had heard. She added, 'If you are asked to bring a pot of blood, drop it on the ground and run away.'

At night they told her, 'Your brother is not well, take this blood to him'. She took the blood and when they said, 'Bring it here, bring it here into the bedroom', she dropped it on the floor and fled away.

She came to a very tall tree. To this tree she said,'If I have truth on my side be small; if I don't, don't.' The tree became small. She sat on top of it. 'Be tall,' she said. The tree became tall again.

Her family were moving to a new place. They were passing under the tree. First came her grandfather. He saw her and said:

> Sule, Sule!
> Sule of the beautiful neck
> Of the iron woman's staff[13]
> Let's walk together
> We will part with a farewell
> Sule, please climb down!

To this Sule replied:

> Grandfather, Grandfather
> Once you were my grandfather
> Now my husband's grandfather
> I will not climb down for you.

He went and her grandmother came. She said:

---

13 Women carry a wooden staff with a carved end at all rituals. See Haberland, 1963:25.

Sule, Sule!
Sule of the beautiful neck
Of the iron woman's staff
Let's walk together
We will part with a farewell
Sule, please climb down!

Sule said:

Grandmother, Grandmother
Once you were my grandmother
Now my husband's grandmother
I will not climb down for you.

She went, and her father came. He said:

Sule, Sule!
Sule of the beautiful neck
Of the iron woman's staff,
Let's walk together
We will part with a farewell
Sule, please climb down!

Sule said:

Father, Father!
Once you were my father
Now my husband's father
I will not climb down for you.

He went and her mother came:

Sule, Sule!
Sule of the beautiful neck
Of the iron woman's staff
Let's walk together
We will part with a farewell
Sule, please climb down!

Sule said:

Mother, Mother!
Once you were my mother

Now my husband's mother
I will not climb down for you.

She went and her sister came. She said:

Sule, Sule!
Sule of the beautiful neck
Of the iron woman's staff
Let's walk together
We will part with a farewell
Sule, please climb down!

Sule said:

Sister, Sister!
Once you were my sister
Now my husband's sister
I will not climb down for you.

She went and her brother came:

Sule, Sule!
Sule of the beautiful neck
Of the iron woman's staff
Let's walk together
Sule, please climb down!

Now she said, 'I will climb down for you because I have no alternative. She climbed down and they went and caught up with the others. After a while she said, 'Father I lost my shoe, let me go back and look for it.' The father said, 'Mother will look for it for you.' 'Mother doesn't know the place where I lost it.' 'I will look it for you then.' 'You don't know the place where I lost it.' 'Then go you two,' said her father and she went back with her little sister.

The little girl asked her, 'Sister how did you manage to climb this tree?' Sule explained and beseeched the tree to become small. When it became so, both went on top of it. 'Be tall,' and it became tall.

Under the tree sat an assembly of elders. The little girl wanted to urinate and asked Sule for permission. She allowed her to. 'Hey men, it is raining,' said one of the elders. 'What do you give if it is not?' they asked him. 'My neck,' he said. They went into the open and there was no rain. 'We will kill you,' they said to the man. The men looked up the tree and saw the girls there. They brought the tree down and took him in. And they lived there together.

D23 The Poor Prince

It is said that a very long time ago there was a king's son. One day he said to his father, 'Father, I want to go to another king's country.' 'Why, my son?' 'I want to see the way the people of that land live.' The king asked his son what he needed for the journey. The king gave him a horse, clothes and money. The special horse he gave his son could fly.

The prince left. He arrived at his destination after a day's flight, but to others that journey takes a month. When he arrived in that country people were gathered in a hall and the king's daughters were choosing husbands. The prince had dropped his own clothes in the forest and put on ragged ones. He entered the hall. The king of that country has seven daughters and the youngest chose the poor man for a husband. The people laughed at him, jeered at him as 'poor, poor'. Even after the gathering had ended, the people on their way home were singing 'poor, poor'. The prince took this lightly; but the princess was angry. She said, 'My God, why do you make me choose this man?' The prince heard her and assured her: 'Wait and I will show you who I really am; I am a king's son.' He said this and struck his tassel against his hand. There appeared a horse with a golden saddle, which she saw and felt happy.

The king gave double-storeyed buildings to six of his sons-in-law and a mud house to the poor man. Soon a war was waged on the king. He summoned all his sons-in-law and gave them arms. Six of them were each given a stallion, and the poor one a limping mule. The others went riding off while he followed them at a distance. They were singing and laughing. They arrived at the battle ground and began to fight. They fought for a long time. But the poor prince has not yet turned up. Later he came, mounted on his golden horse. He descended on the enemy and killed many. The king saw his bravery and gave him his gold ring. The king won the battle and returned home.

The king summoned his sons-in-law and said, 'I have seen all of you fighting. The one on the limping mule could not even reach the battle ground. To whom did I give my ring when his arm was wounded?' The poor man did not say anything to the king. Only to his wife did he tell the truth.

After a period of time the king developed a sickness in his eye. The king ordered his seven sons-in-law to search for medicine. The others were given stallions, and the poor man the limping mule. The prince, when he was about to go, told his wife, 'We will go to my father's land to bring the medicine. I know what I will do. When I come back I will take you with me. Be ready.' Her mother, too, hated her because she had married a poor man.

Astride his limping mount, the prince was jeered with shouts of 'poor, poor' by the others as he left. Once in the wood he summoned his golden horse and changed into his royal attire. He flew to his father's kingdom and arrived in one day while the others travelled for a month.

The prince told his father everything about the country he had been to and what had happened to him. He told his father to give the other men a poison and took for himself the medicine.

After a month the others arrived. The prince went to them and asked them who they were and what they wanted. They told him. Then he gave them the poison. Then he said, 'To show that you have received the medicine, I will make a mark on you,' and he stamped on their buttocks a seal that read, 'the slave of my father'.

On the twenty-ninth day after their departure, the prince started his journey and arrived before them. Hiding in the forest he watched them. They were saying. 'Did a beast kill that boy?' He changed his clothes and mounted the limping mule. They saw and laughed at him. He said to himself, 'I will show you.'

The others came to the king with their drug. They applied the drug to the king's eye. He became mad from pain. The prince gave the medicine to his wife so that she would give it to her father. 'Go away, I am not cured with the one these people brought; is the poor man's medicine going to cure me?' Then the prince touched the king's eye as if by accident and he was cured. Even after he was cured, the king insulted and laughed at the poor prince.

There and then the poor man struck his tassel against his hand. His golden horse appeared. The king saw this and asked him who he was. 'I am the son of a king,' and he told him his story. 'Gather the people and I will show you who really I am.' When all the people were gathered, the prince with his princess appeared sitting on his golden horse. The people cheered him.

Then the prince went to the king and said, 'The men you have sent to bring the medicine have a seal on them that says, "the slave of my father", therefore, give them to me as my slaves.' The king saw that the six sons-in-law indeed bore the seal on their buttocks and presented them to the prince. The prince took them to his father's kingdom and made them till the land.

Chapter 8

Mamaksa: Adults' Tales

M1 *The Six Hunters*

One day Snake, Water, Evil, Fire, Truth and Lion went out for a hunt. They found a camel. Evil said to Snake, 'The Lion is stronger, he can take the camel all for himself. Is there a way to make the camel ours?' 'No.' Then Evil said, 'Do you know what we should do?' 'No I don't.' 'I know,' said Evil, 'When Lion gets under the camel, bite him.'

As he was told, Snake bit and killed Lion. Lion being dead, the remaining five began to follow the camel. But Fire made it difficult for the others by walking in front of them. Then Evil said to Water, 'Please kill this fire. He is making the way difficult for us.' Water fell on Fire to kill him. Fire got extinguished, but Snake too got burnt and died.

Evil, Truth and Water continued to follow the camel. At this time Evil told the others, 'Let's goad this camel towards a cliff and when the camel falls dead we can have it.' So they began to drive the camel towards a cliff. Water, unable to climb up the hill, was left behind and began to go round the foot of the mountain. To this day water runs round the foot of mountains.

Evil and Truth drove the camel half way up the hill. At this point evil said, 'I am thirsty. Let's use a rope to descend into a well to get some water; after one of us has drunk the other will pull up the rope'. Agreeing to this, Truth was tied to the rope first and let down the well. Evil, without pulling up Truth, left her there and went after the camel alone. Evil followed the camel for several days. After these days the camel returned to the well to drink water.

Evil found Truth where he had left her a long time ago. By now Truth was rich, with many cattle. Evil, in great astonishment, asked Truth where she had got all these riches from. Truth replied, 'God gave them to me.'

Evil, wishing to get what Truth had got by doing what Truth had done, went down the well to drink water. There he found Death: 'Why did you come here?' asked Death. 'To drink water,' replied Evil. 'Who are you anyway?' 'I am Evil.' 'Oh! Is that you!' exclaimed Death and killed Evil.

M2 Denial: The Man Whose Buttocks got Stuck

A man prospered and hired a labourer. The labourer worked only for his employer; he had nothing for himself. The man gave the labourer a heifer. The heifer bred and thrived. The employer then expelled the labourer. The labourer said, 'I have cattle here; give them to me.' The employer denied this 'You have no cattle here; disappear.'

The labourer went away after saying, 'I will speak of this to no man, only to God will I tell it.' He went to Golbo [in the southern lowlands]. Golbo was then in the hands of enemies; Borana were not there yet.

Now the rich man's cattle grew in number to nine kraals. At evening times, when the cattle returned from the pastures the man sat on a rock and inspected with pride his nine kraals of cattle. One day as he was sitting on the rock, the rock caught his buttocks. Seeing his buttocks stuck there, the people came to the rescue. Here was a rich man with plenty – here is the milk, here is the butter, here is meat – stuck to a rock and they were unable to remove him.

'You have committed a sin, confess it!' They urged him. The man said, 'The sin I committed – there was one man who used to look after my cattle; it was he who made me prosperous. But I have thrown him away. This is my sin.'

Riding on two horses, messengers were sent to fetch the man from Golbo, and from Golbo they fetched him – the poor man, the one who owns nothing. They said to the poor man, 'We will pick out your cattle amongst these, stand here.' They picked out four kraals of cattle. The rock released one of the buttocks. When they saw one the buttocks still stuck to the rock, they said, 'There is something left still, please speak out.'

The man said, 'There, that big ox is his, I was unable to part with this ox, I love it. Now take it.' When they took out the ox from the kraal, the other buttock came unstuck from the rock and the rich man was able to walk.

M3 The Man Who Denied

The man was rich. A poor young man entered his service, and this young man looked after the cattle. Once when he was grazing the cattle it rained. A small skinny heifer fell in the mud pushed aside by an ox. When the heifer fell, the poor young man lifted it up and washed it. The employer was look-ing from a hiding place. Then he came out and said, 'Young man, you washed the heifer when it fell and also you said of it, 'if you are ruined I am ruined too'. Why?' The poor man answered, 'If she dies, I will not be wanted here; I am poor. That is why I spoke as I did.' 'Take the heifer. I have given it to you,' said the rich man.

The herdsman took the heifer. He fed it. He used to feed it with the milk that was given to him. The heifer grew, bred and filled the cattle enclosure.

By this time the poor herdsman said, 'I want to marry a girl.' 'With what [wealth] will you marry?' asked the rich man. 'The heifer you have given me, which now multiplied enables me to marry,' said the herdsman. 'I have not given it you,' denied the rich man. The poor young man took the case to the elders: 'Borana speak!' he said.

'Do you have witnesses?' the elders asked. 'No.' 'What will prove your case?'

'God and earth. The place where I put the milk pot, the place I put my spear, where the heifer stood when he gave it to me; let him stand there, I will also go and stand where I was then. Let us go to where he gave me the heifer. I have no quarrel with truth,' he said.

They went to the area. The poor man spoke to the place, saying to the earth, 'I have not claimed any heifer that he has not given me; be my judge.' Then the elders again asked the rich man, 'Have you given him the heifer?' 'I haven't,' he said. The elders said, 'Let's go; there is no way we can prove the truth,' and they began to turn away. When the rich man was about to follow them, he found that his feet were stuck in the earth. 'Please come back, come back,' he called the elders. When they turned back he told them, 'It is true I gave him the heifer. Please release me!' he begged the earth. He sprinkled some tobacco [as a thank offering] on the ground and begged the earth for her forgiveness. The earth released him. The poor man was given two herds by the rich man and went away.

M4 The Two Brothers

There is one man who lives with his brother. His brother is rich and he is poor. He has only one ox. He looks after the cattle of his brother for a living. His brother doesn't give him milk when he milks and doesn't give him meat when he slaughters. On top of this the rich brother is not quite happy at the idea of his poor brother owning even that one ox.

Now one day the rich one said, 'There is a place where the hide of a single cattle makes one prosperous.' The poor man killed his only ox, praying, 'My God, at Karrale they say a hide makes one rich. It is my brother who tells me; and I cannot ignore it, though I have only one ox. My God, I am poor; I don't know how I can resist the temptation. God, don't forsake me.'

He killed that ox and left early in the morning. He travelled the whole day and still he had not yet arrived at the supposed place, so he doubted his brother's claim. When it was dark, afraid of the beasts, he climbed up a tree. Men came with many cattle which they had raided and camped for the night under that tree. The man in the tree fell asleep and the hide fell to the ground: *baababababababa*. The raiders, scared by the sudden roaring noise, fled away assuming that they were being attacked. When the poor man woke up in the morning he saw cattle with no-one around. He took them and returned to his home.

The brother saw this and asked, 'Boy, where did you get all these from?' 'Don't talk about it; all your cattle are nothing. Truly a hide is worth a fortune; look, all these just for a single hide.'

The rich brother who saw what happened slaughtered all he had. He prepared many hides and went on his way. After a long journey he arrived at one place and began to call out, 'Buy hides, buy hides!' The people who heard this were saying, 'Go away, what a fool! What do we need hide for?' Everywhere it was like this. He became exhausted and hopeless. And he went back, realizing that he had become the victim of his own malice. At home, the man whom he made to kill his only ox was waiting for him, rich and happy. The evil brother said, 'My brother please forgive me.' And he forgave him.

M5 The Camel that Revealed the Truth

There were two brothers. One of them had eight children, but he was poor. The other one had only a son and an immense wealth – he had cattle, camels, goats and all. Now the man with eight children coveted the wealth of his brother. He wanted to expel his brother out of the land.

One day the rich man was herding the camels with his son. The poor brother came lurking and hid in the bush. Now a camel gave birth. The father told his little son to look after this camel and went to muster the rest. By this time the man in hiding came out and killed the boy. After killing him, he cut off his nephew's hands and put them in a milk pot that he found there on the spot. When the father returned he saw that his son was dead. When he cried the man who killed the boy, his brother, came running.

Now when the elders inquired into the murder case, the brother who killed the boy said 'I cannot help loving my brother; but I know that my brother did not want his son to inherit his property. I think it is he who killed his son. Search for the mutilated hands in the bush, look also in the milk pot.' They searched the whole area and there was none. Finally when they opened the milk pot, behold the handa were there. 'Just as I suspected,' said the man who killed the boy.

The elders deliberated, 'What is the penalty for a man who slays his own son?' 'He must die,' they said. The murderer intervened, 'Don't kill my brother; he has already lost his only child. Banish him out of the land,' he said, wanting thereby to inherit his brother's wealth and his wife too. The elders said, 'If his brother prefers his expulsion to his death let it be so. We will banish him out of the land.'

The victim said. 'If you banish me, I will go; God be my witness.' His wife also left saying, 'I won't dwell among the riches where my son is no more.'

Husband and wife took refuge in the same area. But they didn't talk to each other. He spent the day outside tilling the land and hunting wild animals. At night when he returned he always asked her, 'Any news from God?' And she would respond, 'Let God's breath take you away, shut up!' Always it was like this. They stayed there for eight years in this way.

Now the camel that was born the day the little boy was killed had become pregnant and was about to give birth. When the camel sat down the murderer who had inherited it inserted his hands into the 'birth organ' of the camel to assist it. As his hands were thrust in the camel leapt to its feet and ran away. As it ran in the bush dragging the man, the man was being struck by the trees till his whole body fell piece by piece save his two hands. Many people followed the camel but they were unable to catch up. The camel stopped when it reached the hut where the exiles lived.

There the camel gave birth. First came out two hands and then a baby camel. That night, the husband returning from hunting and asked his wife, as usual, 'Any news from God?' She said, 'May God's breath blow you away; we have a camel here.' The man knew his camel for it had a birth-mark that he saw the day it was born. He took the camel in. He milked it and began to drink the milk, abandoning going out for work.

The men who were following the camel came tracking its footprints. They came to the exile who was drinking milk and asked him, 'Is the camel here?' 'Yes.' 'What did it give birth to first?' 'To those ten fingers.' Then the men said, 'These fingers are your brother's; the one who killed your son and forced you into exile. One kind of nemesis reaches soon, the other takes time. This camel has come to reveal the truth and reinstate you. Now let's go home.'

Husband and wife returned to their home. That night they slept together. Thereafter the wife gave birth eight times and each time she bore twins.

M6 *The Lizard that Entered the Man's Stomach***

(You know Samad Gabra, the one who blesses people, don't you? If Samad comes to anyone's house – be they poor or rich – the owner slaughters a beast for him. Even a person who has only one cow slaughters that one.)

One day Samad Gabra, with his men, came to a man who has only one cow. That night Samad was chewing raw tobacco. He chewed and spat the tobacco beside him. That night a traveller merchant has lodged in that house to pass the night. The man who has slaughtered his only cow collected the chewed tobacco, put it in a bag and gave it to the merchant saying, 'Sell this for me. Don't see what is inside, but sell it for whatever price you get except water.'

The merchant went to market and sold all that he had come to sell, except the bag. Then one man said to him, 'Sell me this bag you have failed to sell.' 'How much will you pay for it?' asked the merchant. 'I will buy it with this thing,' said the customer. The thing was a cat. 'Take it,' said the merchant and exchanged it with the cat. The buyer went with the bag full of chewed tobacco. When he arrived at his home and opened it, it had nothing but chewed tobacco.

On his way back home the merchant lodged in another man's house for the night. The owner of the house was a rich man whose cattle could not be counted. Whenever a baby was born to this man a python came and devoured it. Now on the night the merchant stayed there, the wife gave birth. The python came and the cat killed it. The owner spent the night in terror expecting the python to come and wondering how it failed to come. When it was morning the python was there lying dead. 'Who killed it?' the owner asked. 'This thing,' replied the merchant pointing to the cat.

'Please give me this cat,' said the owner, 'I have lost twenty babies to the python. Give me the cat and I will open one kraal for you [I will give you one kraal of cattle.] The merchant collected the kraal full of cattle and went home.

He arrived at his home and summoned the man who gave him the bag full of chewed tobacco: 'Come and take what your bag has brought for you,' he said to the man. The man came and he gave him only one cow out of the many he got. The man received that cow with gratitude. He had nothing to complain about, after all it was a worthless thing that gained him the cow.

On his way home the man with the cow became thirsty and headed to a nearby house, tethering the cow to a tree. He drank and went back to untie the cow. 'You! Don't untie that cow,' said the man who gave him water. 'Why?' said the cow owner in bewilderment. 'It is me who tied the cow there, it was unable to go with the other cattle because of illness. That is why I tied it there.' said the man who was not the real owner. They argued, then decided to see the elders.

The elders came to inquire into the case. They asked, 'Do you have witnesses?' The traveller answered, 'I don't. But when I tied the cow to the tree a lizard was on the tree, she has seen me.' The elders said, 'Lizard cannot be a witness, you have lost the case. We see the cow is at his door.' The stranger went to his home empty handed.

At night when it was time for the cattle to return home the man squatted to untie the cow. As he squatted the lizard slipped into his belly through his anus. A few days latter the cow gave birth. When the cow gave birth the lizard in the man's belly also gave birth. Thenceforth, every time the cow gives birth the lizard also gives birth. As a result the man's belly ballooned. Finally he began to walk on his knees.

One day a guest came to his home. He killed a calf and left it to his sons to skin it. When they were alone the brothers quarrelled and the elder brother said to the younger, 'Just as Father has slaughtered the cow, I will slay you,' and severed the head of his brother. The mother came, saw and killed the murderer with a knife. Then the father, in anger, killed the mother, his wife.

And now the elders spoke: 'There is some wrong you have done, some sin you have committed that, now, is destroying your family. Confess your sin.' He told them how he had taken the cow that was not his. Then they sent for the true owner of the cow. He came. When he came the sinful man said, 'I will give you your cattle stand here.' The newcomer stood at the door of the cattle enclosure. They began to pick out the descendants of that first cow. When one cow was taken out of the enclosure one lizard came out of the man's belly. Finally when the enclosure was empty, all the lizards were discharged out of his belly. And now he began to walk on his feet.

[Wariyo Guyyo Haro, the father of Jilo Wariyo is the man who told us this *mamaksa* one day.]

M7 The Evil Man Whom the Earth Swallowed

There were two brothers. When the wife of the elder brother died he took another woman so that she would take care of his son, the son born to the deceased wife. After a while this elder brother too died. Now the wife of the younger brother said to her husband, 'I will make you inherit the property of your brother.' 'How can you do that,' he asked her. 'You will see,' she said. Then she went to the elders and said, 'This son of my brother-in-law is inclined to me.' 'What has he done?' they asked her. 'He did something abhorrent [rape],' she accused.

The elders spoke: 'If he has committed such a sin he is disgraced. He will not come to inherit the cattle of his father.' Now the son was disinherited, the uncle acquired all the cattle.

The disinherited son now herded the cattle [of his uncle]. Whenever he returned home he asked the villagers, 'What has God done today?' One day, while the uncle was reading the Koran, his penis sank into the ground. The villagers tried to retrieve it by digging the earth round the sunken penis. When they dug here he cried, 'You pierced me,' when they dug there he cried, 'You pierced me.' As he was crying like this his entire body disappeared sinking into the ground.

The nephew returned from grazing the cattle and as usual asked, 'What has God done today?' They told him, 'The earth has taken away your uncle, the earth simply swallowed him.' By this they realized that the man was a sinner and the boy was reinstated and took back all the cattle.

M8 The Lender

There was a man who, when he heard of a death, used to come and claim that the deceased owed him a debt. He caused much disturbance by telling people that the dead would not be buried unless the debt was paid. They would pay and he let the burial proceed. Always it was like this. He had a mule and there was not a place he failed to go if he heard of the death of someone.

Later, when this man fell ill and died, they dug a grave and went to bury him. His body was carried by his own mule. 'Unload the body from the mule,' they said when they reached the burial ground. By this time the mule squealed *hihihihi,* and ran away with the body. They looked for the mule but they lost her. They searched for the footprints; they couldn't find them. Next morning they resumed the search. They saw the mule in the bushes. But each time they approached her she ran away. The dead man's body was being torn away by the bushes. It was due to the evil he had done. They abandoned the pursuit.

The dead man had eight children. To his children he had said – this is when he was taken ill – 'If I die and if you hear of somebody's death go and claim that the dead owes you money.' The eldest son said, 'Father you have been doing evil things; we will not claim what is not ours.' This was before the death of the man.

Now one day the mule that had run away came back to the village. She had on her back only one hand. 'Unload me, unload me,' she spoke – in those days animals could talk. The elders saw her. They talked among themselves, 'Say, why does the mule came to us with only one hand and urge us to unload her?' 'It is for the debt he has been falsely claiming,' said the mule. Then they buried him – it was not much of a burial, it was only one hand.

Later, the elders deliberated as to the reason why the mule came with only one hand. 'Let's investigate it,' they said. After a while they concluded that: 'The reason why the mule came with only one hand is that, of the man's children – he had eight – only the one had said, 'Father, you have spoken evil,' and it is only this one that will be successful in life and pass his seed across generations.'

The descendants of this boy can be found still, only we do not know them.

M9 *The Eunuch*

There was one wealthy man. Even though this man had got two wives he had no child. Because he was rich he wanted to have children. He went to a diviner and stated his problem. The diviner said, 'In the forest up there there are lions. There is an old lioness that stays all the time in the den. When the other lions go out in search of food you go and get your child from the lioness.'

The man did as he was told and slept with the old lioness. Then the diviner told the man to stay for eight months and to go in the ninth month. In the ninth month the man went to the lioness and found a baby boy crying. He took him to his house and raised him up. The boy, for he had the blood of a lion, became strong. He became a hero.

His father's wife, now he was big and strong, took a liking to him. She bade him to sleep with her one day when the father was not at home. But he refused saying that she was his mother; and even threatened her that he would tell his father on her.

One morning after the cows were milked and the milk drunk, after Borana went to work, the woman told her husband, 'Your son doesn't allow me to sleep in peace. He wants to sleep with me; forbid him.'

The father, the woman's husband, got angry. He wanted to punish his son and told him, 'Tomorrow morning I will circumcise you; wake early, bath and be ready.' The father sharpened a knife and in the morning brought water with *slanum incanum* in it. Then pretending to circumcise his son, he castrated him. The young man became very angry. But he said, 'Since you are my father I will not kill you.'

When the wound healed the young man took his horse and left Borana for Arsi. He didn't want to live in Borana where his status as a eunuch was known. In Arsi he became rich and renowned. The people of Arsi were curious why such a rich and strong man lived without a wife.

They summoned the beautiful women and asked them if the exile ever talked with them. The women said, 'No.' Then they selected a beautiful girl and told her, 'Wash yourself, put on perfumes and when he sleeps sleep with him and try him. If he is a castrated man he will not live in our country, we will kill him.'

The strong man heard the plot and afraid of the people, he married a beautiful girl. But he told her, 'I am a eunuch; sleep with whomever you like.'

Before long the girl who was sent by the Arsi managed to sleep with him. He gave her his back. She told this to the Arsi. When the Arsi were preparing themselves to kill him, his wife heard and warned him. But he said, 'What kind of man is able to kill me?' But the Arsi men, resolved to kill him, ordered a major hunt for big game, in which every participant was required to go naked. Now he realized their intention. That day he spent the night feeding his horse and singing war songs trembling all over with anger:

Awach!
Babb Kelelo Koye
The elephant [ie the great] Lelo Gayya
In the fields the braves share everything
At home is where each heads to his door.

In the morning full of anger he mounted his horse without even untying it, the horse snapped the rope, broke earthen wares, flung the door aside and strode out into the open. As he was galloping, his spear thrust in readiness, the man came across Hare. When he was about to kill her she implored,

'Don't kill me, please.' He said to her, 'Can't you see them trying to kill me by ordering a hunt campaign in which you go naked? I will kill you, I will make a cushion with your hide.' 'Will you spare me if you get back your penis?' Hare asked, and the man agreed. He took her home. She instructed him to bring water with a *slanum incanum* in it. He then went to sleep. Hare spent the night spitting in the water. When he woke up in the morning she told him to wash with the water. When he washed, his penis came out of his body. 'Now go to your wife and beget children,' she told him. He went and he begot a child.

Now that he had got what he had lost, he returned to his father's country. He met his father. They greeted each other. 'Who are you?' asked his father. When he told him his name the father realised that it was his son and died immediately out of shock and terror. The same happened to his mother.

As he was the only son of his father he inherited the four kraals of cattle that belong to his father.

M10 Male and Female

Once a woman and a man argued. The man said, 'Women are more lustful than men.' The woman argued to the contrary. 'I, the woman, do not care that much. But you cannot even stay without sex for a few days.' They took their argument to the elders.

The elders said, 'We will see', and put them on opposite sides of a river. Both were forced to remain naked and both were fed on fat. They sat naked facing each other for many days. He dreamed of a woman and she of a man, but both remained where they were.

But at last the woman became unable to control her urge any longer. Defeated, she called to the man, 'Come, I am overcome.' He refused. To make it worse a worm entered her body and began to make her itch in her vagina. She jumped into the river to get across but the river was in flood and she began drifting away. The man also jumped into the river at this time and rescued her. He brought her to the bank on his side.

The elders had proved who was the more lustful. Today every woman has a worm inside which itches.

M11 The Strong Man Defeated by a Girl**

There was one boy. This boy was herding the calves. The calves got lost and the boy went to look for them. The boy too got lost. The boy and the calves disappeared into a hill. The boy stayed there for about twenty years and became a man. As there was little food, he ate whatever he could get. Now the calves grew, reproduced and became many. The boy had no clothes and walked around naked.

One day some women went to the hill to cut grass. They saw a man on the hill. They returned home and said, 'You know there is a man on that hill.' The men said, 'Could this be true?' and went to look for themselves. When they got there, indeed there was a man on the hill, and there were also cattle on the hill. They sent strong men. The man on the hill attacked them. They were unable to capture him. He struck them with calves. He struck them with three-year-old bullocks. They became tired of it. Then they told the women to perfume themselves and sent them to the hill man. The man saw the women and chased them away. The men came again and again he struck them by lifting bullocks of three years and four years old. They failed to seize him.

Finally they sent a beautiful girl, perfumed all over. The girl came and he chased her. She came back and again he chased her away. But the girl kept on coming back again and again. She came closer and closer and at last when he was tired she succeeded in being beside him. Then she made him sleep with her. The girl stayed there for one day. Now came the men. He struck them with three-year-old calves. Still they failed. Then they retreated back and waited. The girl stayed with the man for three days. After the third day the men came on him from behind. To attack them as usual he went to the four-year-old bullock. But unable to lift it he fell under its weight. Then he went to the three-year-old bullock. Still he fell under it. Now they saw that his power has weakened they fell on him, seized him and made him their captive.

The girl enabled his capture in this way.

M12 The Honey Bird[14]

Once Borana men went to fight and raid cattle. As they were travelling to the enemy territory they heard the honeybird singing. The commander told them to follow the bird and bring back the honey [for the bird would lead them to the bee's nest]. But they refused saying, 'We don't know how far she would take us. Maybe the honey is a long way off and we could fall into the hands of the enemy.' There was no-one among the warriors willing to follow the bird.

Then the commander became angry and he himself followed the bird. The bird perched on a tree where there was honey and the commander returned with it. When the warriors saw that he had the honey, they asked him to share it with them. But he said to them, 'If I were you I wouldn't have asked.' And he ate alone.

When they returned home, the warriors brought a charge against their leader. They told the elders, 'He is our leader, but he refused to share with us the honey, contrary to our custom.' The elders examined the case carefully, and at last they pronounced, 'The bird sang and that is her custom; God gave us the bird to show us where honey is. Therefore you [warriors] should have followed her when your commander told you so. You have behaved contrary to the law when you refused to obey your leader.'

---

14 See also Isack and Reyer, 1989.

To the commander the elders said, 'It is not wise to leave your soldiers without a leader and follow the bird by yourself. You have behaved contrary to the custom. Again, in not sharing what you have got you have done a stupid thing. A Borana doesn't hesitate to share his food and most of all warriors in the fields [or bushes] drink from the same cup. This is a case in which both the accuser and the accused have done wrong. Only the bird has done the right thing. Therefore, this is a case unworthy of deliberation.'

Thus, both parties went home embarrassed.

M13 Rat and Cat

Once rats and cats held a meeting. Cats, intending to eat the rats, said, 'We have found that it is not good to have old people in the land. They are weak and a burden. Go and kill the elderly; we will do the same to ours. Then we will organize a festival to commemorate our accomplishment. Come to the large field for the festival.'

The rats were suspicious and told their elderly ones what the cats had said. Elders of the rats gave the young this advice, 'Tell them you have killed your elderly; go to the festival, but each of you must dig a hole and cover it with grass.'

On the day of the festival both the rats and the cats gathered. The cats were singing, 'Today is the end, today is the end.' On the other side the rats began to sing, when they heard the song of the cats, 'We knew it, we knew it,' By this time some of the cats who had heard the rats' song asked, 'What is this "we knew, we knew"?' The other cats replied, 'Why do you worry? They can't escape us in this large field.' Then when the cats thought it time, they went for the rats. At this time every rat slipped into the hole which it had dug behind its position. The cats who saw what happened cursed, 'These people haven't killed their elderly. This is not the work of young people.'

They say that is why rats live in holes.

M14 The Baboon and the Bee (1)

It was the mountain baboon and the bee that deliberated. Baboon was then a human being. Even today his hands and legs resemble that of men. He belongs to the Galantu clan of Borana. He became poor and disappeared into the forest. There he asked God, 'I became very poor, provide me with food.' 'I will give you food,' said God, 'I have given you honey to live on; go and eat.' Baboon went to eat. He got some and ate. Now Bee, the owner of the honey, spoke, 'Dear have you eaten my honey?' 'Yes.' 'Have you had enough?' 'I am full.' 'What has God told you?' asked Bee. 'He said to me, 'I will make you into a baboon and give you what you will eat. Today go and eat honey." Bee said, 'Now you have eaten me [my honey]. Do you have anything to say?' 'Yes I have. If a person wants an audience with you, at what time are you alone?' Bee answered, 'The person who wants to see me – I dwell in rock cleft and on trees – can see me at noon when the sun is high in the sky.'

Baboon came and attacked Bee [at the appointed time]. Bee counter-attacked. Bee gave Baboon a sting. Baboon ran away. He rolled on soil. He rubbed his buttocks on the ground. It was on that day that Baboon got his bald patch in his buttocks.

Now he returned to God: 'My God, Bee attacked me. While I rub [my buttocks] to the ground I got bruised. It hurts. The wound irritates. What will you give me?' God said, 'For grain I will give you tree fruit, for meat I will give you ants; I have given you also the water well. There is your food; live on these. Did I hurt you?' 'No you didn't.' God added, 'When the water well is deserted drink from it. For a home I have given you the hills. I will make you to bear young ones, you will have them on your back and your belly. Did I do you injustice?' 'Not a bit.' 'Then go in peace,' God said.

It ended thus. That was the day the mountain baboon got its bald patch on its buttocks.

One day a man was digging at a spring. The place was on a mountain ridge. The baboon came while the man was digging and said,

The place you dig this spring is home to me
What made you dig is disrespect to me
If God allows it will be mine.

The baboon came at night drained the water and made the well his home. [Baboons commonly do this.]

M15 The Baboon and the Bee (2)

Once baboons came to the abode of bees. The bees were busy making honey. The baboons asked the bees to give them some honey. 'You can have it,' said the bees. The baboons slipped their hands into the hives. Just then the bees began to bite the hands of the baboons. Baboons ran for their lives. The bees pursued. The baboons rolled over the soil, but the bees didn't cease. They ran – the baboons – they got into a river, and all to no avail as the bees were still chasing them. Then the baboons said to each other, 'Let's defend our-selves with fire.' This time the bees failed to get past the smoke shield.

It was from the baboon that men learned the secret of silencing bees with fire.

M16 The Dik-Dik

God gathered all the creatures of earth and said to them, 'I am to leave earth and ascend to the sky. Before I go I will provide you each with what you will live on.' In front of the gathered creatures he put various kinds of food and left the scene for a moment. There was meat among the food. The dik-dik's eye fell on the meat. Her craving grew and she stole the meat before God returned to distribute the food. The dik-dik ran away with the meat and stopped in the bush to eat it. But just before having a bite, she heard the voice of God and ran away again. She ran and stopped to eat. Again she heard the voice of God, and ran again. The dik-dik was unable to eat the meat she stole.

Finally God appeared to her and asked her why she stole the meat. 'I was tantalized by it,' said the dik-dik. God said: 'Originally I had planned to give meat to you and grass to mankind. But, now that you have taken it before I gave it to you, from this day on you will eat grass and men will eat meat.' And it became so.

That is why today Dik-dik is always on the run, and stops for a moment between the runs. She thinks God is after her and stops to listen.

M17 The Camel's Genitals

God gathered all the animals of the earth to equip them with sex organs so that they could reproduce. Every animal came to God and collected its private parts. When it was the turn of the camel he went past God without stopping to collect his. When God saw the camel has gone past, he picked an organ and threw it towards the camel. It stuck hind-wards.

That is how the genital of the he-camel came to point in the wrong direction.

M18 Leader and Home: The Hares and the Guinea Fowls

Hares and Guinea Fowls were holding an assembly when a man came across. He asked them, 'You who are sitting here, shall I destroy all of you or kill your leaders?'

The guinea fowl said, 'Kill the one leader we have; don't destroy our way of life. If a leader is killed today, the leader is one man, it is this home that gives birth to a leader. A leader will be born but home won't. Kill our leader, don't destroy the herd.'

The hares said, 'Destroy our home; a community who has lost its leader is a lost community. Don't kill our leader destroy our home.'

It became so. Today you don't see two hares walking together; no-one has ever seen this. Their home was destroyed. One hare gives birth in the bush and runs away. But the guinea fowls' home was not destroyed and you see them in large groups living together.

M19 The Power of Harmony

People who travel together must not oppose each other. Two men set out in search of cattle. As they were travelling in the bush one of them said, 'Look, cattle.' The other replied, 'I see.' And they got the cattle. Again as they went one of them said, 'Look, camel.' The other replied, 'I see.' They got the camel. 'Look goats.' 'I see.' They got them. 'Look a dead elephant.' 'I see.' [One points to where there is nothing and says 'look'. When the other agrees 'I see', the non-existent object comes into existence.]

One man saw them and said, 'Please I have no cattle; take me with you. I have no money take me with you.' They refused to take him. He asked them why they refused him. They told him, 'We are afraid that you will oppose us. We don't disagree among ourselves. We agree with each other.' He begged them, 'I will not disagree with you, please my brothers take me.' 'All right we will take you; but don't oppose us. Tomorrow we will go together, be ready,' they said.

They went together in the morning. 'Look cattle!' 'Where?' said the new man and there were no cattle. 'Look camel!' 'Where?' They got none. 'Look goats!' They got none. 'Look honey!' 'Where?' They got honey. 'Look a dead elephant!' 'Where?' he said and they got none.

They returned home that day empty handed. When they got home they told the man to go away from them. They banished him and resumed their old way.

Now: 'Look cattle!' 'I see!' And they got them.

M20 *The Wise, the Coward and the Brave*

Three men: one wise, one coward and the other brave said to each other, 'They say there is a land where humans eat humans. Let's go and see if it is true.' They set out and arrived at the land of the hobgoblin. Two of them stayed behind and the coward entered the house of the hobgoblin. The hobgoblin asked, 'From where did you come?' The coward told him. Then the hobgoblin asked, 'Have you ever heard that in this area humans eat humans?' 'I have, but I am not alone, I have a friend; one man only is no use to you.' 'Go and call your friend,' the hobgoblin said.

He, the coward, returned to his friends. 'Have you seen him?' asked the brave man. 'Yes I saw him. Let's go together again.' The two returned to the hobgoblin's house. 'Where did you come from?' the hobgoblin asked the brave man. 'We heard that you eat men and we came to see for ourselves.' 'Do you have friends?' the hobgoblin asked. 'Yes we have one.' 'Go and call him.'

They went back to the wise man and told him, 'They told us that they will devour us. Once we have come here there is no way we could escape. It is your turn to go, and we came to tell you.'

The wise man came. 'How are you?' 'How are you?' [greetings with the hobgoblin.] The wise one said to the hobgoblin, 'Lay us the mat; we will pass the night here.' The hobgoblin killed a cow for them and they ate. Then said the hobgoblin, 'You have eaten meat, now we too want to have some meat.' He was ready to kill them.

'Just before that,' said the wise one, 'I have news for you, receive it from me. I was in the enemy land fighting a battle. I heard about you and came from there. Do you prefer to eat three of us or do you want many men, captured at the battle and whom they were tired of killing and told us to bring them to you? If you prefer us you can have us.'

'Please, please, get us those men,' said the hobgoblin excitedly.

'Our people are bringing them to you. We will go and bring them in this direction,' said the wise man. They spent the night there. In the morning the wise man told the hobgoblins to ready their knives and they left. The wise one saved the day in this way.

On their way home the wise man asked his friends, 'Who is the best of us?'

M21 *Snake's Water Well*

In the old days there was one snake who owned a water well. A man came and asked the snake to allow his cattle to drink from the well. The snake refused. The man begged the snake [for many days] and, at last, decided to kill him. There is a sycamore tree and the root of this tree descends into the well. The man came with a spear and thrust it at the snake. But he missed the snake and pierced the root of the tree. The snake slipped in to the well. The man retrieved his spear and went home.

His cattle were thirsty and he couldn't find any water. So he came back to the snake and begged him again. The snake said, 'As long as this water well is here you won't cease to beg me. As long as I see the wound of this tree, I won't give you water. Had you not missed me you would have wounded me like this tree.'

M22 *Truth*

One old man had three children. When he was about to die he wanted to put them to a test and reward the one who would tell the truth. He prepared three sacks, filled with Hyena's refuse, ash and honey respectively. Then he summoned his sons.

'My sons, I am going to reward him who speaks truth. Now that I am going to ask you a question please tell the truth. I am going to die. What do you feel about my death?' he asked them.

The eldest son answered, 'Father, your death will cause me happiness. As you have many cattle they will be mine.'

The second son said, 'Father, I will be very sad if you die. I would rather kill myself.'

The youngest son said, 'Father, your death will make me sad. But you haven't yet divided your cattle among us; so it is good if you do so before you die.'

Then the father called the mother, his wife, and said, 'I have put aside for you a sack full of honey. Anyway, what do you feel about my death?' She said, 'If you die, I would like to live only with your eldest son so that we two alone keep all the cattle.'

'All right go and collect your rewards,' said the dying old man to his sons. Each picked what his hands laid on: the eldest son put his hands on the honey sack, since he spoke the truth. The second son picked the sackful of Hyena's droppings. The third one picked the ash sack.

Those who received good things, though they had spoken evil, spoke their heart.

M23 I Am More Beautiful

The baboon and the hyena argued about who was more beautiful. The baboon said, 'I am more beautiful.' The hyena also said, 'It is me who is more beautiful.' They argued. 'Then,' they said, 'Let's look for some one who settles the matter for us.'

There was one rich man who owned many goats and a large farm. They went to this man. 'Uncle,' said Hyena to the man, 'Uncle, Baboon claims that he is more beautiful than me; but it is I who am more beautiful; we came here looking for a judge, please tell us who is more beautiful.' The man, the judge, found himself in great trouble. If he said the hyena was more beautiful, the baboon would destroy his harvest. If he said the baboon was more beautiful the hyena would devour all his goats. So he devised a strategy. He told them, 'Both of you stand turning your face away from me. The one whose behind I pinched is the one who is more beautiful.' Then when they turn their faces he pinched both at the same time. Immediately they ran away happily; each saying to himself, 'He pinched me, I am more beautiful; he pinched me, I am more beautiful.'

In this way the man saved himself from trouble.

M24 The Fattest Giraffe

The fox said to the lion, 'Uncle Lion, please kill for me the fattest giraffe.' The lion said, 'The giraffes live in the bush, they flee away when they see me. I never see them. Therefore I don't know which is the fattest.' The fox said, 'I will tell you what to do.'

The fox dug a pit and made the lion lie on his back in it. Then she covered the lion with grass, leaving his teeth out. Now only the lion's teeth were visible. Having done this, the fox went to the giraffes and told them, 'I saw something never seen before: The earth has brought forth teeth. Come and let's kiss it.' All the giraffes came and in turn began to kiss the teeth. Now came the biggest giraffe. The fox had told the lion earlier that she would give him a signal when it was the turn of the fattest giraffe to kiss his teeth. When the giraffe came and kissed the teeth of the lion, Fox gave the signal and the lion grabbed the mouth of the giraffe and killed it.

In this way the fox and the lion ate the fat giraffe together.

M25 *Rules of Conduct (Hates)***

The old man said, 'I hate something regarding being one [regarding the number one]. I hate a man who travels alone.

'I hate something regarding being two; I hate a man who marries a girl while possessing only goats with two teats.

'I hate something regarding being three; I hate a man of thirty who doesn't own the three sweet milk givers [cattle, goats and camels].

'I hate a fourth thing; I hate a man of forty who doesn't pull apart people who are fighting.

'I hate a fifth thing; I hate the man of fifty who speaks evil.

'I hate a sixth thing; I hate a man of sixty who can not detect a lie.

'I hate a seventh thing; I hate a man of seventy who leaves his own bed and goes to another woman's bed.'

After the old man had said these things, the others asked him, 'Why did you talk like this?'

The old man answered, 'The reason I hate a man that travels alone is that, a man who travels alone can get hurt, lost or die; there will be no one who will call help for him. That is why I hate it.'

Then they asked him, 'Why do you hate the man who marries a girl while possessing only goats with two teats?'

'A man who marries a girl,' he answered, 'while possessing only goats with two teats, well either the goat is cut short from being barren or from disease. That is why I hate it.' He continued:

'A man of thirty who doesn't own the three sweet milk givers – if there is something wrong with the cattle, he solves his problems with the camels; if there is something wrong with the camels he solves his problems with the goats. But the man who doesn't own these three, if he doesn't come to realize their importance at this age [thirty] he will not learn at any age. That is why I hate it.

'A man of forty who doesn't pull apart men who fight, will not come to pull them apart at any age. If he doesn't feel responsibility at this age he will remain so in the future.

'A man of fifty has gone half way through life. He holds an equal position in an assembly, he is equally an elder. If he speaks evil, he loses his position. If he still speaks evil at this age, he will not learn to avoid it at anytime.

' A man of sixty who cannot detect a lie, who is not mature enough at this age; he will not attain that quality hereafter.

'A man of seventy who leaves his bed behind for another woman's – his bed knows his secret. Iit says, 'he is senile'. By going to the bed of another woman he adds shame upon shame, for that bed too will come to witness his senility.

M26 *Arero Bosaro and his Wife***

[It is Golicha Dida Ketelo who told me this *mamaksa*.]

Arero Bosaro was a soothsayer – the one who prophesied that the Borana would begin to raise camels like the Gabra and goats like the Rendile. Arero Bosaro quarrelled with his wife. Her name was Adi. Arero then spoke to his wife as follows:

You Adi, I am tired of telling you to build a pen for the newly born calves.
If you build one you don't rail it, I am tired of you;
If you rail it you don't plaster it, I am tired of you;
You Adi, do you think I don't know you? What I fail to know is where you are from.
I don't know if you were brought up as a village dog.
I don't know if you were brought up as a strayed donkey.
You are feeble,
With bone's like an elephant's.
Elephant eater like Wata
Hovering over a Wata like a vulture.

When he was insulting his wife like this the small boy who was sitting by his side said, 'Granddad, why do you insult Grandma like this?'

Arero said, 'I am right to insult your grandma. I am tired of telling her to wash the utensils; she will end up washed off by her neighbours [meaning that they will avoid her] – your grandma who doesn't even remove the ticks off the cattle.'

M27 *The Man who Saved his Lover*

The man quarrelled with his wife and set out for big game to prove his might. He killed a giraffe.[15] Instead of returning to his home he went to the house of his lover, Debbo. When he arrived at his lover's house, her husband was beating her. The husband was saying, while beating, 'You have a lover, confess it.' The hunter, the lover, heard this as he arrived at the back of the house and stood there waiting. He became tired of waiting for the beating to end. He saw that the woman was resolved not to betray her lover despite the hard flogging she was receiving. Then, out of his compassion for his lover, he took on the recital of the warriors' chant:

I have anointed my Dalacha [name of the horse on which he killed giraffe] with blood and *fito* [oil with which a hero is anointed]
Debbo refused to confess, honouring her name, risking her life
The husband whips her with a leather thong to force her to confess.

---

15 Borana are ambivalent about giraffe hunting which does not carry the prestige nor trophies of big game hunting. There are many songs about giraffe hunting. See Baxter, 1986.

I protect your name, Borana will guard your life.
Confess with the help of God.

M28 *The Brave Novice Hunter*

There was a young man. His father loved him very much. But his age-mates
scolded and despised this young man who was cherished by his father. They
despised him on grounds of cowardice. Even his younger brother had killed
something. This young man, even though he had never been away from
home, knew everything. The father heard about the contempt for his son by
the age-mates. He said to him, 'You boy, I know it is me who sired you. How
come your age-mates despise you?'

Now the young man didn't say anything. He went out to hunt elephant.
The other youths, who were quite brave hunters and killers, followed him
to see what would become of him. In the bush the young man found a herd
of elephants and charged them single-handed. He struck one of them on the
head, in the belly – everywhere. But the elephant was too much for him. The
age-mates were watching him quietly. He fought like a man. Even though he
had never been out hunting they realized that he was brave and strong after
all. Now when the young man discovered that he couldn't kill the elephant
alone he began to recite a war chant while still fighting:

> I struck its head
> And call on the the leader of my age-mates,
> I struck in its belly
> And call on the age-mates who have guts,
> [Your] mother's son calls for help
> While delivering blows.

Now when he sang like this, all the others came to his help. His age-mates came
and charged, and his Mother's son, his younger brother, too came to his help.

M29 *The Husband who Ousted the Lover*

The man's wife had used to be visited by her lover. The husband told her
lover to leave his wife alone. But the lover refused: 'I can't leave this woman;
I love her.' The lover even ousted the husband and compelled him to leave
his home. In those days when a Borana was forced to leave his home, he
went into the bush, killed a beast and returned home singing [about] his feat
of bravery. Now when this man was made to leave his home he set out to
kill a beast. He went to kill a warthog. He found this warthog and killed it.
He came back home. He sang:

> *Awach!*
> It is smaller than the bull and bigger than the bullock

My hunt-mates failed to identify my warthog
It is larger than the small and smaller than the large
My hunt-mates failed to name my spear
He didn't ask for her hand
He didn't pay the bridewealth calf
I failed to say why the womanish-man is here.

When the woman and her lover heard this, the lover went away in shame and the woman loved her husband again.

M30 *The Wisdom of Liban Wata*

The day the Gada leader and his clan officials were camped at El Dall a Somali came to them. He asked, 'I want Liban Wata to be my godfather [guardian]. Is he here?' 'Here he is,' they told him. The Somali went to Liban Wata and said, 'I want you to be my godfather, let's go inside.' And they went together to Liban's house. On their way they stopped under a small tree. It was the Somali who said, 'Let's stop here for a moment; there is something little we should talk about,' and he sat down. 'Oh,' said Liban, 'For yourself you sit in the shade and you tell me to stand out here. What if the something little you say is a ploy just to fish something big out of me?'

'Allah! He knew it,' said the Somali and they walked towards home. 'My friend,' said the Somali, 'What I came about is this riddle which nobody could solve. Two people saw it, ten collected it, thirty ate it and only one person swallowed it. What is the meaning of this riddle?' asked the Somali.

Liban answered, 'The two who saw are a pair of eyes, the ten who collected are the fingers of two hands, the thirty who ate are teeth, the one who swallowed is the soul [the man].'

'Allah! I cannot bear your wisdom,' said the Somali and went.

Chapter 9

Arga-Ageti: Myths and Legends

A1 *Adem and Hawey*

God first created Adem and Hawey. Then he made a tree for them with two branches. On one limb he put sweet fruits, meat and honey – for them to eat. On the other he put a fruit which kills if eaten. He warned them not to eat this fruit which causes death.

Adem and Hawey lived together. One day Adem left Hawey telling her he would be back soon. At this time Shetan [Satan] came to Hawey and asked her where Adem had gone to. 'He just left telling me he will be back soon,' she told him. Then Shetan said, 'Adem has gone to see another beautiful woman.' Hawey said, 'But God created no other woman besides me. Where did he get another woman?'

'There is a beautiful woman,' Shetan said.

'Show me.'

Shetan took Hawey to a pond and told her to look into it. When she looked she saw her reflection in it. Taking her own reflection for another woman, she became quite furious and pledged to kill Adem.

When Adem returned she asked him about the other woman. He said it is not true, but Hawey didn't believe him. So she demanded of him to take an oath by eating the forbidden fruit. She gave him the fruit and when he put it in his mouth God seized Adem's throat before he swallowed it. The fruit remained on Adem's neck and became the *kookkee* (Adam's apple). That is why only men have a *kookkee*.

God cursed Hawey for what she had done: 'Give birth with pain; let blood spill out of you. Let the male have authority over you. Go down! [i.e. be weaker]. Sleep [live] under the male; let the burden of work be upon you.'

It is for this reason that women live under men.

A2 *Sule and God's Rod***

It is Sule who brought God's rod (the rainbow) into existence. Sule was the beautiful girl married to a lion. In those days the lion was human. Only poverty drove him into the bushes and there he became a beast. Somebody

132

killed the lion that was Sule's husband. She went searching for him. She came to one house, stopped, and told the owner, 'I'm looking for my husband.' The man said, 'I have not seen your husband; come in and sit on that hide.' 'Of what is this hide?' Sule asked [she saw that the hide was a lion's]. 'Just a cattle hide, sit on it,' the man said.

She sat on it. Losing all hope of discovering her husband, she wept:

> He whose man casts shade
> Courts me under it,
> He whose teeth are [always] washed with blood
> Has come to see his blood spilled.
> My husband
> The mountain dweller
> Scatters the many,
> My husband!
> He of the thirty teeth
> To whom thirty men are no match.

When she cried like this sitting on her husband's skin, God revealed himself to her: 'Why are you crying?' 'I lost my husband.' 'Shall I rejoin you with him?' asked God. 'Rejoin me.' The hide ascended to the sky carrying her.

Now, our God has a wife. While he was going to her Sule barred the way by holding her wedding sceptre in front of God. God became very angry, 'Why do you impede me?' He said and brought strong wind: *bobobobobo*. Storm originated on that day. And Sule's sceptre became the rainbow (God's rod). God's anger became thunder. He was furious and said, 'How come you bar me from my wife and hold your sceptre in my way. From now on I've made you woman, I've made you to be less than man.'

A3 The Mule

Long ago at the beginning of creation sky and earth were very near to each other. They talked to each other. They talked through the medium of rain. In those days it rained constantly – summer and winter.

The mule was sick of the rain and told it to stop: 'Why do you always rain? Stop it!' The sky refused to stop. So then the mule kicked the sky. God became angry and cursed the mule: 'Be barren!' From then on, the sky receded higher up, and rain ceased to fall constantly.

A4 Wayu Bano: The Conceited Man

God used to live on earth. One man asked God to give him peace. God said, 'I won't.' 'Why?' asked the man. 'Man is not capable of handling peace.' Then the man asked God to give cattle [wealth]. But God refused and turned the man out. The man was not ready to give in that easily, he would go to God's wife. On his way there he saw a donkey rolling, and passed by saying, 'What on earth was that!'

The man went to God's wife and asked her if her husband was in. She said, 'Yes, the donkey you saw now is he.' 'I saw not man but donkey,' he said and asked her what he came for. She said, 'Your first request was right; one has to ask God only for peace and love and not for wealth. Go and tell him that you don't want any wealth but peace.'

The man went to God and said, 'I don't want any cattle, goats or camels; I only beg you to give me peace.' Then God asked, 'Who told you to ask like this?' 'No-one.' God realized that this was the work of his wife. He became very angry. His anger was demonstrated in the form of a storm. The storm we see today was created then. God reproved his wife for telling the man the secret. But to return to the man, God gave him peace.

When the man got peace his few cattle thrived and multiplied. The man became very rich and grew very proud. One day as God was playing *sadeeq* [a board game] with him, the man said, 'Of the two of us, who is wealthier?' God said, 'I don't know; but we will see. Tomorrow, I will bring together my cattle and you will bring together all your cattle.' The man said, 'How can I bring all of them into one place? What land could take all my cattle?' 'I will cut back the forest and prepare a large enough field,' said God. The vast field at Dida Liban was made that day.

The next day the man came with all his cattle. Next came God bringing with him his cattle, which are lions, snakes and hyenas. God mixed his with the man's. The lions, snakes and hyenas at once killed all the man's cattle. Only one he-goat escaped death.

The man saw what had happened and said, 'God, I have seen that you are mightier and wealthier. You made the mule barren. You have made me empty. Now what am I to do with this one he-goat?'

'I will bless this he-goat for you; put it to graze on a hill. The cattle I have taken from you will not be given back to you. I will bless and sanctify this he-goat; I will give it a name.' And God blessed the goat and left the world.

War came upon the man and he sacrificed the goat and prayed for victory. That goat is Wayu Bano. Today when the Borana go to war they sacrifice a he-goat and call it 'Wayu Bano he-goat.'

The man got many spoils from the war, though he was unable to handle peace.

A5 *Gada and Gadayo Galgalo*

The first man whom God created was a Borana called Boficho. Boficho had two wives. The senior was Borana and the junior was Guji. The senior wife became jealous of the younger one and wanted to kill her. One day when the second wife went to look after the cattle, the first wife, (the senior one) gave her son, Gadayo, a pointed rod to kill the second wife. As he had been instructed Gadayo flung the rod at her from his hiding place. She came home groaning where Boficho, her husband, removed the rod from her body. Then he whipped Gadayo.

The senior wife, seeing the failure of her first attempt, pursued a second. She made a spear and gave it to Gadayo. She told him to stab the young woman, slipping the spear through the adjoining wall. Gadayo did as he was told and the woman was killed. This was the first appearance of death.

Due to the introduction of death and the killing of each other, all the people under Boficho said, 'If we began to kill each other we do not want to live together; we will go our own way.'

One group of people gathered under a sycamore tree and said, "We are Borana'. Another sat under *birbirsa* tree and called themselves Guji. And in this way the Konso sat under a rock, Somalis settled by the river, the Darasas sat beside an ant hill and others crossed the sea and became white people. So the family of man disintegrated.

Gadayo ran from the face of his people. He travelled for a long time. As he went God appeared to him disguised as a toddler. After exchanging greetings God [the small boy] asked him where he was going. Gadayo went on without replying. He went on. And once again God, now as an old man, appeared to him. He asked him the same question. This time Gadayo replied, 'I am looking for God.' 'Why do you search for God?' 'So that he will give me food, drink and wealth.' The old man gave Gadayo many cattle. Gadayo slaughtered a cow, ate and continued on his journey. As he went the cattle disappeared one by one until one cow remained.

Now he met an old man who asked him where he was going. Gadayo told him his purpose. The old man asked Gadayo to give him the cow. He gave it to him. Then the old man advised Gadayo: 'If you find God, ask him not for wealth but love.'

Gadayo resumed his journey. He met with God, who appeared to him as an old man. 'Where do you go?' asked the old man. 'To God.' 'Why?' 'So that He may give me love; the love of men, women,and children. To ask him for law and custom which I could live by.'

And God declared to Gadayo, 'I give you love; be sweet. You will be father to your people. You will bless them. You are the reconciler and the judge.' Gadayo asked, 'I am alone; where are the people I will be father to?'

'Go back to the country where you killed your mother. There you will find the children of the woman you killed, the children of your father. Rule over them.' After this God gave him a book (law) by which he would live. So he returned to his homeland.

On his way back Gadayo met the old man who had given him counsel. The old man asked him where he came from. Gadayo said, 'I am the father of Borana. I return after receiving law and authority.' Then Gadayo gave the book to the old man.

The old man gave the book to the Borana who were under the sycamore tree. They were living together with cattle and a cow ate the book. They told what happened to Gadayo. He told them to slaughter the cow and the content of the book was found imprinted upon its intestine. From that day on, when the Borana want to know about something, they sacrifice a cow and read its intestine.

It was in this way that Gadayo received the Gada law.

A6 *God and the Poor Man*

The man was poor, with many children and few cattle. He went to God to ask for cattle (look, this story is about the origin of our traditions). He went. He was to say to God, 'I have got many children, but I don't have enough cattle to feed them, please provide for me.'

God's children were performing some kind of ritual when the poor man came. They were at the entrance. When the poor man came they asked him, 'Father, where are you going?' 'To your father; is he at home?' 'Yes, why?' He declined to tell them and went in.

He found God and said, 'Father prosper me, make me well.' God said, 'Go away; I have made you well, I have prospered you. Go.' He kept coming to God for many days. He had only seven cattle and each time he returned home from visiting God he found one cow dead. He would skin it, eat the meat and return to God. 'Father prosper me.' 'Go I have already prospered you.' Always it was like this. Now the man was left with only one cow.

As usual he met God's children at the gate. 'Father where are you going?' they asked him. 'To your father.' 'Why?' This time he responded, 'I am poor I have got many children and nothing to give them. That is why I keep coming.' Then the children advised him, 'Don't talk like this to our father. Ask him for love; love to the old, to the young, to the big, to the small. Ask for grace and blessing. But don't ask for any cattle.'

He went in to see God and said, 'Father bless me, establish my love with Sabo, establish my love with Gona [the two exogamous moieties]; with friends, neighbours and all; with the grass and all. Make me sweet.'

'Who taught you to talk like this?' asked God. The man hid the truth and said, 'No-one but myself.' (Look now sleep is about to be created.) 'You lied to me,' said God and killed the man. He stayed for a while after killing him and then woke him up. He had only made him sleep, you know. It is in this way that sleep has come on us. Now God asked him again and the man spoke the truth: 'Your children taught me to speak in this way.'

Then God gave the man a honeybird: 'Take this,' an eagle, 'Take this also,' a fox and a cattlebird [tick bird]. The honeybird leads to where honey is found. The eagle shows where a dead elephant is lying [for its tusk]. The fox shows where water is found and the cattlebird [which always sits on the back of cattle] leads to where cattle are found.

Now the man got everything. He had been left with only one cow and now he got everything he needed – cattle, camels, elephant's tusk.

It is in this way that sleep has come on us.

Then God told the man how he should pray and perform rituals: 'Perform your rituals during the night times.' The man got everything. All the people loved him. He was greeted by young and old alike; *'abbo yoyyaa, abbo yoyyaa'*, a salutation of affection.

A7 Disintegration of the Oromo

Guji, Borana, Arsi and Wallega – these were one people, one family. It is Hawey who bore them. Her husband is Adem. Only Hawey and Adem were living in the land. There was none other. Hawey gave birth to four children: Boran, Guji, Arsi, and Wallega. Wallega was the youngest.

One day there came Shetan (Satan). He said to Hawey, 'Hawey, your husband visits another woman; why do you live with him?' 'Which husband of mine? How can there be another person in this world besides the two of us?' 'Come I will show you.' He took her to a river and she saw her reflection in it. Adem came home. She said, 'You sleep with another woman in secret.' 'What woman?' 'I have seen her.' 'What has happened to you? Is there another person other than you and me?' he said. She brought him to the water. 'There you both are!' she said showing him the reflection. She killed herself.

The brothers grew up. They quarrelled one day, and the eldest one struck the youngest. The others intervened: 'What is the matter?' 'I will kill him.' 'How will you kill him?' '[He will be dead] like our mother'. But they were unable to quell them. Borana killed Wallega. Now Wallega had one son.

'If we have come to such an end, we have to separate,' they said. Each ran away from the other. Arsi went facing Makka Madina. Borana went towards the east. Guji took to the north, and Wallega the way to the west. Then Borana said, 'I am Borana.' When they asked him why he said so he answered, 'Because my mother bore me under the *boror* tree.'

Now one man, whom the Arsi today venerate and call Shekana Hussen (see Aguilar 1998; Baxter 1990) – this man, God loved him. Shekana Hussen was Borana, from the Matari-Gadula clan. He was in Agal. Today they venerate him at this place. Sitting quietly he beat a drum *dum dum dum*. The people went and saw him. One boy thinking he was a sorcerer pierced him with his spear. Shekana Hussen left the place trailing his blood. From Agal by way of Borbor he came to El Dal. Dragging his leg he went and stopped at Afattu Qalliti. There he found a sheep. He sacrificed it. The places that today we call Arer, Sasaq, Debano and Yoyo are the places where his blood fell on the ground.

He traveled onwards. On his way to Makka Madina at one place he observed that he only saw women. He cursed the place: 'In this country God has made all people women, and dogs to be men.' To this day in that land women sleep with dogs and bear humans.

Shekana Hussen arrived at Makka Medina and summoned together the dispersed brothers. 'You are brothers; live together, be one,' he told them. They have never become one: 'Since a brother has killed his brother; since we have changed we could not live together.' They remained enemies.

A8 *Mother Abanoye***

Mother Abanoye was wise, wise and brave. They elected her as their leader and in her reign women became superior to men. When they camped it was the husband who carried the babies, it was the men who built houses, and after completing the houses they also built the stock enclosures.

So when things kept on getting worse, the men held a council. But they were not able to devise a way out of their problem. They said, 'In what way can we subjugate women?' No solution was found.

There was a poor man. He had neither father nor mother. One day he saw the elders going by and he asked them from where they were coming. 'The poor fool!' the men said and went past without answering him. They were discussing the tyranny of Abanoye's regime. After they had gone past, one of them returned and talked to the boy. The boy asked him, 'What is it you were talking about?' The man replied, 'We have failed to subdue this woman Abanoye. We carry the babies, when we camp we have to build the kraals and even if it is already dark by the time we finish building the kraals we have yet to build houses. We are tired.'

'I will tell you what to do,' said the boy, 'Get a knife; when you are about to move to another place, and when the women tell you to carry the babies, tell the mothers that you are not going to carry the whole baby; and that you are going to cut the baby into two parts so that you and the mother each carry half.'

This was agreed upon.

The next day was the day of the move to a new area. Now every man said: 'I will not carry this baby all by my self. Let's cut it into two and carry half each.' When the men said this the mothers said, 'No, no! Don't cut my child; I will take care of him.'

That day they camped and went to the poor boy. 'Have you camped?' he asked them. 'Yes.' the boy told them. 'Now build only the kraals. Don't build the houses. At night make love to your wives in the open field.'

At night all the people were by the fireside. Then while half of the men were sitting there, the other half asked their wives to make love to them there and then. The women said in horror, 'No! Look here. People are watching us, what will they say?'

Now the next morning the women thought that in case something happened as on the previous night, it would be wise to build houses and they cut wood and built houses. The men said, 'Now we are relieved of these two jobs.'

Abanoye, the chief continued to give them, the males, a hard time. She presented riddles: she asked them to bring a hide that had a hair on both sides. They couldn't find one and they went to the poor boy. He told them take her a donkey's ear. When Abanoye saw them succeed, she thought of some task they could not accomplish. She ordered them to come with a sackful of fleas. The men went to the boy. The boy told them to collect a sack full of ass's dung and suspend it over the hearth. They did as they were told and took the sack to Abanoye. She opened the sack and there it was full of fleas. Had they failed to accomplish these tasks they would have received severe punishments and humiliation, for she was such a person.

Finally the boy advised the men, 'Dig a pit and cover it with grass as camouflage. Then put Abanoye's chair on the edge of the pit and you sit circling the pit. Decline every thing she demands. Make her angry. You know that when she is angry she moves her chair to and fro. That will send her down the pit.'

They dug the pit and covered it. Then they sent for her with the message, 'Come immediately, we are faced with a serious matter.' Abanoye was asleep at home by that time. They know her eagerness for news and her determination to make sure that nothing took place without her knowledge. So they wanted to put her to disgrace, presuming that she would come running out naked. But when Abanoye was sent for to come soon, she said, 'I am faced too with an equally serious matter. What has past has past; what has come, we will consider. Together. Handle it well until I come. I am dressing myself.' For she was wise and she had understood their intention.

Now she came to the assembly place and they put forth an issue. When she suggested some idea everybody opposed her. People were speaking from every direction. In anger Abanoye began to move her chair in every direction. And when she moved the chair forward a little bit too far, she fell into the pit. While she was falling down the pit she raised her voice and pronounced her last will, her last declaration to her fellow women. She said:

Women!
Lie be yours, deception be yours
Sip from the milk of your husbands
When they tell you to do something add something to it
Seduce men into love making
Lie!
Deceive!

Crying she went down to the bottom where she died.

Now men became the superiors. But from that day on women began to lie. When you come from outside she tells you lies. When you are to beat her she implores you. And everything that Abanoye wanted women to be, they became. Abanoye has done this for revenge on men.

Abanoye was such a clever woman until she was outwitted by the ingenuity of the poor boy.

A9 Dido Gawole the Strong Man**

Dido Gawole was strong. One cannot find a brave and strong man like him. Wise too he was. At that time the Borana were fighting the Arsi. They used to fight with shield and spear. In battle even fifty men couldn't be a match for him. He was full hearted. When he fought, if he missed with his lance, he struck and killed with his shield. Such was the man Dido Gawole.

A poor man called Obolo entered this brave Dido's service as a servant. Obolo didn't wear any cloth. He was naked. The only part he covered was his arm. Dido saw Obolo and said to his wife, 'What is this creature, throw him out. Here we have such a thing but what is it?' When Dido said this Obolo also said, 'Here we have such a thing and what is it?' Obolo repeated everything he heard. He did this to feign foolishness.

'Hey, what kind of man are you?' asked Dido.

'Hey, what kind of man are you?' mimiced Obolo – [it was a ploy, a ploy to kill Dido].

'Please throw out this good-for-nothing.'

'Please throw out this good-for-nothing.'

He was always like this. 'Forget him; the fool,' said Dido.

Sitting without any cloth on by the fireside Obolo stirs milk. Dido had a horse. When the horse came in Obolo stared at the horse. It was Dido's wife who finally spoke: 'Dido, I am afraid of this man. When the horse comes in, see how this dirty man stares at it. This is terrible, I am afraid,' she said. 'Forget this fool, what can he do to my horse?' dismissed Dido.

While Dido was assuming that Obolo was nothing but a fool who stirred the milk, naked with legs stretched apart, one day Dido's wife saw the erected penis of Obolo. She wanted to sleep with him and she did so. Women are terrible, you know. And then she put clothes on him.

Dido saw that Obolo had a cloth on. He asked his wife who made him put it on. She answered, 'He is a dirty man. It is not good for our name to have in our house a poor man who is naked.' She said this because she loved Obolo now. She lied.

Now that he had developed intimacy with the wife, Obolo asked her how he could kill Dido. 'That is easy,' she said, 'First he takes out the cows into the fields; at this time he carries spear and shield. Then he returns and takes out the oxen; this time also he carries spear and shield, he is never off his guard. Then he takes out the calves; this times he puts down the spear and shield and carries a cane. You can kill him then.'

Now Obolo wanted to go back to his homeland and come with warriors. When he was about to go he said to Dido's wife, 'I will go, and return with an army in five days.' Then Obolo went away stealing Dido's horse.

'Where is the man,' Dido asked.

'The man has disappeared. Forget him the fool, who would care to know where he has gone to.'

Dido said, 'That is fine it is good of you to banish him.'

On the morning of the fifth day Dido first took the cows to the fields carrying spear and shield, then he took out the oxen carrying spear and shield. When it came to the turn of the calves he picked up his cane and went out. Obolo was expecting this moment. Obolo's men at once jumped on Dido from their hiding place. Dido defended himself. He lifted the calves and struck the enemy with them. He killed and killed and killed. The enemy were saying, 'What is this who kills with calves?' Now in the middle of the fighting Dido called on his wife, 'My wife, hand me my shield, hand me my shield.' His wife threw the shield calculating so that it would not reach Dido. When Dido stretched himself to get hold of the shield, the enemy got an opportunity to hit him. He died.

Among the Borana there was one brave man like Dido. He was Boru Madha Daday, the Aba Gada. Dido and Madha didn't like each other. But now when Dido died, Madha ceased to play and to laugh. He was sad and angry at Dido's death. One day while playing sadeeq [a board game] he sang:

Ohohohohooo!
Obolo bare-chested
Dido of decorated chest
Dido is nowhere
The wings of the vulture descended on him
While alive he made me lifeless [dried up]
Now my dead brave one has tied me
like a dry burden [leather sack].

He said this [in anger] and broke the *sadeeq* board. Then he told the men to prepare for war.

They went to fight. There was one man, a young boy whom they called Dido Muke. He wanted to go to war. 'You are young, don't go,' they told him. But he wouldn't listen. He wanted to avenge Dido's death.

They arrived at the battlefield. The Arsi had also come. This Obolo has a warrior's armlet, for he was quite a brave warrior. Now he had added Dido's armlet to his arm so he barely managed to lift up his left arm. They fought and fought and fought. But the young man Dido Muke was not fighting. What was he waiting for? He was waiting for Obolo. As he was looking for Obolo, he saw him coming to him. He charged him with his spear. Obolo fell. Dido Muke told him to stand up. 'I can't, have mercy on me,' Obolo begged. Dido said, 'Mercy for Dido's killer?' and slashed Obolo's arm.

The Borana won and took the spoils (cattle) and returned home. When they arrived at their camp they told each other not to divide the spoils and to head all the cattle in one direction. In the direction the cattle were heading they dug a pit and buried Dido's wife up to her neck. Then they let the cattle run over her. The cattle brushed by and trampled on her until nothing was left of her head.

This is how Dido was killed and his wife punished.

A10.1 Dido Gawole: His Childhood**

As a child when Dido fought with other children he was not in the least afraid. Nor did he retreat. The father saw this and thought, 'This boy is impossible, wait, we will see how far he is courageous.' Dido used to tend the calves. One day he returned from his duty and as usual asked for water. The father and the others had taken two water pots and in one they put a francolin and shut it in. They placed the pot with the francolin closest to the direction Dido would be coming from. When Dido asked for water, they told him to drink from the pots. He reached for the pot that was nearer to him. When he opened the pot the francolin rocketed out. During this unexpected occurrence Dido smashed the pot to pieces. [This proved that indeed Dido was never surprised or startled]. They said, 'Don't provoke him ever.'

A10.2 Dido Gawole: His Childhood

Dido belonged to the Karrayu clan. At that time Karrayu and Warajida clans used to play a game hitting each other with a mud ball. Dido was then quite a young man. When the two clans played this game it always ended in many wounded Karrayu men while the Warajida went unharmed. For this reason, the Warajida bullied the Karrayu by saying, 'People of fragile skull' (*Galalacha mataa busuuqqee*).

When Dido began to play this game, and he saw that men of his clan received wounds while the others did not, he asked himself why. He contemplated and finally discovered the rivals' tactics. The Warajida were inserting a stone in the mud ball. So at the next game he told his clansmen to do likewise. When the game started, blood began to flow from the heads of the Warajida. Now the secret was discovered, the Warajida ceased to play the game. They also stoppped calling the Karrayu 'people of fragile skull'.

Dido was such a wise one even in his youth.

A11 Dido Muke the Young Warrior

[I was told this story when I asked why Dido Muke wanted to avenge Dido Gawale.]

There are two other Didos besides Dido Gawole: Dido Muke and Dido Abasabe. This was when Dido Muke was a very young man.

One day Dido Gawole's wife said to her husband Dido, 'Dido I want to have a lover [besides you].' Dido said, 'Why? Is there some thing you lack?' 'I only wanted to add pleasure upon pleasure; I lack nothing.' 'Then,' said Dido,' Is there someone in your mind?' 'Yes, Dido Abasabe,' she told him.

Dido was not happy about this. He said, 'He is a coward, why do you only see that he is handsome?' He declined her choice. When she asked him for his preferences, he suggested Dido Muke the young man. 'Why do you insult me Dido,' she said, 'Why do you insult me? He is only a kid. Am I going to sleep with a toddler?'

Now Dido wanted to show her that his choice is the right one. He told her to prepare the mead (*daad'i*). He said, 'Now this man of your choice is a coward. I will give him this mead and he will get drunk. If he wants to uri-nate, he will do it on the door stones, for he will not go far in the darkness. I will show you your lover's cowardice.'

They brewed the mead and summoned their friends. They prepared two types of mead – one strong and the other of low quality. The wife's choice, Dido Abasabe, came first and they served him with the low quality mead. He drank and soon began to behave erratically. Even the low-quality mead he had consumed had made him drunk. The young Dido Muke came and they gave him too the ordinary mead. Dido Muke tasted, spat it out and said, 'Why do you insult us Dido? Why do you hurt us? Why make us drink this kind of mead?' He was beside himself. Then they served him with the high quality mead. He tasted it and said, 'Now this is a real mead.'

Later that night Didi Gawole asked his wife, 'Whose choice is right, yours or mine?' 'It is rather strange. This small boy amazes me,' she said in defeat. Dido's admiration for the young man doubled. He said to wife, 'Now take a bath, prepare yourself and wait for him.' She washed and perfumed herself.

Dido Gawole was sitting outside under a tree shade discussing things with the elders. Dido Muke was also there and Dido said to him, 'Please young man, I forgot my tobacco at home; run and fetch it for me.'

Dido Muke went. When he came into Dido Gawole's house, Dido's wife was ready for the young man. He asked her for the tobacco. But she said, 'Go up there and rest on that bed, I will join you there.' 'What!' he said, 'Are you trying to make an ass out of me? It is not for me to sleep where Dido has slept.' He went away.

Dido saw him come out. He said, 'Friends, the boy we have sent has not returned with the tobacco. I don't know what has happened, let me go and see.' He came to his wife and asked her what has passed between them.

'That kid is impossible. He reproved me. I don't think he will see my face again,' she said. Dido proudly asked her, 'Whose choice is right, yours or mine?' 'Yours.'

They settled the matter. This was the man who avenged Dido's death and killed Obolo.

When they fought to avenge Dido's death, didn't this boy kill the murderer? It was he who killed Obolo. After he killed Obolo, he called Madha, the chief, and told him to sing the killer's song. 'What am I to say, it is not I who killed Obolo.' 'Sing!' 'But I have not killed.' Dido Muke said to this, 'It is you who killed Obolo; had it not been for you who organised this campaign Obolo would not have died.' And Madha sang.

It is in this way that Dido Muke forced Madha to sing the killer's song: but it was Dido who killed Obolo.

A12 Dido Gawole and Madha

Dido Gawole was brave. He became defiant and refused to listen to the others, and the chiefs became discontented with him. Madha was the Aba Gada and Dido didn't obey his orders. The chiefs and the elders assembled together and deliberated on whether to sentence him to death. The man, Dido, was clever and he discovered their plot. One day as they were discussing Dido's case, one of them saw something and pointed to the others, 'Look an ostrich is coming.' Another man saw and said, 'It is not an ostrich, it is a man.' As they were arguing, 'It is a man, no it is an ostrich', the figure came nearer and became distinguishable. It was Dido. He was sitting on his black horse wearing white garments and that is how he came to look like an ostrich. When Madha saw that it was really Dido he said, 'My friends, let me defecate,' and went into the forest. He became afraid. Today that place is called 'the hollow land of Madha's faeces' (*Daambal udaan Madhaa*).

Dido arrived and dismounted from his horse. He was furious, shaking in anger. He grabbed a tree with his hands to tie his horse to it, and the tree was uprooted. He tried another tree and this other one too got uprooted. He tried this, he tried that and all was the same. He was shaking so violently that he uprooted the trees. He became tired of the trees and tied his horse to the tuft grass *caqoorsa*.

Then he turned to the elders and said:

What a deceitful assembly
What a fool assembly
Which agreed on his death.
Without enquiring about Dido

Listening to the defendant before sentencing him to death was thus started.

The chiefs didn't let the matter go. They hardened against him. The people were on ritual pilgrimage and they travelled to El Dalo. Dido didn't camp with them. He went further past and camped alone at Gaftiro bordering the Arsiland. It was there that the Arsi warrior Obolo entered Dido's service and later killed him.

A13 Enaye: Betrayal

Enaye was rich and a great warrior. When he took a rest, he used to sleep on his wife's lap out in the open in front of his house. The enemy wanted to kill him and approached his wife. They asked her, 'When is your husband off his guard?' She told them, 'He usually sleeps on my lap; you can kill him then.'

When Enaye slept on her lap she tangled and twisted his hair with a tuft of grass. The enemy came on the appointed hour. When she saw them she withdrew her legs. When Enaye heard the footsteps and tried to lift his head he found that his hair was tangled with the grass. He struggled, but the grass was so firm. They killed him there.

The people discovered the wife's betrayal and seized her. They dug a hole and buried her up to her neck. The Gada assembly were then at El Dall. Enaye was rich and they drove the big oxen to her. The oxen ran over her and trampled over her head.

A14 The Ambusher Shanu Qaru

Shanu Qaru was a great ambusher. One day he went to kill a Guji man. The man was grazing cattle. Shanu, from his hiding place, was waiting for the moment the man would be off his guard. For the whole day Shanu followed him. But the man didn't put his weapons down even for a moment.›

At sunset the man took the cattle home. Shanu followed. The Guji man's camp consists of only two huts belonging to his two wives. The Guji entered his house, asked for water and sat down. He had a baby son called Aga [meaning rock]. Aga woke up when he heard his father's voice. Aga had a bell on his arm. The mother handed the boy to his father and went out to bring in the calves. After a while the father put Aga on the bed and went to his second wife's house.

Shanu saw the man leaving and slipped into his house. He took the little boy out of his bed and sat on the chair the father had been sitting on carrying the baby. The mother came with the calves. Assuming the man with her son was her husband she went out again to bring the remaining cattle. Now Shanu left the house taking the baby with him and hid behind the fence.

When the mother returned she saw that her husband was not in. She looked on the bed and also saw that her son was not there. She went to the house of her co-wife and asked her husband whether Aga was with him. 'No, he is in bed,' he said. 'He is not there,' she said. They began to search in all places in utter bewilderment. Amidst this confusion Shanu pinched the baby's ear. The baby cried. When they heard they ran towards him. At this time Shanu sang:

> A rock (*aga*) has a cleft
> Aga has a bell
> Those who look for Aga
> Shanu Qaru has it.

Immediately after saying this Shanu killed Aga and ran away. The parents who saw Shanu run away pursued him crying, 'Catch Shanu, catch Shanu!' People from other camps heard the cry and came out demanding: 'Where is Shanu, where is Shanu?' Shanu himself speaking in the Guji dialect was crying, 'Let Shanu not escape,' while running.

They let him escape thinking he was one of them. Shanu was such a man and he died only recently [in 1982].

A15 Liban Wata the Wise and His Only Error

Liban Wata the Aba Gada was a wise man. He solved every puzzle and won every dispute. Many men tried many times to outwit him without success. But one day he said, 'I am wise, I am strong. No-one can say of me, "he lost." There is no problem that remains unsolved by me.' Then a man called Madha replied, 'Are you cattle who solve every problem? [We know that] only cattle are the solution to every problem. Are you cattle?' [There is a saying, 'There is no problem that cattle do not solve.] Liban Wata failed to answer this.

It was on that day that he made his only error.

A16 Wale Wachu: His Exile and Return**

Wale Wachu was the Aba Gada [1772–80]. The people of his assembly (*yaa'a*) developed a grudge against him. His wife, whose name was Asa, warned him that the people of his generation set (*luuba*) were displeased with him. He said, 'They are not unhappy with me, they love me like themselves.' 'I will show you [with a sign],' Asa said. 'I will tell you what to do. Now I will buy you the best tobacco from Moyale, I will buy *magaado* [salt chewed with tobacco] from here. I will send for the best *jimaa* [a leaf that is chewed as a stimulant, also known as *chat* or *miraa*] from Boye. When you are at a meeting hold out the tobacco so that they can see it. Unwrap the salt before their eyes and chew the tobacco with it. You know men of our assembly, they ask for something they like from someone they love. If they love you, they will ask you to share the *jimaa* with them. They know the quality of your tobacco and it is only you who has it. Watch carefully what will happen.'

The next morning he put on his clothes, wrapped his tobacco, wrapped his salt and went to a meeting. All the elders and officials of his assembly came for the meeting. Wale began to chew the *jimaa* leaf, holding it out visibly. He found that no-one asked for it. He chewed the tobacco and added the salt to it. He found no-one who would raise the subject [of sharing]. They spent the day discussing the issue of the meeting. They returned home.

Wale was a great man. His wife was a great woman. He said to her, 'I have proved what you have said. You know our people, no one had asked me for the *jimaa* I chewed it all alone. I chewed the tobacco alone. I ate the salt alone. Not even a single person asked me to share with him. I discovered the truth of what you have said.'

Now it was time to move into another area. As he was the leader, he had to lead the move. He told his children to drive the transport camels further away where no-one could find them. At night when the disappearance of Wale's camels was learned of, the assembly was told that tomorrow's journey was cancelled. But Wale disagreed. He said, 'We should not fail to move, we should not fail to observe the custom. The camels will come by themselves. You have to go. I will follow.' They agreed and packed. When they were just about to move, they found Wale's camels and brought them home.

He told the assembly to be on the move while his camels were being loaded. As the assembly could not start the journey without Wale's presence, he mounted his horse and led them [saw them off].

He led them up to Gaftiro and returned, pretending to check if his loaded camels had caught up with the group. While turning back, he kept asking whether they had seen his camels. 'We didn't, we didn't,' they were saying. Asking in this fashion he went away from the assembly.

Earlier he had already told his family to move in another direction from where the assembly was heading to. And now he went to them. He caught up with his family at Fulo. He left the calves and went with the rest. [The calves cannot go quickly, indicating that he hurried ahead.] He passed the night across the Hadhesa. He rose early in the morning and went by the way of Malka Farda Wale. When he reached Wallenso he left the steers and resumed the journey with the rest of the cattle, which by now consisted of mainly cows.

Now the assembly camped and asked each other, 'Have you seen Wale?' No-one had seen him. They realized that he had run away. They selected thirty strong men to pursue and bring back Wale. The pursuers turned in their tracks. They took Wale's track. They arrived at Walda Jaru. They saw the calves [Wale had left behind] and killed them. They arrived at Wallenso, saw the steers and killed them too.

When Wale got his cattle and camels across a river, the pursuers arrived from behind. Wale and his wife took counsel. She told him, 'You know your horse is a brave horse – a warrior. If they get your horse, it is as if they have got you. They will not pursue you. Tie this horse by the riverside and let's go away.' He tied the horse and went away.

When the pursuers came to the river they saw the horse there. They stopped and talked among themselves. 'We will not kill it,' they said, 'This horse is a warrior, I have seen him killing this, I have seen him killing that. We won't kill him; let's go on,' they said. There was one man among them – Wale's brother. This man said, 'If we kill his horse he will come out,' and he killed the horse. All the men who were there had horses. They knew what a horse meant to a man. They got angry at what this man did and said to each other, 'We have transgressed a custom that we shouldn't by killing this horse.' Then they decided to return home, abandoning their chase.

Back at the camp they reported, 'We have killed his horse, but we lost him.'

Wale arrived at Moyale. At a place called Dambi Hidi Mata, he made a ritual sacrifice. His cattle grew in number. There he performed every ritual that has to be performed. His cattle filled three kraals. From there he went to Dibbe and camped there. He built his home at El Babo. His cattle became six kraals.

By the time Wale's kraals had become six kraals the assembly were starving. However much they ate, their hunger could not be satisfied. They finished all their cattle. There was no milk and they began to eat wild fruits.

A pregnant woman who was collecting fruits fell from a tree. She moaned, 'What a curse.' Another woman who had been under the tree remarked, 'Is it today we are cursed? We were cursed the day Wale disappeared from among us.' A man overheard them and told it to another man. The whole assembly heard it, and talked over it. Finally they decided to search for him and ask forgiveness. They selected thirty men and sent them out to look for Wale.

The men came to El Babo where Wale had settled. Wale's wife saw the men coming and said, 'Look Wale, men of your assembly are here.' 'Go and greet them,' he said. She went to them and asked them, 'Don't you greet Wale?' 'We are afraid of him.' She assured them. They came in. 'Wale we came looking for you; we greet you,' they said to Wale. Wale told his wife, 'I have to water the cattle, show them in.' She showed them in.

She gave the thirty men thirty pots of milk. It didn't even wet their tongues. She roasted them thirty pots of coffee. It didn't even wet their tongues. She killed a big ox. It didn't even wet their tongues. They simply sat there, the same before, the same after.

Wale returned at evening. She told him, 'I gave then thirty pots of milk; it did them no good. I roasted thirty pots of coffee; it did them no good. I killed an ox; it did them no good. Here are your men.' Then Wale brought them a young steer. He asked them to come and bless it. They blessed it. He slaughtered it and told his wife to roast the liver. The men were given the

roasted liver and they become unable to finish even half of it. They were satisfied. They passed the night there. On the next day they asked him to return
with them.

They returned together. When Wale returned to the assembly they were
in the situation they had been in before. Wale had already seen it; he gave
them a cow each. They killed and ate the cows. He gave them some more
and they ate those too. He was tired of it. [He had given them to breed from
and replace their herds.] He gathered them and performed a prayer ritual.
After the ritual he gave then a heifer each. It was these heifers that bred and
multiplied.

Then he waged war on the Guji. They raided cattle. 'We will not divide
the spoils,' he said. They did as he told them. They brought the cattle to their
camp. All their wives came out and divided the cattle among themselves. It
was on that day the expression, 'capturing by [a woman's] waist band' was
coined (*anfalaan boojuu*). The men didn't get a single cow.

Wale again waged battle against the Arsi. They raided cattle. Now he
told them to share. They divided the cattle. And abundance reigned.

A17 Malda Doyo the Weak Boy Turned Great Warrior

There was a young man whose name was Malda Doyo Boso. He was a weak
boy. His father was a strong warrior. One day the father asked the mother,
'Am I the father of this boy? Why doesn't he hunt. How come he doesn't
know how to recite war songs?' The mother answered, 'It is true you are the
father of this boy. The day I conceived him, you were not at home. I was
preparing yoghurt for you. That day I was draining the water out of the
yoghurt. I drank too much of the milk-water. I didn't know the day of your
return; but unexpectedly you returned on that day. That night I conceived
this boy, and that is why he became weak.' 'If he is really my son, he will
react to what I apply to him,' said the father.

The father isolated his son and built him a hut. There he killed an ox for
him. The son ate (finished) the whole of it. Again the father killed another
ox. The boy ate half of it. And at this time father and son heard men chant-
ing war songs. 'What are they singing Father?' Malda asked. 'Sleep quietly,
you don't know what they are singing,' said the father by way of scolding.
The young man became angry. He pushed aside his father and hastened to
where they were singing. He joined the singers and when his turn came he
sang the war song without any mistake.

After the singing the men prepared to go to war. Malda also said to his
father, 'I will go with them.' 'What do you know about war? Sit quietly,' the
father said. Malda in anger demolished the fence and followed the warriors.

They went to a place called Barraq. Now Malda had never been to war
or hunting big game. But when he saw a herd of elephants, he asked, 'Is this
the one to kill?' 'Yes,' they said. Leaving the others behind he ran and

charged the elephants alone. He killed three. Then he asked the warriors, 'Does one get anointed by killing this?' 'Yes.'

Then they came to a place called Rappi. There they came across mountain baboons. He chased the baboons and killed many. They went then to the land of the enemy. He killed many enemy warriors.

They returned home. By the time they arrived at their village it was early morning. Malda sang:

> At Barraq he danced with elephants
> At Rappi he danced with baboons
> Dancer Galgalu Malda Doyo Boso.

The father heard the song. He heard his name and his wife's name being mentioned. He said to his wife, 'Wake up, put on your clothes.' 'Why?' 'Our name is being mentioned; I don't know if it is positively or negatively.' When they went out they saw their son coming carrying the spears he has captured. From then on he became a great warrior.

A18 Malda Doyo the Merciful

Malda Doyo became a brave warrior. In those days the Borana were fighting the Arsi. The Arsi were led by Manno Jarso. Both warring parties were heading towards each others' territory and on their way they became tired and rested. Malda was the commander of the Borana warriors. He was surveying the area. There Manno, with the Arsi, was also on a reconnaissance mission. The two bumped into each other. 'Who are you?' 'I am Borana, and you?' 'I am Arsi.'

Malda asked the Arsi, 'What are you doing here?' 'I am the commander, I walk in front of my army.' 'I am too a commander,' said Malda. 'Aren't we going for each other?' asked the Arsi.

They fought. They wrestled. The Arsi knocked down the Borana. 'I am going to castrate you; pull apart your legs,' said Manno the Arsi. 'Don't do it, please have mercy on me,' entreated Malda. 'Why should I?'

'It is the vulture that consumes the castrated. We are both commanders who came across each other, please don't.'

'Yes I will,' said Manno.

'If you have to, I will pull my legs well apart for you. Help me to my feet.'

The Borana rose to his feet and suddenly grabbed the Arsi. They fought. The Arsi fell down and the Borana, Malda, was on top. 'I will castrate you,' said Malda.

'God doesn't allow the expected to happen as the unexpected, don't castrate me.' Malda said, 'You were about to castrate me, and now I will do it to you.' 'All right let it be.' 'But I won't,' said Malda and took the man into captivity. He took him home. He killed an ox for him and then let him free.

At another time the Arsi killed a certain Borana. The man he killed was Malda's relative. Now Malda organized an operation to avenge the blood of his relative. Just like the other time the Arsi, Manno, and Malda met alone. Malda in anger sang:

Avenging castration with castration
Tears with tears
Revenge makes the brave weep
And the coward suffer.

Now the Arsi too became angry. They fell on each other. Malda was on top. He killed and castrated Manno.

A19 Iddo Saffale

The Borana, who were divided into the two moieties – Sabo and Gona – used to perform rituals and wage wars separately. When the Gona perform the fire-making ritual (*uuchuuma*) before going to war or conduct ceremonies, they lean their spears on a man. They select a strong man from Sabo for this purpose.

The Sabo became sick of it and refused to carry Gona spears. The two came at odds. The Gona said let's fight each other. As both were Borana they could not use spears. So they agreed to use balls of mud. Now the Gona smuggled stones into the mud balls. They began to throw them at each other. The Sabo were getting wounded while the Gona were not. For this the Gona used to ridicule the Sabo as, 'Sabo of the fragile head'. The Sabo talked among themselves: 'How come we get wounds while they don't.'

Now among the Sabo, one man, Iddo Saffale, came to the Gona and asked them to lean their spears on him. They took it as a gesture of reconciliation and leaned on him all their spears. Now that they were bare handed, Iddo struck the Gona with their own spears. He killed many. This took place at the water well of the Gona clan named Oditu. Iddo confiscated the Oditu well, which is the one found at El Dharitu. Until today this well had been owned by the Digalu-Titi, which is Iddo's clan. From that day on the Gona stopped saying 'people of the fragile head'. They also abandoned the habit of leaning spears on Sabo men.

A20 Jarso Wada and the Battle of Malka Halu

In the old days people used to wage battles on the counsel of a diviner. Once the Arsi people went to fight the Borana. The Arsi raiding party was led by three war chiefs. They came to Boranaland. They searched for Borana camps but they failed to locate them. At that time the Borana population was small and you could not find them everywhere. The Arsi searched for the Borana by going as far as Yabelo and Mega. Unable to find them they turned back.

They told their diviner that they had failed to locate the Borana. The diviner said, 'How come you didn't find the Borana? Does that mean the river has ceased to flow in the saltland? Does the fig tree cease to stand on top of Walmal?' The diviner was telling them where the Borana had camped. The Arsi returned again to the Borana territory.

While the Arsi were on their way, the Borana diviner envisioned their coming. He said, 'The Arsi raiders are coming. The enemy will destroy you. They have the fig trees on top of Walmal, and the river at the saltland for a sign, a landmark. Cut and burn the trees. Change the direction of the river that flows into the saltland. Besides, there is one man that saves Borana – Jarso Wada of the Hawatu-Walensa clan. He is in Taltale, fetch him. In this battle the raiders, the Arsi, will take the cattle and destroy the people. If Jarso takes part in this battle he will die, but he will take back the cattle and save the people. And the enemy will be totally destroyed.'

This is what the Borana diviner foretold. The Borana went to Jarso Wada and told him all. 'You will not return alive, but if you fight the people will be saved and the cattle regained.' Then Jarso said, 'If my own life can buy [or save] the lives of many Borana, I will die for the people, but I will make a will.'

'What is your will?' they asked.

'The Borana will not be destroyed if my life can save the clan. Let the cattle of my family drink from any well, even in the dry season no well owner should turn them away. Second, whenever a *haayyuu* [judicial elder] is to be elected, let my clan never enter into competition with other clans; give the *haayyuu* to my clan.'

They accepted his will. And up to today one *haayyuu* is given to the Hawatu-Wallensa clan. His descendants' cattle drink from any well.

Now the Arsi came. The Borana had destroyed the fig trees and redirected the river. The Arsi found the Borana, however, and they fought. They fought and fought for five days. On the sixth day the Arsi won and took away the cattle. When the Arsi, with the cattle they raided, arrived at Webb, they said, 'Webb, saltland (*sodda*) had led us to you in peace; now fate is on you. Webb see us to our home.' Thus they prayed and left Webb. They reached Arero. They prayed, 'Arero, Webb has led us to you. Fate is on you, see us to our home.'

The Borana warriors, led by Jarso Wada, were quietly following the Arsi. The diviner had warned the Borana not to attack the Arsi while they were calling the name of God [while praying]. So, the Arsi were blessed in every land they spent the night at. The Borana simply kept following them. Now the Arsi went past Arero and arrived at the Dawa river. There they said, 'Dawa, fate is on you, destroy our enemy.'

Now the Borana diviner said, 'This time they have not called on God. They are speaking evil; fall on them.' At Dawa river they fought and fought and fought. In the midst of the battle the cattle rushed back towards home.

Human blood was flowing into the river like water. It was on that day that the place was named ' the dyed river bank'. Jarso Wada died in the battle, after killing many, many people. He gave his life for his people.

A21 Dawwe Gobbo, the Spy Aba Gada

Dawwe Gobbo was an Aba Gada [1706–14]. It was the dry season. Water and grass were scarce. At that time the fertile areas were controlled by the Wardai people.[16] The grass was like honey there and the Wardai wells were full throughout the year. Dawwe's heart was set on that land. He deliberated with his people and then went to the Wardailand. He took off all his clothes, his warrior's armlet and his *kallachaa* [a metal phallic-like emblem of head-gear] and entered the Wardai territory disguised as a fool. The Wardai took him for a crazy man, and he behaved as one. He always repeated what others had said. One of the Wardai chiefs took him in.

At the chief's house, where he stayed, Dawwe had nothing to do except rolling in dust, eating ash, parroting everything addressed to him. He was a perfect lunatic. But the wife of the chief observed something unusual about him. Whenever he saw the chief's horse and spear he stared at them for a long time, his face assuming a thoughtful composure, as if in lust or as if he were nostalgic for something associated with them. She told her husband, 'Maybe this man is not crazy after all.' But the husband didn't give weight to her suspicion. However, after close observation she concluded that the crazy man was only masquerading. Then she told Dawwe, 'I don't know when you are going to come for us, but I know you will come; and when you come, spare me.' Dawwe didn't say anything except repeating her words as usual.

One day when all the male adults were out of the village, Dawwe revealed to the woman his real identity. He then made love to her. He was about to return to his kingdom. He told her, 'I will come shortly; put on your roof a white hide so that my men won't touch you.' Then Dawwe took the chief's spear and his horse and fled to his land.

Soon the men came and discovered his disappearance. The wife told them that he had gone with the horse. They pursued him but in vain. The horse Dawwe took, the chief's horse, was such a special breed no-one could catch up with it.

After six months Dawwe, who knew all the secrets of the Wardai, came back leading Borana warriors. They easily destroyed the Wardai villages. Many villagers were killed, many fled. But most of the women did not run away and the Borana took them and made them their wives. They became Borana and the land too became the Borana's.

---

16 The Wardai (Orma), as Borana call them, controlled most of the grazing from the Ethiopian escarpment to the coast at that time. The Oromo-speaking Orma are now restricted to the Tana River area of Kenya.

A22 *Prophecy*

Five men went to Dhadacha Yaya and Waqole Bora [who were at that time retired Borana chiefs] to ask them about the future. As they went they came across a sheep that suckled a warthog. One of them, seeing this spectacle, said, 'I saw something never seen before,' and he returned home, for he considered it a bad omen. The rest [four] went on. As they went, according to some they came across owls, and according to others across bulls. [This is an interpolation of the narrators: 'according to some' refers to the four characters in the tale.] Some say: 'While the owl that was struck went unharmed, the one it touched with its blood died.' Others say: 'While the bull we struck went unharmed, the one the wounded bull's blood contaminated died.' One of them said, 'I saw something never seen before and turned back.' The remaining three went on. Now they came across three wells. The middle one was empty, The others were overflowing. Water flowed from the right-hand well to the left one without entering the middle well. One of them said: 'I have never seen anything like this before.' And he turned back. The other two came across an emaciated horse which stood in the midst of green grass. One of them said: 'I am afraid this is something never seen before,' and he too turned back.

The fifth man, who was left alone, arrived at his destination. He explained to Dhadacha and Waqole that they were five in the beginning and how the rest went back. They said to him: 'We know what you came for. Tonight we will play riddles; listen to us.'

That night they began to play riddles:

'Lie chased away truth; truth hasn't escaped neither has lie returned. Solve my riddle if you can.'

'Lawlessness chased away law; law hasn't escaped neither does lawlessness return [from the chase]. Solve my riddle if you can.'

'Spearhead has become butt and butt has become spearhead. Solve my riddle if you can.' They played for most of the night.

Now when it was morning they asked the guest what he had seen on his way. He told them.

They interpreted it thus: The sheep that suckled warthog does mean that, even if for a single day Wata [an outcast group of hunters[17]] will rule over Borana.

The owl that was struck and continued, while the one that was touched by the blood died, says that a time will come to say, 'This is the man who killed my brother.' You will be unable to take revenge.

The story of the wells foretells that you will cease to think of your brother and favour strangers.

The starved horse you saw in the midst of overgrown grass is about the time that will come to pass when many cattle [or wealth] fail to sustain even the children.

---

17 See Kassam, 1986b; and Bashuna, 1993.

A23 The Origin of the Qallu

The first Qallu came from God. He descended from the sky. He was first discovered by a Wata hunter. Near the Qallu were three black cows. A ram and a bamboo container with a snake and a whip [*liico* carried by married men at most rituals]. He wore on his head a *kallachaa* and checked turban. The Wata hunter who first saw him called the Borana to show them. The Borana, who were of the Karrayu clan, came, and when they saw the matter they sent the Wata away. They recognized that the Qallu was from God. They begged him to come into their village. He refused. Finally they sent the Qallu a girl who was of the Metari-Meta clan. Then they waited for three days. After the third day the men returned and this time the Qallu spoke to them [some say the girl appeared with him], and said 'God bore me; only along the road of prayer have I come.' Then they took charge of the Qallu and all that was with him. The girl became his wife. He became the Qallu of the Karrayu and of the Sabo moiety as a whole. To this day the Qallu of the Karrayu marries a girl from the Metari-Meta clan, that is a member of his own moiety [thereby breaching the rule of exogamy and so manifesting his freedom from social rules]. This is how the Karrayu gained their Qallu.

The Qallu of the Gona moiety is from the Oditu clan. He does not come from the sky, from God. He has human parents. Once there was severe drought. The leaders were about to perform the *muuda*, or anointment ceremony. So they told the people not to leave the shrines in search of water and grass. But the leaders did not come soon and the people were unable to wait. The drought was severe and the cattle were infested with ticks. One by one all the clans left, until at the end only the Oditu remain. When the leaders came to the shrine they found only the Oditu. Among the Oditu they elected one man and anointed him as a Qallu. Today the Oditu say, '*obsan qaallooman*', which means that only those who have the patience can become Qallu.

Part Three

Stories in Borana

Chapter 10

Selected Narratives in Borana

D1 *Geedaaloo Cubbu*

Duri duri, leenca, soosso, geedallo, ookko, uummo fi waraabeessi walti naqatan jedhan. geedalloonif soossoon loon tiksuf bahani jedhan. Yoo tiksanu geedalloon soossoon, 'koottu ollaa kanaa bishaan nuu kadhadu,' jedheen. Hin kadhadhu soosso arganne jedhani na fudhatu," jette. 'Kenni soossoon keenya, kenni soossoon keenya jedhe si fudhadhaa,' jetteen. soossoon kaate itti dhaabatte. Jarri soosso arganne jedhani fudhataniin. Galgala galnaan,' soossoon mee?' jedhaniin. 'Ollaa kana bishaan kadhadha jette otoo ani hin deemiin jedhuun deemte namni fudhateen,' jette. Itti dhaabatan. Horii gula Yaa'ani. Amma geedalloon ookko walin tiksan. 'ookko, koottu ollaa kanaa bishaan nuu kadhadhu,' jetteen. 'Ookko arganne jedhani na fudhatan, hin fedhu,' jetteen 'Ookkoo keenya kennaa, Ookkoo keenya kennaa jedheen si fudhaa kootti,' jetteen. kadhani itti dhaabatan. Ookkoo kaan in fudhatan.Galgala galanii, 'Ookkoon mee?' jennaan, ' ollaa kanaa bishaan kadhadha jette deemte namni fudhate, ' jette. In Calliisan. Ammaan tana uummoo waliin tiksani. uummoon, 'hanphee in nyaana,' jettee, otoo ishiin hin nyaatiin uummootti kennitee jennaan uummoon afaan ishii walitti qabatte. Amma fuula looni bahani. 'Isii uummoo,' jennaan 'hm' jette. 'Abuyyoo leenca akkeesitaa? You ani galgala gale siif hin himiin!' jette. You loon galanu geedalloon dura ceete leencatti himte. 'Mee yaamiin,' tana. 'uummoo!' jedheen Leenci. 'Hm,' jette. 'Ati na akkeesitaa?' jedhee dhaye ijjeese.

Amma boruu waraabessaan waliin tiksani. Sa'aan leencaa dhaltee jennaan, 'Koottu in nyaana jibicha,' jetteen. Jibicha kaanin in nyaatan. 'Geedalloon dhiiga callaa dhugde.Jibicha nyaatani kuruphe qabani galani. Leenci, 'Sa'aan maal dhale?' jennaan jibicha jedhaniin.

Yoo inni laalu kuruphee. 'Enyutu nyaate?' jedhe. 'Waraabeessatu nyaate,' jette geedalloon. Waraabeessi kaan, 'Dhayi nu laali,' jennaan leenci geedalloo dhaye dadhabe. Waraabeesa dhaane jennaan manyeen keessaa jige. 'Jibicha kiyya nyaatte,' jedhe waraabeessa dhaane ijjeese.

Leencaan Wal tiksani. Geedalloon eerbee kalaada fudhatte gaara irra koorte. Leenci gaara jala taa'a, ishiin gaara koorte:

'E! abuyyoo, abuyyoo leenca
Koormi kiyyaaf koormi kankee walhadhani
Qoomaan dhowwi, qoomaan dhowwi,'

jettee dhagaa guddaa irraangadee gadhiiste. Leenci qoomaan dhowwinaan
dhagaan kaan irra ce'ee macare ijjeese. Geedalloon akkana nama cufa fixxe
horii kaan cufa fudhatte.

D9 *Diidoo Filince*

Mucaa tokkoon maqaa Diid' Filince jedhan. Mucaan kun abbaa hin qabu,
haadha qaba. Horii Booranaa tiiksa. Loon diiram bobbaase. Ijoolle ollaatiin
waliin oolu. Lafti baalii [ayyaana] ijoolleen daabbo guurratte boqootaatti
dachaate nyaatti. Inni hin qabu, dhoqqe wayaatti guurrate dhufe.'Kiyya kunoo
gulana nyaana qara keessan nyaadhuu?' jedhee in nyaate. 'Kee kenni,' Yoo jed-
hanuun, 'eegaa loon facaase deebi'a,' jedhee itti dhaabate. Achuumaan itti
dhaabate. Ijoolleen muumme hin qabu reebuum reebde qabde. Boollo Waraa
beessaa keessa keette.

Loon in galan. Haati mucaa galagala dhabde. I joolle gaafannaan, 'egii
boruu hin garre," jette. Haati barbaada litti dhaabatte. Raasaa keessa
deemte. 'Diid Filince, Diid Filince!' jette yaamte. Waraabeessi ishii jala
deeme caqasa. Waraabeessi boollo dura dhaabbatee, 'Diida Filince!' jedhe
yaame. Haadha se'ee 'yoo' jedhe bahe. Waraabeessi duugda irra keeyyate
itti dhaabate. Fagaate jennaan irraa busee, 'Ani amma waraabeessa, siin
nyaadha,' jedheen. 'Na nyaata beenu gooli [fiira] kan kee cufa yaammadhu
walin na nyaattu,' jedheen. Inni biraaa itti dhaabate jennaan dhagaa guuree
dhaddacha dheeraa koore.

Waraabeessi gooli guurree deebi'ee jennaan dhabe. Muka jala ejjee 'Diid
Filince!' jedhe yaame. Mucaan in dhowwaate. 'Gadi bu'ii, si nyaadha,' jedhe
waraabeessi. Mucaan, 'Na nyaatta, afaan bani utaalee keessa sii bu'aa,' jedhe.
Afaan keessa dhagaa itti darbate. Waraabeessi in du'e. Goola waraabeessaa
cufa fixee dhagaan irraa obbaa'e. Waraabeessi tokko callaan haafe. Kun jalaa
deemu didnaan mucaan akka gadibu'u hin qabu achuumatti haafe.

Namicha tokko ka diiram qotiyoo bobbaafatu arge. 'Abboo kottu ilma
sii ta'aa, waraabeessa kana narraa ijjeesi,' jedhe. Irraa ijjeesee ka'ee gala-
teen. Niiti isaatiin mucaan kun ilma keenya jabeessi jedheen. Boruu diiram,
'koottu fuula obruu si garsiisa deebite sanyii naa fiddaa,' jedhee agarsiisee
sanyii naa fudhii jedheen.

Galee haadhaan, 'abbeen korpeessa lachuu qaliiti foon nuu eergi jed-
heera,' jedheen. Qaltee isaaf itti kennite. Inni amma baduuf waan ka'eef
kanuum warreegate ka'ee itti dhaabate.

Baduum badee, fagaatee jaarsa fardaan deemu argee jennaan dubbise.
Namichilleen hejjee dubbise. Namichi fincaaniif gooree jennaan farda anatu
harkaan sii qabata jedhee fudhate. Farda gubbaa bu'ee itti dhaabate.

Ammallee jaarti qoraan cabsituun bahe. Jaartiin, 'Koottu, guddoo kiyya qoraan kana narra kaa'i,' jette. 'Farda kiyya essatti hidhadhaa?' jedhe. 'Farda mukatti hidhadhu,' jette 'Aadaan mukatti hin hiitu, miila namaa malee,'jedhe. 'Miila kiyya irra hidhadhuu narra kaa'i' jette Miila kaan xur-risee muka gubbaa kaa'ee, haada otoo hin hiikiin farda gubbaa bahee itti dhaabate. Jaarti kaan lafa irratti harkisee ce'uum ce'ee ijjeese.

Galgala lafti halkanoofnaan ollaa biyyaatiin bahe. Jaarti kaan duduuba kaa'ee ollaa Booranaatti seene. 'Jaartiin kun fayyaa miti dhiibu keesa in kaa'a, farda moonaatti naa hidhaa, 'jedhe. Bulani baraaqa ka'ee farda laalla'a jedhe gadibahe. Jaartiin reenfa, yaa doote, ofumaa dhiibu keessa ciifti. Akka isiin doote in beeka gadibhe iyye. Ollaan dhufnaan, 'Kunoo warri kun jaartii dhukubsattu kana ijjeese, anille baqadhee diiram bahe iyye,' jedhe. Dubbatani in kaffalchisaniif. Diiram ka'ee itti dhaabate.

Warra horii gurguruun bahe, gurguurtuun kaan otto muka jala ciiftu duubaan dhufee mukarratti koore. Koraa fardaa fuudhee itti gadhiise. Wanniin 'bobobobobb!' jennaan gurguurtuun kaan in baqatte. Horii warraa guurratee gale.

D13 *Bulguun Niiti Awwaalte*

Duri duri, wari sadii – abbaa, haadha, ilma – jiru jedhan. Lafa kana bulguun jira jedhani. Abbaaf mucuan loon tiksu. Abbaan haadha irratti balbala cufe akkana jedhan: 'Hancaa hin hancisiin, qilqille hin goosiin, gundoo hin mid-hiin,' jedheen. Achii mana gubbaa uree ka'ee biraaa deeme. Nitiin waan inni hin hojjatiin jedhe cufa hojjatte.

Bulguun dhuftee, 'Afaan balbalaa essa?' jetteen. Maal jette? Jennaan, 'Dhaamsa warra keessani sitti hima, afaan balbalaa essa?' jetteen. 'Koori gubbaan bu'ii' jetteen. Koorte gubbaan buute. 'Sin nyaadha moo qoteen si awwaala?' jette bulguun. Qoti na awwaaliin tana. Qotte garaacha moona keessa awwaalteen.

Bulguun ofii okolee liqimsitee teesse. Abbaan gale. You gale ishiin in teessi. Barcuma kiyya natti kenniin tana. Irra ceceete. 'Isii niitiin in maraatte, isii niitiin in maraate?' jedhe. Barcuma kaan kaaste itti kennit 'Ciicoo kiyya miyyu naa kenni,' jedheen. Irra ceceete. 'Isii nitiin in maraatte, isii nitiin in maraatte?' In baateen.'Itiille kiyya naa haafiin,' tana. Itiille isaa hin beektu, irra ceceete, irra ceceete. 'Isii niitiin in maraatte, isi niitiin in maraatte?' In baate. Baate hafte.

Mucaan, 'Abboo, wanniin kun ayyoo miti, wanniin kun ayyoo miti, jedhe.' 'Ijooleen in maraatani?' jedhe abbaan.

Godaanuuf ka'ani. Ishii farda irratti fe'ani.Goromsi tokko koyeessa, daddeebite. Fuula niiti awwaalan in qotte. Qotumm qotte, qotuum qotte dhagoode ol muldhiste. Abbaan You gaddeebi'u haateen tana. Qotee bolloo keessaa fuudhe. Itti dhaabate. In iyye:

'Waariyoo, Waariyoo
Wanniin sun bineensa
waraana farda irra kaa'ii
waraana farda irra kaa'i.'

Jedheen 'Maal jette, Maal jette?'

'Farda Kora irraa dabu dhowwaa [2]
Haate farda irraa dhaqu dhowwaa [2]
E Waariyoo waraana farda irra Kaa'aa
Wanniin kun bineensa, waraana!'

Otuuma akkana jedhu duubaa dhaqabee, waraanaan *'tubuq'* godhe farda
irraa kaase.

D18   *Ogoraan Gurra Inleensaa Qabe*

Inleensaaf Bununni waliin dhimaltu dhaqan jedhan. Inleensi karaa ogoraa
bahe jedhani. Ogoraan gurra qabe jedhni. Bununuun irraa baasu dadhabde.
Bununuun gaalaan bahe. Gaalaan akkana Jetteen:

'Gaala! Gaala!
Naaf inleensi walti dhimaltu dhaqne
Inleensi karaa ogoraan bahe
Ogoraan gurra qabe
Macare irraa baasu dadhabe
Gaalan, irraanaa baa baasi'

'Hin baasu, ani dhale bira ejjaa!' jedhe gaalli. Bununuun namaan bahe:

'Nama! nama!
Naaf inleensi walti dhimaltu dhaqne
Inleensi karaa ogoraan bahe
Ogoraan gurra qabe
Macare irraa baasu dadhabe
Gaalaan irraa naa baasi jedhe
Dhale bira ejjaa jette
Nama, gaala naa elmii!'

'Okoleen mee?' tana. [namatu jedhe.] Bununuun okoleen bahe:

'Okolee! Okolee!
Naaf inleensi dhimaltu dhaqne
Inleensi karaa ogoraan bahe

Ogoraan gurra qabe
Macare irraa baasu dadhabe
Gaalaan irraa naa baasi jedhe
Dhale bira ejjaa jette
Namaan naa elmi jedhe
Okoleen mee? jedhe
Sitti yaa elmanu!'

'Hin elmanu; You ani ajaa'e maaliin na qoraasatin?' jette Okoleen.
'Baddanaan si qoraasina,' jedhee baddanaan bahe:

'Baddana! baddana!'
Naaf inleensi dhimaltu walin dhaqne
Inleensi karaa ogoraan bahe
Ogoraan gurra qabe
Macare irraa baasu dadhabe
Gaalaan irraa naa baasi jedhe
Dhale bira ejjaa jette
Namaan naa elmi jedhe
Okoleen mee? jette
Okoleen sitti yaa elmanu jedhe
Maaliin na qoraasitan jette
Baddana, qoraassiin, tana.

'Siif hin qoraassuun,' tana, 'You ani boba'e ag dabre maaltu na dhaamsaan,'
tana. Bununuun itti dhaabate. Waaqaan bahe:

'Waaqa! Waaqa!
Naaf inleensi walti dhimaltu dhaqne
Inleensi karaa ogoraan bahe
Ogoraan gurra qabe
Macare irraa baasu dadhabe
Gaalaan irra naa baasi jedhe
Dhale bira ejjaa jette
Namaan naa elmi jedhe
Okoleen mee? jette
Okoleen sitti yaa elmanu jedhe
Maaliin na qoraassitan jette
Baddanaan si qoraassu jedhe
Maaltu na dhaamsaa jedhe
Waaqa, roobi dhaamsi.

'Yoo ani roobee lafa tana cufa miisise maaltu na dheeda?' jedhe waaqni.
Arbaan bahe:

'Arba! Arba!
Naaf inleensi dhimaltu waliin dhaqne
Inleensi karaa ogoraan bahe
Ogoraan gurra qabe
Macare irraa baasu dadhabe
Gaalaan irraa naa baasi jedhe
Dhale bira ejjaa jette
Namaan elmi jedhe
Okoleen sitti yaa elmanu jedhe
Okoleen maaliin na qoraassitan jedhe
Baddanaan si qoraassu jedhe
Maaltu na dhaamsaa jedhe
Waaqaan roobi dhaamsi jedhe
Maaltu na dheeda jedhe
Arba, ati dheedi.'

'Gaaf ani dheedee bokoke maaltu garaa na fallaansaa?' Waraanaan
bahe:

'Waraana! Waraana!
Naaf inlleensi dhimaltu waliin dhaqne
Inleensi karaa ogoraan bahe
Ogoraan gurra qabe
Macare irraa baasu dadhabe
Gaalaan irraa naa baasi jedhe
Dhale bira ejja jette
Namaan elmi jedhe
Okoleen mee? jette
Okoleen sitti yaa elmanu jedhe
Maaliin na qoraassitan jedhe
Baddanaan si qoraassu jedhe
Maaltu na dhaamsaa jedhe
Waqaan roobi dhaamsi jedhe
Maaltu na dheeda jedhe
Arbaan dheedi jedhe
Maaltu garaa na fallaansa jedhe
Waraana, garaa fallaansiin,' tana.

'You ani jalaa miiladhu maaltu na qajeelcha?' jedhe Waraanni. Bununuun
tumtuun bahe:

'Tumtu! Tumtu!
Naaf inleensi dhimaltu waliin dhaqne

Inleensi karaa ogoraan bahe
Ogoraan gurra qabe
Macare irraa baasu dadhabe
Gaalaan irraa naa baasi jedhe
Dhale bira ejja jette
Nammaan elmi jedhe
Okoleen mee? jette
Okoleen sitti yaa elmanu jedhe
Maaliin na qoraassitan jedhe
Baddanaan si qoraassu jedhe
Maaltu na dhaamsa jedhe
Waaqaan roobi dhaamsi jedhe
Maaltu na dheeda jedhe
Arbaan dheedi jedhe
Maaltu garaa na fallaansa jedhe
Waraanaan garaa fallaansi jedhe
Maaltu na qajeelcha jedhe
Tumtuu, ati qajeelchiin.'

Tumtuun, 'Toole, in qojeelcha,' jedhe.

Tumtuun waraana qajeelche, Waraanni garaa arbaa fallaanse, arbi marga dheede, bokkaan ibbida dhaamse, baddanni okolee qoraasse, okoleetti namni gaala elme, gaalli ogoraa gurra inleensaarraa baase.

D19 *Tuqaan Dooqaa Ofii Barbaaddu*

Duri duri, tuqaan dooqaan ishii badee jennaan mucaa Garbicha jedhaniin waliin doqa kaan barbaada dhaqxe. Mucaan doqa kaan argatee galaana keessa duraa buuse. Tuqaan abbaa mucaa bira deemte, 'Abbaa Garbiichaa, Garbichi kan kee dooqa kiyya galaan keessa narraa buuse, dhaani naa fusi-isi,' jette. Abbaan Garbichaa in didee.

Yoo didu, tuqaan hiddii diidaa bira deemte, 'Hiddii, hiddi diidaa, obruu abbaa garbichaa dheedi,' jetteen

'Obruun Abbaa Garbichaa mal ta'e? jette hiddiin.

'Abbaan Garbichaa, Garbicha ofii dhaane dooqa tiyya naa fusisu didee.'
'Hin dheedu,' jette hiddiin.

Amma tuqaan gara Waataa deemtee, 'Waata, hiddii iddi,' jetteen. 'Hiddiin maal ta'e?' jedhe waataan. Tuqaan:

'Hiddiin obruu Abbaa Garbichaa dheedu diddee
Abbaan Garbichaa, Garbicha ofii dhaanee dooqa
tiyya naa fusisu didee.' Jette.

'Hin iddu,' jedhe waataan.

Yoo inni didu, ibidda bira. dhaqxe. 'Ibidda, goonphe Waataa gubii,' jette. 'Waatni [Waataan] maal ta'e?' jedhe ibiddi. Tuqaan:

Waataan hiddii iddu didee
Hiddiin obruu Abbaa Garbichaa dheedu didde
Abbaan Garbichaa, Garbicha ofii dhaane dooqa tiyya naa fusisu dide.

'Hin gubu,' jedhe ibiddi.
Bisaan bira deemte, 'Bisaan, ibidda dhaamsi,' jette. 'Ibiddi maal tae?'

Ibiddi goonphee wataa gubuu didee
Waatni hiddi iddu didee
Hiddiin obruu Abba Garbichaa dheedu diddee
Abbaan Garbichaa, Garbicha ofii dhaane dooqa
tiyya naa fusisu dide.

'Hin dhaamsu,' jedhe bisaan illeen.
Arba bira deemte. 'Arba, bisaan xuuxi,' jette. 'Bisaan maal ta'e?'

Bisaan ibidda dhaamsu didee,
I biddi goonphe waataa gubuu didee,
Waatni hiddii iddu dideeWaatni hiddii iddu dideeWaatni hiddii iddu
dideeWaatni hiddii iddu dideeWaatni hiddii iddu dideeWaatni hiddii
iddu dideeWaatni hiddii iddu didee
Hiddiin obruu Abbaa Garbichaa dheedu diddee,
Abbaan Garbichaa, Garbicha ofii dhaane dooqa
Tiyya naa fusisu dide.

'Hin xuuxu,' jedhe arbii.
Jirmii bira deemte. 'Jirmii,garaa arbaa baqaqsi.'
'Arbii maal ta'e?' jedhe jirmiin.

Arbii bisaan xuuxu didee,
Bisaan ibidda dhaamsu didee,
Ibiddi goonphee waataa goboo didee,
Waatni hiddii iddu didee,
Hiddiin obruu Abbaa Garbichaa dheedu diddee,
Abbaan Garbichaa, Garbicha ofii dhaane dooqa tiyya naa fusisu dide.

Jirmiin ille, 'hin baqaqsu,' jedhe.
Antuuta bira deemte. 'Antuuta, jirmii jala duuli.'
'Jirmiin maal ta'e?'

Jirmiin garaa arbaa baqaqsu didee, Antuutni, 'jirmii jala hin duullu,' jedhaniin.

Ijoolle bira deemte. 'Ijoolle, antuuta laawween ijjeesaa.'

'Antuutni maal ta'e?'

Antuutni jirmii jala duulu diddee
Jirmiin garaa arbaa baqaqsu didee,
Arbii bisaan xuuxu didee,
Bisaan ibidda dhaamsu didee,
Ibiddi goonphee waataa gubuu didee,
Waatni hiddii iddu didee,
Hiddiin obruu Abbaa Garbichaa dheedu diddee,
Abbaan Garbichaa, Garbicha ofii dhaane dooqa tyya naa fusisu dide.

'Hin ijjeesnu,' jedhani. Gaada biraa dhaqxe. 'Gaada, ijoolle ijjeesi.'

'Ijoolleen maal taate?'

Ijoolleen antuuta iddu diddee,
Antuutni jirmii jala duulu diddee,
Jirmiin garaa arbaa baqaqsu didee,
Arbii bisaan xuuxu didee,
Bisaan ibidda dhaamsu didee,
Ibiddi goonphee waataa guubuu didee,
Waatni hiddii iddu didee,
Hiddiin obruu Abbaa Garbichaa dheedu diddee,

Abbaan Garbichaa, Garbicha ofii dhaane dooqa tiyya naa fusisu dide. 'Hin ijjeesnu.'

Loon bira dhaqxe. 'Loon sooma gaadaa irra oriyaa cabsaa,' jette. 'Gaadi maal ta'e?'

Gaadi ijoolle ijjeesu didee,
Ijoolleen antuuta iddu diddee,
Antuutni jirmii jala duulu diddee,
Jirmii garaa arbaa baqaqsu didee,
Arbii bisaan xuuxu didee,
Bisaan ibidda dhaamsu didee,
Ibiddi goonphee waataa gubbuu didee,
Waatni hiddii iddu didee,
Hiddiin obruu Abbaa Garbichaa dheedu diddee,
Abbaan Garbichaa, Garbicha ofii dhaane dooqa
tiya naa fusisu dide.

'Hin cabsinu,' jette loon.Waraabessa bira dhaqxe. 'Waraabessa, loon nyaadhu.'
'Loon maal ta'an?'

Loon sooma gaadarra gubachu didanii,
Gaadi ijoolle gubchu didee,
Ijoolleen antuuta iddu diddee,
Antuutni jirmii jala duulu diddee,
Jirmii garaa arbaa baqaqsu didee,
Arbii bisaan xuuxu didee,
Bisaan ibidda dhaamsu didee,
Ibiddi goonphee waataa gubuu didee,
Waatni hiddii iddu didee,
Hiddiin obruu Abbaa Garbichaa dheedu diddee,
Abbaan Garbichaa, Garbicha ofii dhaane dooqa
tiyya naa fusisu dide.

Waraabessi akka warra kaan hin didne, ittum ce'e 1oon qabe. You loon
qabu loon sooma gaada irra qubatan; gaadi ijoolle gubate, ijoolleen antuuta
kaan ijjeese; antuutni jirmii jala doole; jirmii garaa arbaa baqaqse; arbii
bisuan xuuxe; bisaan ibidda dhaamse; ibiddi, goonphee waataa gube;
waataan hiddii idde; hiddiin obruu Abbaa Garbichaa dheede; Abbaan
Garbicaa; Garbicha kaan dhaane dooqa kaan galaana keessaa fusiseef.

D20 *Sulee Midhaaddu*

Duri duri, ijoollee lamatu jira. Ijoolleen kun abbaaf haadhaan tokko.
Ijoolleen kun abbaaf haadha irraa baddee warra bulguun baate. Bulguun
mana hin jirtuyyu. Ijoolle lamaan kana keessaa intalli tokko maqaa lama
qabdi – tokko Sulee, tokko Qaroo.
   Qaroon warra bulguu seentee ishiin koosi hsrtii, intala kaaniin, maqaan
Gawwilee, 'Ati annan raasi,' jetteen. Isiin annan raastee [Curristee], Qaroon
ille koosii hartee jennaan bulguun warratti gale. 'Ahaa, hojjattu arganne,'
jettee waliin himte.
   Leencaan warri jaala, leenci mana bulguu kaan dhufe. Bulguun leencaan,
'Nama akkanaa argadhe, tokko midhaaddu, intala kana narraa kadhadhu
fudhii soddaa waltaanaa,' jedheen. Leenci kaan kadhate Sulee fudhe. Sulee
amma leenci fudhee, leenca bira galte. Abbaan ijoolle intalti Sulee jedhan
leenci fudhe qabaa kan jedhan dhagayee ijoollee kaan barbaada dhaqe.

D22 *Sulee Midhaaddu*

Mucaan tokko jira. Abbaa isaatiin, 'Abboole, intala akka sulee keenya midhaaddu naa barbaadi,' jedhe. Barbaadu dhaqe. Dhabe gale. La dhabeen
tana. 'Sulee keenya si fuusisa, na dhukube jedhiiti dhiibu keessa gali,' jedheen – abbaan. Dhaqee dhiibu keessa taa'e. Intala diqqo tokkootu jira,

dhaqe Sulee bira, 'Addaa Sulee, ani waan siin jedhan siti himaa, re'ee kana naa elmi,' jetteen. In elmiteef. 'Guyyaa kana akkana siin jidhani, yoo dhiiga geessi siin jedhan lafa buusi biraaa deemi,' jetteen.

Galgala, 'Addaan kee fayyaa miti, hoodhu dhiiga kana geessi,' jedhani itti kennan. Achiin deemte. 'Mee, mee?' jedhani jennaan gadi gadhistee baqatte. Kaate badde. Muka dheeraa tokkoon baate. Muka kaaniin, 'Ani yoo dhugaa si yaamma'e naa gabaabadhu, si yaamnaan naa dheeradhu,' jetteen. In gabaabbateef. In koorte. 'Naa dheeradhi,' jette. In dheerateef.

Warra kaantu godaane. Godaane jala yaa'e. Dura akaakuun jala bahe. [akkana jedhe]:

'Sulee, Sulee!
Sulee moorma faayaa
Ka siiqqe sibilaa
Waliin yaana miila
Garagar banaan dhaamsa
Sulee, naa bu'ii!' jedhe.

Akkana jennaan Suleen:

'Akaaku, akaaku!
Ati dur akaaku kiyya
Amma akaaku dhirsa kiyya
Siif hin bu'uu!' jette.

Biraa dabre. Akkoon jala bahe:

'Sulee, Sulee!
Sulee moorma faayaa
Ka siiqqe sibilaa
Waliin yaana miila
Garagar baanaan dhaamsa
Naa bu'ii!' jetteen.

Suleen:

'Akkoo, akkoo!
Duri ati akkoo kiyya
Amma akkoo dhirsa kiyya
Siin bu'uu!'jetteen.

Biraaa dabarte. Abbaan jala bahe:

Sulee,Sulee!
Sulee Moorma faayaa
Ka siiqqe sibilaa
Waliin yaana miila
Gargar baanaan dhaamsa
Naa bu'ii!

Suleen:

Abbo, abbo!
Duri ati abboo kiyya
Amma abbaa dhirsa kiyya
Siin bu'uu!

Haadhatu jala bahe

Sulee, Sulee!
Sulee moorma faayaa
Ka siiqqe sibilaa
Waliin yaana miila
Gargar baanaan dhaamsa
Naa bu'ii!

[Suleen]:

Ayyoo, ayyoo!
Duri ati ayyoo kiyya
Amma haadha dhirsa kiyya
Siin bu'uu!

Mucaa tokkootu isii jala bahe:

Sulee, Sulee!
Sulee moorma faayaa
Ka siiqqe sibilaa
Waliin yaana miila
Gargar baanaan dhaamsa
Naa bu'ii!

[Suleen]:

Addaa, addaa!
Duri ati addaa kiyya

Amma ati sayyu kiyya
Siin bu'uu!

Obboleessa kaantu jala bahe:

Sulee, Sulee!
Sulee moorma faayaa
Ka siiqqe sibilaa
Waliin yaana miila
Gargar baanaan dhaamsa
Naa bu'ii!

'Silaa sii bu'aa waan godhu hin qabu,' jettee buteef. Kaate itti dhaabatte.
Warra kaanitti dhaqabani. 'Abbo, Kopheen koo narraa bu'e, gaddeebi'een
barbaada,' jette Suleen. 'Haate siif yaa barbaadduun,' tana. 'Haateen fuula
hin beektuun,' tana. 'Ani siif yaa barbaaduun,' tana. 'Ati fuula hin beektuun,' tana. 'Addaa guddoon siif yaa barbaaduun,' tana. 'Inni fuula hin
beekuun,' tana. 'Beenu, lamaan keessan barbaadadhaa,' jedhaniin.
   Kaate gaddeebite – obboleessa waliin. Addaa, akkamiin muka kana
kortee?' jedheen obboleessi. 'Waan dhugaa si yaammannaan naa
gabaadadhu, si yaammamaan naa dheeradhu jadheetin,' jette. In jetteen. In
gabaabateef. In korani. 'Naa dheeradhu,' jetteen. In dheerate.
   Amma warri kaan gaadisa yaame. Koratu jala taa'e. 'Addaa fincaan na
muddee,' jetteen. 'Fincaa'i' jedheen. In fincoofte. Warri kaan, 'dhiiroo,
bokkaan la roobeen,' tana. 'Yoo bokkaan kun roobu baate maal si gonaan,'
tana. 'Na ijjeesaa,' jedhe. Gadi bahan. Bokkaa kaan dhabani. 'Si ijjeesnaan,'
tana. Amma yoo ol laalanu warri ka tataa'u kana. Gurratani ka'ani yaa'ani.
In galataniin.
   Akkasiin warri sun galate.

M6 *Qarcoon Garaacha Namaa Seente*

Saamad Gabraa ka eebbaa [ka eebbisu] In beektu miti? Saammad Gabraan
kun yoo warra namaatti qajeelu – otoo deega dureesa – hin jedhiin loon
qaluuf. Tokko ille ka qabu yoo Saammad itti qajeele in qalaa.
   Amma yeroo tokko Saamad baalli fudhate dhufe. Nama sa'aa tokko
qabuun nama isaa qabate itti qajeele. Sa'aa kana itti qale. Saammad buna
nyaata, tamboo nyaata; nyaate alalaa isaa armuum buusa. Namichi
Saammadiif sa'aa qale – ollaan isaa gurguurtu – alalaa kana guure subbatti
naqee hoodhu naa gurguuri jedhe itti kenne. 'Waan subba kiyya keessa jeru
saaqxe hin ilaaliin, bishaan callaan naa hin bitiin [hin gurguu riin] malee
waanuum argiteen naa gurguuri,' jedheen.
   Amma namichi gabayaa deeme waan inni qabate cufa gurguure yoo
jedhu namichi tokko, 'Abboo subba lafatti haafe kana naa gurguuri,'

jedheen. Maaliin bittaa jennaan wanni na jala deemtu kanaan jedhe.
Wanniin qaxurree. Qaxurree kaan fudhate itti dhaabate. Namichi alalaa
bite yoo saaqe ilaalu alalaa; waan itti godhuun hin qabu. Namichi kaan
qaxurree qabate mana namaatti bule. Abbaan manaa dureessa- ka loon
lafatti olanu – namichi kun [dureessi kun] yoo ilmi isaa dhalate cufa
jawween dhufe mucaa dhalate kaan nyaata. Amma gaafa namichi [gurgu-
urtuun] achi bule nitiin duressaa deette. Jawween in dhufe. Dhufnaan qax-
urreen kaan 'qabb' goote. Abbaan manaa bo'aa, 'jewween Ammaa amma
dhufa' otoo jedhu, 'hardha akkam haafe' otoo jedhu lafti bariite jennaan
yoo laalu bineensi kunoo ka ciisu kana. 'Isii, maaltu ijjeese?' jennaan,
'Kunoo wanni kanatu ijjeese,' jedhe nammichi. 'Waan kee kana, karra
tookko sii bana, naa kenni,' jedhe dureessi. Itti keenne. Namichi karra
baneef. In gale.

Mana ofiitti galee, abbaa alalaa kaan yaame, 'Koottu, waan alalli kan
kee fide fudhadhuu, ' jedhe. Deebana kaan ofumaa dhimmate goromsa
tokko callaa itti kenne. Alalaa tambootu biteef. Waan tuffatuun hin qabu,
namichi goromsa kaan qajeelfate. Goromsa kaan qabate otoo deemu dhee-
botee jennaan warra biyyaatiin bahe. Goromsa mukkatti hidhee bishaan na
obaasaa jedhe warra kaaniin. Dhugee gaddeebi'e. Yoo Gaddeebi'ee
goromsa hiikuuf jedhu namichi bishaan isa obaase, 'Abboo goromsa kana
hin hiikiin,' jedheen.

'Maal?'

'Goromsi kuusa fuudhe loon biraaa cite, hin hiikiin,' jedhe. ['goromsi
kiyya' jedheen.]

'Ani goromsa kana gaafadheen galfadhaa,' jedhee abbaan goromsaa
biyya itti baase. Jaarrotiin bahani dhugaa qabdu jedhaniin. 'Dhugaa hin
qabnu, duuba yoo ani goromsa kana ass hidhu qarcoo takkatu muka
kanaraa taa'a' jedhe. 'Qarcoon dhugaa siif hin taatu, goromsa dhabde;
deemi karra nama keessaa,' jedhaniin jaarroleen.

Ka'ee qajeele. In gale. Galgala loon galani jennaan namichi goromsa
dabaan fudhate kaan goromsa loonitti gadhiisuuf quphane yoo hiiku qarcoon hudduutti seente. Amma goromsi in dhalte. Yoo dhaltu qarcoon
garaacha namicha keessaa ille tokko dhalte. Goromsi lama dhalte. Qarcoon
lama dhalte. Goromsi sadii dhalte. Qarcoon sadii dhalte. Yoo goromsi
dhaltu cufa qarcoon in dhalti. Amma namichi in qarbaa'e. Amma duuba jilbaan deeme.

Guyyaa tokko keessummaan dhufe waati tokko qalaa jedhe itti kenne
biraaa deeme. Waati kaan qalani. Yoo qalanu mucaan goddoon, 'akka
abboon waati qale anilee si qalaa,' jedhe mucaa maan'aa mataa irraa
mure. Haati kana laalnaan, nyaaphichi na galaafate jette utaalte haadaan
ijjeeste. Abbaan achii dhufe 'bade!' jedhe haate yoo dhawu ishiin illeen in
doote. Amma jaarrotiin bahani,'cubbuutu akkana Si tolche, dubbadhu,

cubbu kaan,' jedhaniin. Duri akkana ta'e jedhe dubbate. Namicha kaan
[Ka abbaa goromsaa] yaamaa jedhani deemani fidani.Yoo dhufu,'Loon
kun keeti, sii banaa, karra keessa ejjii,' jedheen. Amma yoo inni karra
keessaa loon tokko baasu qarcoon tokko kessaa baati. Ammas yoo tokko
baasuqarcoon tokko keessaa baati. Yoo loon moonaa obbaa'anu namichi
ka hejju kana- ka jilbaan deemu kaan. Waariyoo Guyyoo Haroo –
abbaan Jiloo Waariyoo –isatu akkana nutti mammaake. Cubbu lagad-
haan kana.

M11 *Mucaa Gaara Irra Jiraatu*

Duri mucaa tokkotu jira. Mucaan kun jabbiyyee keessa jira. Jabbiyyeen
badnaan inni jabbiyyee gula bade. Jabbiyyeen gaara irratti baddee in dhabn.
Mucaa kaan walumaan dhabani. Gara ganna didamaa raasa keessa taa'e.
Waan inninyaatu hinjiru – wam arge nyaata. Amma jabbiyyeen kaan riim-
tee jennaan horuum hortee dhalte. Mucaan ofirraa wayaa hin qabu qullaa
deema.

   [Gaafa tokko] nadheen marra [marga] haamuuf gaara kaan irra bahani.
Yoo laalan namatu gaara irra deema.'Beekta namatu gaara kana irra
deema,' jette himite. 'Wa- nniin dhuguma moo?' jedhanii biyyitti itti yaate.
Yoo itti yaa'anu namatu gaara gubbaa taa'a. Loonti gaara gubbaa jira.
Dhiira itti ergani. Dhiira kaan in hadha, in dadhabni. Lamacha looniin
hadha, sangaa saddeet jiraattiin hadha – in dadhabani. Yoo jibbaatan nad-
heeniin 'qayyi naqadhaa,'jedhani ndheen gula yaa'ani. Nadheen dhuftee
jennaan ofirraa hadhe. Jabbiyyee sadii jiraattiin hadha, afuur jiraattiin
hadha. Namayyuu fixee dadhaban.

   Amma dubra qayyi naqachiisani, dhadhaa dibachisani itti eergani.
Dubartiin kaan dhawattuum dha'atti, inni ofuum irraa hadhaa; ofuum irraa
eega. Adoo ittuum deebi'u, ittuum deebi'u, booda itti dhiyaatte. Dubra kaan
waliin ittuum qabatani. Wal baratani. Dubrtiin kaan biruum oolte. Amma
jarri itti dhufani. Jabbiyyee sadii jiraatiin haadha, in dadhabani. Dubra kaan
bira marsanii, guyyaa sadii bira oolte. Achii yoo yu eegee itti dhufani jabbiyyee lama jiraattiin jala jiga – in dadhabe. Jabbiyyee sadii jiraatiin jala jiga
– in dadhabe. Mucaa akkanaan qabatani Booranatti galani.

M25 *Jibba*

Jaarsi Akkana jedhe:
   'Ani wa tookko jibba – nama tokkicha ka qophaa deemu jibba.
   'Ani wa lama jibba – nama re'e mucha lamaa intala fuula itti fudhe jibba.
   'Ani wa sadii jibba – mucaa ganna sodoomaa ka sadeen annan mi 'aa'an
[midhaa'aa] hin qabne jibba. 'Ani wa afuur jibba – nama ganna afuurtamaa,
namni biraa wal didaa, nama sun gargar hin baasiin jibba. An wa san jibba
– nama ganna sanataama duubi cuulsu duubat.' 'Ani wa jaa jibba – nama

ganna jaatamaa, namni sobee jennaan sooba sun ka hin beekkanne jibba. 'Ani wa toorba jibba – nama ganna toorbaatamaa, ka itiille ofii gubbaa deeme itillee nadheen dhibii barbaada dhaqe jibba.'

Yoo akkana jedhu, 'Ati maaliif akkana jette jedhaniin.'

'Nama tokko qophaa ka deemu waan an jibbuuf yoo qophaa deemu in cabaa, in baqaa, in du'aa; namni iyyuuf hin jiru. kanumaaf jibbe,' jedhe.

'Nama re'e mucha lamaa intala fuula itti fuudhu maa jibbitaa?' jennaan jaarsi, 'Nama re'e mucha lamaa intala fuula itti fuudhu, yokan citte dhabani yokan cittoon dhabani; aganumaaf jibbaa,'jedhe. 'Mucaa ganna soddoomaa maa jibbitaa?' jennaani

'Namni ganna soddoomaa ka sadeen annan midhaa'an hin qabne, yoo loon keessa rakkate gaala keessa rakkoo baha, yoo gaala keesa rakkate re'e keesa rakkoo baha; yoo waan kana tokko ille hin qabne lubbuu ofii malee hormaata inni eggatu dhibiin duubatti hin haafne, agnaaf jibbaa.

'Namni ganna afuurtamaa, namnii wal didee nama sun gargar hin baasne, ganna dhibiin inni gargar baasu hin jiru.'

'Namni ganna shantamaa, gannaa qixxee, [Shantamatu irra hafe], Koraa qixxe, sa'aa qixxe, namaa wal qixxee. Yoo cubbu dubbate, yoo waan hin jirre dubbate. Waan kuncufa irraa cita waan kana duuba inni cubbuu lagatu hin jiru jechuudha.'

'Nama ganna jaatamaa sooba namarraa hin beekkattiin, ganni dhibiin kan inni beekkatu duubatti hin haafae – yoo ganna kanatti hin biilchaatiin.

'Namni gana toorbaatama ka itillee offii irra ka'ee itillee nadheen biyyaa itilleen isaatu in arabsitiin – 'dhiira miti' jette, yaa jaare. Yoommoo itillee nadheen dhibii dhaqe jibba jibba irratti dare jechuudha – itilleen sun itti *masakartti.* [Witnesses]'

M26 Areero Bosaro

[Dhiyoo kanna Golichi Dida kateelootu mammaaksa kana naa mammaake]

Areero Bosaro, ka akkana way raagu kun: 'ka gaalloolle Gabra ta'e, re'e Reendila ta'a' jedhu kun – jaarti isaatiin wal didan jedhan. Jaartiin isaa maqaan Adii, Areeroon jaarti isaa akkana jedhe:

'Adii, loon kiyya lafatti hin dhaliin, dhaqooba jaari jedhee si dhdhabe;
Jaartu hin danqartu, si dadhabe,
Danqartu hin dhobiftu, si dadhabe
Isii Adii, natu si hin beeknee? Manatu si hin beekne malee,
Mana kan saree susuukaa, si hin beeknee malee,
Mana kan harre gummuuraa taatu si hin beekne malee,
Lafee ille akka arbaa,
Arba nyaattu akka Waataa
Waataan martuu akka suubbo alaatti.'

Yoo inni akkana jedhee arbsu mucaan diqayyaan ka bira taa'u, 'Akaaku, ati akkoo maaliif akkana arrabsitaa?' jedhe gaafate.

Areeroon:

'Baga arrabse akkoo tan tee,
Qodaa hin goofsiin jedhe dadhabe, ona ollaa
Goofanii. Akkoo tan tee ka
Yoo namni way dubbatu mataan rimuu,
Ta reefensii loon silmii irraa hin buqimne, ' jedhe.

A2 *Sulee – Ulee Waaqaa*

Uleen Waaqaa Sulee gula dhufte. Sulee leencatu fudhe. Leenci gaafas nama; iyyummaaf bade bineensa ta'e malee. Leenca kaan namni in ijjeese. Suleen dhiirsa ishii barbaada namaan baate. 'Dhirsa kiyya dhabe,' jette.

'Dhirsa kan kee hin garre, kunno gogaa sun irra taa'ii,' jedhaniin.
'Gogaan kun maalii?'
'Gogaan lakki namuuma, irra taa'ii,' jedhan. La dhirsa dhabde, yaadatu garaa keessa mure, inbootte:

Goofaree gaaddisaa, deemmaa na daaddisaa
Ilkaan qariifaan dhiiga
Dhiigi duraa hin baane.
Dhirsi kiyya
Buultiin godee gaaraa
Lolee goduu baasaa, dhirsi kiyya!
Ka gaadee soddoomaa
Ka soddooma dhirri hin geeffanne.

Rabbiitu itti dhufe duuba. 'Ati maaliif akkana taata? ' jedhe.
'Dhirsa kiyya dhabeen akkana ta'aa,' jetteen.
'Fuula takkaan [tokkoon] isan galchu ree?'
'Fuula takaan nu galchii,' jette. Gogaan ol dabre [akka irra teeetti].

Rabbiin keenya amma niitii qaba. Yoo inni gara niitii isaa deemu Suleen ofirraa dhoorte – ulee ishii dura qabatte. 'Maaliif na dhoorte!' jedhee dalane. Bubbee fidee bubise. 'Boobobob' jedhe. Uleen waaqaa amm achirraa dhufte. Bubbeen ille achirraa dhuftee, mandisuun dalansu waaqaa taate.

Waaqi ka dalane, 'Ati akkam nadheen na dhoortee siqqe na dura qabdaa?' jedheeti armaan deebi'ee, 'Nadheen gadi namaa si tolchee!' jedheen.

A8 *Haadha Abanooyye*

Haati Abanooyyeen qaroo. Qaroomtee jabaatte. Amma yoo moo'aa fila-tanu ishiin mooti taatee nadheen biyya moosifte. Yoo godaananu ijoollee dhiiratu baata. Yoo qubatanu mana dhiiratu jaara. Moonaa looni ijaartee irra deebitee mana jaarti – dhiirti. Amma dhiirti waan kana dadhabee in korate. Yoo koratu walii hin galu in dadhabe. Nadheen kana maaliin jala deebisna jedhe dadhabe.

Mucaa tokkotu iyyeessa – haadha hin qabu, abbaa hin qabu – guyyaa tokko yoo warri tokko karaa galu mucaan kun garamii galatan jedhee gaafateen. 'Mucaan iyyeessi kun maal jedhaa? Dhiisaa daallee kana,' jedhani biraa dabran. Yoo dabranu warra kana keessaa namichi tokko itt gore. Namcha kaaniin,'maal dubbatan?' jedhee gaafate – mucaan. 'Abanooyye kana dabsachu dadhabne; ijoollee goddaanaa in baannaa, you qubatani dallaa looni jaara, dalla yoo irraa baanu aduun la dhiitee, deebinee mana ijaarra – in dadhabnee,' jedhe. 'Mala kiyya fuutu?' jedhe mucaan, 'Yoo goddaana [godaanuuf] kaatanu billaa fudhaa, ijoollee miila gargar qabaati gargarii murrannaa [haadha waliin] jedhaan' jedhe. Amma yoo boru godaanu ka'anu dhiirti cufti, 'Ijoollee kophaa baachu hin danda'uu, gargarii qoodana,' jedhe. Yoo akkana jedhu nadheen, 'him barbaadu, Ijoollee kiyya naa kenni,' jettee fudhatte. Amma in qubate – godaanni. Egii qubatan mucaan akkana jedhee itti hime; 'Dallaa looni callaa jaaraa, mana hin jaarinaa bulaa; yoo halkan geette nadheen diida irratti qabadhaa refaan,' jedhe.

Yoo dhiirri diiduum irratti nadheen kaan qabu, nadheen ceertee didde. Ibiddi in booba'a, tokko you qabu tokko biraa taa'a. Nadheen namni na argaa jette didde.

Amma nadheen boruu kaate, 'Akkam dhirsi kyya otoo namni na arguu na waliin raffaa?' jette ganama kaatee muka muurtee mana jaarte. Kana lamaan akkanaan jalaa bahani.

Waan dhibiin Abanooyyeen ka dhiiraan dhibde, waan hin jirre fidaa jettiin: 'Kophee ka gama lamaan riffeensaa fidaa,' jetteen. Dhabani jennaan guurra harree muranii qorani fidani. 'Kana na jalaa baatanii, amma subba tafkii miyyuu fidaa,' jette. Jarri kaan amma mucaa bira deemee gaafate. Inni waan jedhee, 'Udaan harree guuraa, ibidda gubbaati hidhaa, [achii] itti geessaa,' jedhe. Yoo udaan harree subbati guurani ibidda gubbaati hidhanu subbi kaan tafkii miyyuu ta'e. Itti geesani.(otoo kana fidu baatani qixaatiin isaan argatu jabduuyu).

Amma kana jalaa banaan mucaa biraa deemani. 'Waan isan taatanu,' jedhe mucaan, 'Waan isan taatanu, balee qotaa, canaa jala kaa'aa, bobeessa naanneessaa, achii kora yaamaa, dubbi moormaa,' jedheen. Abanooyyeen barcuuma guddaa qabdi, kora yaamani jennaan dhuftee barcuuma irra teesse. Balee dura teessisaniin. Warri kaan balee gama taa'e. Abanooyeen kana fidaa, kana fidaa yoo jettuun, 'hin fidnu, guyyaa cufa fidnaa? 'jedhani moormaniin.Yoo ishiin dalantee barcuuma irra dadeemtu balee keessa buute.

Buute jennaan otuum balee keesa gadi fiigdu, 'Nadheen!' jette yaamatte:

Nadheen!
Sooba hyyeetti, sosoobu hayyeetti
Annan abbaa warraa mataa irraa qiqqicuu bhayyeetti,
Jaala barachuu hayyeetti,
Takka sin jedhan takka jala kaa'uu hyyeetti
Sooba hayyeeiti, sobaat hayyeetti ...'
jette nadheenitti dhaamsa dbarsite dabarte.

Amma nadheen dhiira jala deebite. Duuba dhaamsa Abanooyyeef – nadheen soobu jalqabde. Yoo amma ati lolaa kaatu si sooban, yoo ati tokko dubbatte, dubbi tokko jala dhaabdi. Nadheen kanaaf akkana taate.
    Abanooyyeen akkanaan qaariite.

A9 Diidoo Gaawwale

Diidoo Gaawwaleen jabaa. Jabaa akka isaa hin arganu. Qaroo illee. Bara sun Arsiin wal haadhani – waraana wantee qabatani. Yoo itti gabba'u namni shantama isa hin buusu. Hin riifatu. Yoo wal darbatani wal dhaban, wantee kaaniin fixa.
    Amma duuba namichi iyyeessa tokko Oboloo ka jedhan dhufee Diidooti gale. Namichi Oboloon kun qullaa deema. Diidoon niitii isaatiin, 'Waan kun maalinni? waan kana armaa balleessi. Wanni akkan jiraa maalinni?' jedha. Yoo inni akkana jedhu Oboloonis 'Wanni akkana jiraa maalinii,' jedha. Beeke akka daalle of taasisee waanuum namni jedheen deebisee jedha. Yoo, 'Aboo ati maalinni?' jedhaniin innille, 'Aboo ati maalinni?' jedha. 'Haardhaa! Inille, 'haardhaa!'
    'Dhiiroo waan baddu kana asii balleessaa!' – Diidoon.
    'Dhiiroo waan baddu kana asii balleessaa!' – Oboloon.
    Hojiin isaatu Kanuuma. 'Ay, daallee; dhisi,' jedhe Diidoon. Oboloon quallaa taa'a. Nadheen biraa taa'e annan raasa. Diidoon farda qaba. Farda galchani, okaa itti kennani, yoo fardi '*Ihihihi!* 'jedhu, Oboloon '*Ihihihi!'* jedha. Duuba, farda kana akka malee ilaala.
    Niiti Diidootu dubbate duuba: 'Diidoo, nama kana soddaadhe, yoo fardii kun dhufu, namichi gadhe kun farda akkam ilaala? soddaadhe!' jette.
    'Dhiisi daalle kana, farda kiyya maal irraa ilaala?' jedhe diidoon.
    Diidoon, 'namichi, annan raasaa, callisee bargaafate qullaa taa'aa,' otoo jedhuu, niitiin Diidoo nafa Oboloo laalte barrachuu feete. Koottu wajjin rafnaa jettee in barratteen. (Nadheen balaa mitii!). Booda wayaa itti hodhiite. 'Eentu wayaa kana hodheef?' jedhe Diidoon. 'Isii abboo, iyyeessi ka akkanaa ka mana keenya jiru, qulaa deeme maqaa nu balleessa,' jette. Amma la jaalatte, in soobdi.
    Amma niiti wajjin waligalani jennaan Oboloon, 'dhirsa ke kana yoo marriyachu fedhan atamitti marriyatan, yoom dagata?' jedhee gaafate – Diidoo ijjeesu fedhee. 'Maal dhibdi, yoo inni loon bobbaasu waraana-wantee qaba,

yoo sangaa duraa banu waraana-wantee qaba, yoo jabbi gorbaa bobbaasu qoyee qaba, yoo kana biyyee kaa'u malee maaltu jira!' jetteen. Amma Oboloon in bade. 'Namichi kaan mee?' jedhe Diidoon. 'Namichi bade dhiisi, daallee, gara inni deeme maal beekna!' jette nitin. 'Baga daaraa baafte, yaa badullee,' jedhe Diidoon.

Amma Oboloon yoo badu niiti Didoon akkana jedhee itti hime[tureeyu]: 'Ani bulti shaniin dhufa, duula fudhadhe dhufa, attille itillee adii mana irra keyyadhu,' jedhee deeme – akka duulli ishi hin ijjeesin. Bultiin shan sun in geette. Diidoon sangaa bobbaase; wanteen bobbaase. Yoo fuula jabiin geettu qoyyee fudhate. Yoo sun Oboloon duula qabatee eega, irra bu'e. Diidoon jabbi kaan anphaare [hanphaare] nama heddu fixe. Ag' fixee, ag fixee, ag fixe. 'Namni jabbiin dhaanu maaliini!' jedhan. Diidoon niitii isaatiin, 'Niitii kiyya, wantee naa darbii, wantee naa darbi, wantee na darbii,' jedheen. Wantee kaan irraa gorssiitee achi dhofte. Diidoon wantee kaan harkaan qabadha yoo jedhu in ijjeesaniin.

Nama jabaatu jira duuba – ka akka Diidoo – Madha jedhuun. Jarri duri wal hin jaalatu. Amma Diidoon du'ee jennaan Madhi hin kooblu, hin taphatu. Amma Madhi yaa'i waame. 'Ani saddeq dhaha, na bahaa,' jedhe. In bahan. Madhi saddeeq dhahaa in geerrare:

Oho ho ho!
Oboloo qooma diidaa, Diidoo qooma looti
Diidoon bade koola rummichi rige
Yoo jiru na goggogse
Donaan jabaan koo goggoogaa natti hidhe.

Akkan jedhe sadeeq dhaane cabse. Achii yaa'a kaaniin, 'Amma waan taatanu, boru balbaleetti labsina karaab sadii hidhaa,' jedhe itti hime.

Dulli in bahe. Nama tokkotu jira duuba – ijoollee. Diidoo jedhuun – Diidoo Muuke.[Mucaan kun ani in duulaa jedhe ka'e]. 'Gurbaa ati ijoollee, hin duuliin,' jedhaniin. Dideee, 'in duulaa!' jedhee duule. Haaloo Diiddoo duulu fedhe.

Amma Arsii waliin walti dhufani. Oboloon kun arboora qaba, ka Diidoo dabalee naqatee harka isaa ol fuudhu hin danda'u. Wal hadhan, wal hadhan, wal hadhan. Diidoo Muukeen calliise dhaabate egga. Oboloo eega. Duula kaan keessa otoo Oboloo laalu Oboloon dhufe – arboora isaa akkan saaqqatee. Diidoon waraana itti darbate. Oboloon in kufe. Diidoon, 'Ka'i!' jedheen. 'Hin danda'u na boojji,' jedhe Oboloon. 'Haaloo Diidoo si booj- jaa?' jedhe harka isaa mureen.

Booranni Arsii fixe jennaan, danaba kaan, 'Danaba hin goorsiinaa,' jed- hanii walitti qabanii, niiti Diidoo karaa loon galu keessa lafa qotani mataa ishi gad awwaalani danaba irratti offani. Qeencaan ciranii, qeencaan ciranii lafee ille irraa balleesani.

A10.1 *Diidoo Gaawwalee – Yeroo Ijoollumaa*

Diidoo Gaawwaleen gaafa ijoolle jiru, you ijoolle diiqqo faana wal dhaanan ille hin rifatu. Homaa hin dheetu. In dadhabaniin. Amma abbaan, 'Mucaa kana la dadhabne, eegaa, mucan kana waan inni keessa jiru laalla,' jedhe. Amma Diidoon jabbi tiksa. Tikaa gale, 'Bisaan natti kenaa,' jedhe. Butte lama ka bisaani wal biraa dhaabani butte tokko bishaan itti naqani. Tokko gororri qabani keessa kaa'anii itti qadaadani. Yoo inni dhufu butte ka gororrin keessa jiru gara inni dhufuti dhaabanii, 'Achi keessaa dhugi,' jed-haniin. Inni eeboteera, butte kaan buqqisee kookki fudhate. Gororriin yoona '*barrrr*' jette baate. Yoo isiin *barrrr* jettu inni '*hirrrr*' jedhee butte kaan dhayee cacabse. Achii akka inni janna beekani, 'Lammeesso Diidoo hin soobinaa,' jedhani.

A16 *Walee Waacu*[18]

Walle Waacuun Abbaa Gadaa. Amma yaa'iin itti hammaate jennaan niitiin walee – maqaan Asaa – akkana jetteen, 'Walee yaa'iin kun sitti hammaate,' jette.

'Hin hammaanne; maal natti hammaataa, akkuum fedhe na jaalataa,' jedhe [Waleen]. 'Milikeet**[19] sii godha (akka itti beektuun), tamboo boran-daadi moyaalee sii bita, jimaa ka Boyee, lattu sii buqqisa. Ati saaboo keeyadhu, yoo kori bahe badoo keessatti ballisi, tamboo bordandaadi tana nyaadhu, akkana ballisi, magaado ille ballisi, kurfeefadhu, akkana cirrisi. Lubi [luba] keenya ka atti beektu, hin obsu jimaa kana keenni siin jedha – yoo si jaalate. Tamboo dansaa kana beeka, situ irra qaba, waan kana si irratti hin qabu, yoo keenni jedhan laalladhu.' jetteen.

Amma ishiin yoo akkana jettu Waleen hidhaa isaa keeyyatee, saaboo kaan keeyyatee, magaadoo kaan hidhatee, tamboo isaa hidhatee koratti gabbahe. Yaa'iin cufa in bahe. Hariyaan luba issaani cufa in bahe.

Waleen jimaa kaan qaqabate. Nama 'natti keenni' jedhuun dhabe. Tamboo kaan nyaate. Magaado itti kureefate. Nama tokko ka dubbissun dhabe. Yoo kana koruum oolani; wacaa oolani. Achii Walleen manatti gale. Niitiin mootu, inni moo'aa, 'Waan ati jette la arge. Lubii keenya ka atti beektu jimaa naa keenni hin jeenne, kophum kiyya fixe; tamboo kana ofu-maan nyaadhe; 'lubii keenya (keessaa) namnii tokko natti keenni hin jenne, magaadoo kana natti kenni hin jenne; waan ati jette la argeen tana. ['yaa'iin akka natti hammaafe arge.']

Inni Abbaa Gadaati – amma yaa'iin godaana la buufate – Waleen guyyaa ijoollee isaatiin 'horroo kana ooffaa, achi fageessaa,' jedhe qara itti hime. Galgala in lalabani: 'Gaalli Waleen hin galle yaa olleen; tana. Hin oolanu,

---

18 Wale Wachu was an Aba Gada whose office term was 1772–30.
19 sign

aadaan hin oolchitu, 'gaalli illee ofumaan gala, banaa,' jedhe Waleen. 'ee!' jedhani banani. Yoo bananu gaala isaa oofani galchani.

Waleen, 'Gaala kiyya naa fe'aa, ani godaana qajeelcheen deebi 'a' jedhe farda isaa qabatee – godaana yaa'a isafu lalaba – dura bahe. Lalabee qajeelee, yaa'a qoggeelchee Gaattiroo gadi buuse. Achii, 'Godaana kiyya maal gartan? Goodaana kiyya maal gartan?' jechaa deebi'e. 'Hin garre' jed- haniin. Itti dhabate.

Amma warratti qara itti himee [ture], karaa Fulloon bahee itti dhaqabe. Jabbii gorbaa ass kutee biraaa dabre. Itti dhaabate. Halkan itti qabee Hadheesasa gama bule. Boruu ka'ee Malkaa Farda waleetiin dhaqe. Walleensa geenyaan ammallee ka raaba kute.

Warrii kaan [Yaa'iin] amma in qubate. Walgaafate. 'Walee gartani?' 'hin garree.' 'Walee gartani?' 'hin garree.' Jedhan. 'In beeknaa la dheete.'jedhan. Achii dhiira tolchani itti eergani. Faana ofii deebi'ani. Faana isaa fudhatan. Waldaa Jaarrutiin bahan. Jabbi kaan argan. In tuman. In dabre. Walleensoon bahe [bahan]. Sangaa kaan tuman. You inni malkaa loon buuse taakisiisu jarri la dubaan dhaqabani.

Yoo kana isaaf niitiin wal mariyatan. Niitiin isaa akkana jetteeni 'Boroor kana [farda walee] namni tuqu hinjiru, haraka isaa hin qabatanu, Boroor malkaati hidhi, yoo Boroor si jalaa hafe si hin barbaadanu, biraaa taakki,' jetteen. Yoo jarri bu'anu Boroorri ka hejju kana. Itti baafate. 'Hin gabb- ifnu,' jedhe, 'Boroor eenyutu gabbisaa? Abboo wanniin kun dhiira; gaafa akkanaa kana ijjeese, gaafa akkanaa kana ijjeese°.hin gabbifnu. Hin ijjeesnuun,' tana.

Amma obboleesatu arma keessa jira. [A man whom Wale's brother had once slept with his wife] Namichi kun, 'Boroor yoo ijjeesne Waleen in baha,' jedhe. Inni deeme farda Walee ijjeese. Yoo kana namni cufti ka farda yaab- bate beeku, namicha ijjeese kaan la oode. Jarri kaan, 'Aadaan hin dabartu, egii fardi kun dabarte …' jedhani irraa galan. Galani, 'Boroor la gabbifne, inni la taakkee,' jedhani warra yaa'atti dubbatan.

Waleen deemee Moyaaleen bahe. Fuula Dambii Hidda Mataa jedhanitti dhibaayyu bahe. In hore. dhibaayyu baha; waan aadaan jilaa tolfatu inuum tolfata; loon isaa karra sadii taate. Artii deebi'ee Deeba qubate. El Baabbo gubbaa taa'e. Qodaa tolchee arma taa'aa karraa sadii itti daree jaa ta'an.

Yoo loon Walee jaa ta'an, yaa'iin kaan in beela'e. Nyaatan[illee] homaa keessa hin buu'an. Lafti biyyaa nagaa, jarri in sabdaa'e. Horii dhabe. Nadheen amma gaalle koorti – annan hin jiru- wanni kaan gurratti. Guyyaa tokko niitii tokootu – ka garaacha qabdu – muuka irraa dhaqatte. You muuka irraa dhqattu, 'Waan baddiin tana' jette. Kaan, ka bira hejjitu, 'haradha badnee? Gaafa waleen nu keessaa bade badneen,' tana. Namichi tokko kana dhagaye. Waan dhagaye warra dhibiitti dubbate.Walti haasa'an; wal gaafatan. Achii, 'haa barbaadnuun,' jedhan. Dhiira tolfate. Fuula inni qubate quba qaba, El Baabbo dhufe.

Jarri yoo El Baabbo dhaqabu niitiin Walee ka dhoqee gubbaa hejjitu warra kaan argite. 'Walee kunoo yaa'iin keessan arma ciisa, beeketaa?' jeetten. 'Beenu dubbisi,' jedhe Waleen.

In deemte. 'Isin maaliif Walee nagaa hin fuune?' jete. 'In sodaanne.' 'Hin sodaatinaa, koottaa nagaa fudhaa,' jette.

'Jaal Walee, si barbaada yaana, nagaa sifunaan' tana 'Loon hin dhugne, in obaafadha, kaasi beeni galiin' jedhe Waleen niiti isaatiin.

In galatteen. Dhiira soddoomaa[f] qoodaa soddooma itti fuute. Hin lulluqanne. Eelee soddooma itti qalte. Hin luuluqanne. Loon kaan dura galan. Sangaa itti qalte. Hin lulluqanne – in ciisa. Waleetu galgala gale. Niitiin, 'Qodaa soddooma itti fudhee- hin lulluqanne, eelee soddooma itti qalee – hin lulluqanne, sangaa itti gale – hin lulluqanne; lubbii keessan ka ciisu kana,' jette Waleetti himte. Amma Waleen ka'aa dhiiroo jedhe jibiicha itti qale. 'Kotta ariiradhaa,' jedhe. In ariirate. In qale. 'Tiruu keessaa fuudhaafi dhaabaaf,' jedhe. Yoo dhaaban namni tokko cinaacha tokkoon dabru dadhabe. In quufe. Hin bullee, 'Amma in gallaa, nuun galiin,' tana. [Waleen ka'e warra waliin gara yaa'a deebi'e].

Yoo Waleen galu warri kaan akka kaan jira, nadheen akka kaan jirti – oduu la dhagaye- itti qoode. Qalani nyaatan. Ammalle itti deebise. Ammallee in qalani. Yoo kana in jibbaate. 'koottaa,' jedhe dhibaayuun bahe. In eebbise. Dhibaayuun galee itti deebise. (in qoode.) Raaddi kun in horateef. Amma duula lalabani. In duulan. Gujiitti duule. Danaba galche. 'Hin qoodannu,' jedhee Waleen. Beenni gaafas dubbii Abaa Gadaa hin dabru, 'Hin qoodannu offaa.' jennaan offani galani. Warratti galee Waleen nadheen lubaa cufa baase. Itti keenne. Cufa gargar qoodani. 'Anfalaan booja'an', jechuun gaafas baate. Tokko illee dhiirti hin dhabe. Galfatee amma ille garagale.

Amma ille duula lalabe. Gamatti duule. Arsii irraa galche. 'Kottaa qodadhaa,' jedhe. In qoodan.

In quufan.Amma ille garagale. Amma illee duula lalabe. Gamatti duule. Arsii irraa galche.

In qoodan. In quufan.

Bibliography

Abdulkadir Hajji Jama (1982), *Some Cultural Elements as Reflected in Somali Folktales*, Unpublished MA Thesis, Addis Ababa: Institute of Language Studies, Addis Ababa University

Aguilar, Mario (1998) *Being Oromo in Kenya*, Trenton, NJ and Asmara: Red Sea Press

Andrzejewski, Bogumil Witalis (1962), 'Ideas About Warfare in Borana Galla Stories and Fables', in *African Language Studies*, Vol.3, 116–36

Anozie, Sunday O. (ed.), (1982), *Phenomenology in Modern African Studies*, New York: Conch Magazine

Arewa, Ojo and Gregory Shreve (1982), 'Phenomenology and the Ethnography of Speaking Folklore', in Sunday O Anozie (ed.), *Phenomenology in Modern African Studies*, New York: Conch Magazine

Asmarom Legesse (1973), *Gada: Three Approaches to the Study of African Society*, New York: The Free Press

Bartels, Lambert (1982), *Oromo Religion, Myths and Rites of the Western Oromo of Ethiopia: An Attempt to Understand*, Berlin: Dietrich Reimer Verlag

Bascom, William (1965), 'The forms of Folklore', in *Journal of American Folklore*, Vol. LXXVIII, 3–20

Bashuna, A. B. (1993), 'The Waata hunter gatherers of Northern Kenya' in *Kenya Past and Present*, 25, 36–8

Bassi, Marco (1996), *I Borana; una societa assembleare dell'Ethiopia* by, Milan: Franco Angeli,

Baxter, P.T.W. (1965), 'Repetition in Certain Borana Ceremonies', in *African System of Thought*, London: International African Institute

—— (1966), 'Stock Management and Diffusion of Property Rights Among the Borana', in *Proceedings of the 3rd International Conference of Ethiopian Studies*, 116–27. Addis Ababa

—— (1986), 'Giraffes and Poetry: Some Observations about Giraffe Hunting among the Borana', *Paiduma*, 32: 45–63

—— (1987), 'Shaikh Nur Hussein of Bale', in A. El Shaied, *The Diversity of the Muslim Community in London*, 139–52. London: Ithaca

Ben-Amos, Dan (1982), *Folklore in Context: Essays*, New Delhi: South Asian Publishers Pvt. Ltd.

Boswell, George and J. Russell Reaver (1962), *Fundamentals of Folk Literature*, Oosterhout: Anthropological Publications

Cerulli, Enrico (1922), 'The Folk-Literature of the Galla of Southern Abyssinia', in *Harvard African Studies*, Vol. 3, 9–228

Coffin, Tristram (ed.) (1968), *American Folklore*, Voice of America Series III, USA

Cotter, George (1990), *Salt for Stew: Proverbs and Sayings of the Oromo People with English Translation*, Debra Zeit, Ethiopia

Dahl, Gudrun (1990), 'Mats and Milk Pots: the Domain of Borana Women,' in Anita Jacobson-Widding and W. van Beek (eds), *The Creative Communion*, 129–36. Uppsala: Studies in Cultural Anthropology

Desalegn, Seyum (1986), *E.Cerulli's Folk Literature of the Galla of Southern Abyssinia: A Critical Evaluation*, Unpublished M.A. Thesis, Addis Ababa: Institute of Language Studies, Addis Ababa University

Dorson, Richard (ed.) (1972), *Folklore and Folklife: An Introduction*, Chicago: University of Chicago Press

Dundes, Alan (1964), 'Texture, Text and Context', in *Southern Folklore Quarterly*, XXVIII (quoted in Ben-Amos, 1982)

Fekade Azeze (1984), 'Ethiopian Oral Literature: A Preliminary Review and Bibliography', in *Proceeding of the 8th International Conference of Ethiopian Studies*, Addis Ababa

Finnegan, Ruth (1966), *Limba Stories and Story Telling,* Oxford: OUP
—— (1992), *Oral Traditions and the Verbal Arts,* London and New York: Routledge
Georges, Robert and Alan Dundes (1963), 'Toward a Structural Definition of the Riddle', in *Journal of American Folklore,* No. 76
Goldstien, Kenneth (1964), *A Guide for Field Workers in Folklore,* Hatbro: Folklore Associates Inc.
Gragg, Gene B. (1982), *Oromo Dictionary,* East Lansing and Chicago: Michigan State University
Haberland, Eike (1963*), Galla Sud-Athiopiens,* Stuttgart : Kohl Hammer Verlag
Hailu Araya (1972), *Ten Semantic Categories Most Reccurrent in Ethiopian Folk Poetry, Their Socio-Linguistic Bases,* Doctoral Dissertation, Washington DC: Georgetown University
Helland, Johan (1980), 'Social Organisation and Water Control among Borana', in his *Five Essays on the Study of Pastoralists and the Development of Pastoralism,* 48–78. Bergen: Sosialantropologisk Institutt
—— (1997), 'Development Interventions and Pastoral Dynamics in Southern Ethiopia', in Richard Hogg (ed.), *Pastoralists, Ethnicity & the State in Ethiopia,* 81–103. London: Haan
—— (1998), 'Institutional Erosion in the Drylands: the case of the Borana pastoralists', *EASS-REA* Vol XIV, No 2
Hymes, Dell (1971), 'The Contribution of Folklore to Sociolinguistic Research', in *Journal of American Folklore,* No. 84, 42–50 (quoted in Arewa and Shreve, 1982)
Isack, H. A. (1986), 'People of North Kenya', in Margaret Sharman (ed.), *Kenya's People,* Nairobi: Evan's Brothers
Isack, H.A. and H.U. Reyer (1989), 'Honeyguides and Honey Gatherers: Interspecific Commmunication in a Symbiotic Relationship', *Science,* Vol. 243, 1343–7
Iser, Wolfgang (1974), *The Implied Reader,* Baltimore: Johns Hopkins University Press
Jaenen, J Cornelius (1956), 'The Galla or Oromo of East Africa', in *Southern Journal of Anthrophology,* University of New Mexico
Kassam, Aneesa (1984) *La geste de Renard, Variations sur un conte Gabra, Etude linguistique,* PhD Dissertation; Paris: University of Paris III
—— (1986a), 'The Fertile Past: the Gabra concept of oral tradition', *Africa* 56:2, 192–209
—— (1986b), 'The Gabra pastoralists/Waata hunter gatherer symbiosis: a symbolic interpretation', in F. Rottland and R. Vossen (eds), *Afrikanisele Wildheuter,* Hamburg: Buske
Leus, Ton (1999), *Mammaassa Booranaa,* Yaballoo, Ethiopia: Dhadim Catholic Mission
Levi-Strauss, Claude (1963), *Structural Anthropology,* New York: Basic Books Inc.
Lindfors, Bernth (ed.) (1977), *Forms of Folklore in Africa,* Austin: University of Texas Press
Mangesha Rikitu (1992), *Oromo Folktales for a New Generation,* London: Mengesha Rikitu
Melakneh Mengistu (1990), *The Major Themes and Motifs of Southern Agaw Folktales,* Unpublished MA Thesis, Addis Ababa: Institute of Language Studies, Addis Ababa University
Okpewho, Isidore (1980), 'Rethinking Myth', in *African Literature Today,* No. 11. 5–23
Praetous, Franz (1889), *Eine Galla-Fabel,* Leipzig: Zeitschrift Afrikanische Sprachen
Propp, Vladimir (1968), *Morphology of the Folktale,* Austin and London: University of Texas Press
Scheub, Harold (1977), 'The Technique of the Expansible Image in Xhosa Ntsomi Performances', in Bernth Lindfors (ed.), *Forms of Folklore in Africa,* Austin: University of Texas Press
Sharman, Margaret (ed.) (1986), *Kenya's People,* Nairobi: Evan's Brothers Ltd.
Shibeshi Lemma (1986), *A thematic Approach to Famine Inspired Amharic Oral Poetry,* Unpublished MA Thesis, Addis Ababa: Institute of Language Studies, Addis Ababa University,
Sumner, Claude (1992), 'Oromo Wisdom Literature: Oromo Folktales', Unpublished Manuscript
Tesfaye Gebre Mariam (1990), *A Study of Major Themes in Jablawi Folktales,* Unpublished MA Thesis, Addis Ababa: Institute of Language Studies, Addis Ababa University
Thompson, Stith (1946), *The Folktale,* Los Angeles: University of California Press
Wilding, Richard (1982), 'The Liban Myth and the Enigmatic Cowmen', in *Proceedings of the Annual Seminar of the Department of History,* 265–279, Debrezeit
Wood, John (1999), *When Men are Women: Manhood among the Gabra nomads of East Africa,* Madison: University of Wisconsin Press.

Index of Headings and Subheadings

A formal index has not been included in view of the study being clearly organized into three main parts, with a detailed list of contents, and the arrangement of the text by topic and story; these features, along with the following reference to headings and subheadings within the text will, we hope, combine to serve the reader in finding his or her way around the work.